THE POLITICS AND POETICS OF CAMP

'What *is* Camp? *Is* Camp gay? *Is* Camp political?. . . These questions demand attention, and my own Camp response would be: **only her hairdresser knows for sure**."

from Chapter 2

The Politics and Poetics of Camp is a radical reappraisal of the discourse of Camp. The contributors look at both the meaning and the uses of Camp performance, and ask: is Camp just a style, or a witty but nonetheless powerful cultural critique?

The essays investigate Camp from its early formations in the seventeenth and eighteenth century to its present manifestations in queer theatre and literature. They also take a fascinating look at the complex relationship between queer discourse and decidedly un-queer pop culture appropriations on film and the stage.

The Politics and Poetics of Camp is an incisive, uncontainable and entertaining collection of essays by some of the foremost critics working in queer theory, from a number of disciplinary perspectives. This book makes a well-timed intervention into an emerging debate.

Moe Meyer is Mellon Fellow in Contemporary Arts Criticism at the California Institute of the Arts. Contributors include Gregory W. Bredbeck, Kate Davy, Thomas A. King, Margaret Thompson Drewal, Chuck Kleinhans and Cynthia Morrill.

THE POLITICS
AND
POETICS OF CAMP

Edited by Moe Meyer

London and New York

First published 1994
by Routledge
11 New Fetter Lane, London EC4P 4EE

Simultaneously published in the USA and Canada
by Routledge
29 West 35th Street, New York, NY 10001

© 1994 Moe Meyer

Typeset in Bembo by Witwell Ltd, Lord Street, Southport
Printed and bound in Great Britain by T.J. Press (Padstow) Ltd,
Padstow, Cornwall

British Library Cataloguing in Publication Data
A catalogue record for this book is available from the British Library
Library of Congress Cataloging in Publication Data
The politics and poetics of Camp / edited by Moe Meyer.
p.   cm.
Includes bibliographical references and index.
1.Homosexuality. 2. Homosexuality—United States. I. Meyer, Moe.
HQ76.25.P65   1994
305.9′0664—dc20   93–18913
ISBN 0–415–08247–1. — ISBN 0–415–08248–X (pbk)

It's embarrassing to be solemn and treatise-like about Camp. One runs the risk of having, oneself, produced a very inferior piece of Camp.

Susan Sontag, "Notes on Camp," 1964

CONTENTS

PLATES

CONTRIBUTORS

Gregory W. Bredbeck is Associate Professor of English at the University of California, Riverside. His most recent book is *Sodomy and Interpretation: Marlowe to Milton*. He is currently preparing a new book entitled *Stone/Wall: Representational Histories of Queer Identity*.

Kate Davy is Associate Professor of Drama and Women's Studies and Associate Dean of the School of Fine Arts at the University of California, Irvine. She is the author of *Richard Foreman and the Ontological-Hysteric Theatre* and editor of *Richard Foreman: Plays and Manifestos*. She is preparing a book about the artists affiliated with the WOW Cafe in New York.

Margaret Thompson Drewal is Associate Professor of Performance Studies at Northwestern University. She is co-author, with Henry John Drewal, of *Gelede: Art and Female Power among the Yoruba*, and the author of *Yoruba Ritual: Performers, Play, Agency* (Indiana University Press, 1992).

Thomas A. King is Assistant Professor of English at Brandeis University. He is preparing a book entitled *The Tactical Body: Staging Identity in London, 1660–1740*.

Chuck Kleinhans is Associate Professor of Radio, Television, Film at Northwestern University. He is editor of *Jump Cut*, journal of film theory and criticism, and is preparing a new book entitled *Mass Culture and Countercultures: The Dialectics of Media and Change*.

Moe Meyer is Mellon Fellow in Contemporary Arts Criticism at the California Institute of the Arts. He is preparing a book entitled *Oscar Wilde's Body: A Study in Containment and Camp*.

Cynthia Morrill is a graduate student in the Department of English, University of California, Riverside, where she is completing her dissertation, "The Performance of Queerness."

ACKNOWLEDGMENTS

I would like to thank especially Martin Worman and Thomas A. King for our many discussions of Camp that inspired this project. Special thanks to the Center for Interdisciplinary Research in the Arts (CIRA), Northwestern University, Evanston, Illinois, for sponsoring our Camp Theory Symposium, April 1992.

I thank the University of Michigan Press for permission to reprint Kate Davy's "Fe/male Impersonation: The Discourse of Camp," from Janelle G. Reinelt and Joseph R. Roach, eds, *Critical Theory and Performance* (1992).

I also thank the Athletic Model Guild for the generous permission to use Robert Mizer's "Curry and Rightmire" on the cover. As well, I thank the following for their permission to use the photographs in this collection (in order of appearance): Genyphyr Novak, Chicago; Special Collections Department, Northwestern University Library, Evanston, Illinois; National Portrait Gallery, London; Musée du Louvre, Paris; the Newberry Library, Chicago; Donna Ann McAdams, New York; John Stern, New York; Mark Avery, Milwaukee; and the Liberace Foundation for the Performing Arts, Los Angeles.

INTRODUCTION
Reclaiming the discourse of Camp
Moe Meyer

In the last decade, Camp, or queer parody, has become an activist strategy for organizations such as ACT UP and Queer Nation, as well as a focus in utopian movements like the Radical Faeries. As practiced by these contemporary groups, Camp is both political and critical. Defying existing interpretations that continue to define Camp as apolitical, aestheticized, and frivolous, the contributors to this volume, prompted by its recently foregrounded political usages, attempt a reappraisal of the phenomenon. These writers suggest that Camp is not simply a "style" or "sensibility" as is conventionally accepted. Rather, what emerges is a suppressed and denied oppositional critique embodied in the signifying practices that processually constitute queer identities. Accordingly, the contributors to this volume operate from shared beliefs concerning the construction of Camp. These are: Camp is political; Camp is solely a queer (and/or sometimes gay and lesbian) discourse; and Camp embodies a specifically queer cultural critique.[1] Additionally, because Camp is defined as a solely queer discourse, all un-queer activities that have been previously accepted as "camp," such as Pop culture expressions, have been redefined as examples of the appropriation of queer praxis. Because un-queer appropriations interpret Camp within the context of compulsory reproductive heterosexuality, they no longer qualify as Camp as it is defined here. In other words, the un-queer do not have access to the discourse of Camp, only to derivatives constructed through the act of appropriation.[2]

The use of the word "queer" to designate what is usually referred to as "gay and lesbian" marks a subtle, ongoing, and not yet stabilized renomination. It is used by some of the writers in this volume for various reasons. "Queer" does not indicate the biological sex or gender of the subject. More importantly, the term indicates an ontological challenge to dominant labeling philosophies, especially the

1

medicalization of the subject implied by the word "homosexual," as well as a challenge to discrete gender categories embedded in the divided phrase "gay and lesbian." Because Camp, as we are defining it in this volume, gains its political validity as an ontological critique, and because its reconceptualization was initiated by observations of queer activist practices, the term "queer" may be the best descriptor of this parodic operation.

The reappropriation of the once derogatory term "queer," and its contemporary use as an affirmative self-nominated identity label, is far from clear in its current applications. Two writers who have attempted to define this term, Teresa de Lauretis (iii–vi) and Simon Watney, both do so by juxtaposing it with and in opposition to the labels of "gay and lesbian." I think that this logic is inadequate to the task of clarifying the meaning of "queer". Watney, in particular, identifies the emergence of the label as a generational phenomenon, one used by younger gay men and lesbians to differentiate themselves from what appears to be the bourgeois assimilationism rampant among some segments of the gay and lesbian community and to signify that those who have come out in the era of AIDS are somehow different from those who have not. The flaws in this kind of argument should be apparent: first, it indicates that what is at stake is a critique of class, not of sex/gender; second, it conflates middle-class with middle-age and assumes a unified understanding of the terms gay and lesbian and a singular lifestyle on the part of those who have reached a certain age; and third, it reveals itself as based in the ageism that has been so detrimental within the gay community. If the term queer is indeed based within imagined generational difference, then I would suggest that it signifies nothing more than a potentially destructive, divisive, and ageist maneuver that, in the end, serves to interrupt the continuity of political struggle through an ahistoricizing turn. But once the uncritiqued ageism of current definitions has been revealed and discarded, what remains – the critique of class – is of definite value and can be used to formulate what might be at stake in both the terms "queer" and "Camp."

What I would offer as a definition of queer is one based on an alternative model of the constitution of subjectivity and of social identity. The emergence of the queer label as an oppositional critique of gay and lesbian middle-class assimilationism is, perhaps, its strongest and most valid aspect. In the sense that the queer label emerges as a class critique, then what is opposed are bourgeois models of identity. What "queer" signals is an ontological challenge that displaces bourgeois notions of the Self as unique, abiding, and continuous while substituting instead a concept of the Self as performative, improvisational, discontinuous, and processually constituted by repetitive and stylized acts. Rather than some new kind of subject constitution that emerges as the result of a generation-specific response to the AIDS crisis, queer identity is more accurately identified as the praxical response to the emergence of social constructionist (sex/gender as ideologically interpellated) models of identity and its, by now overly rehearsed, oppositional stance to essentialist (sexual orientation as innate) models, thus historically situating queer identity in an epistemological rift that predates the advent of AIDS.

Queerness can be seen as an oppositional stance not simply to essentialist formations of gay and lesbian identities, but to a much wider application of the depth model of identity which underwrites the epistemology deployed by the bourgeoisie in their ascendency to and maintenance of dominant power. As such, the queer label contains a critique of a more vast and comprehensive system of class-based practices of which sex/gender identity is only a part. The history of queer practices, as Thomas A. King charts in chapter one of this volume, is a critical maneuver not limited to sexualities, but is one that has valuable applications for marginal social identities in general. Broadening the scope of the queer critique in this manner also constitutes a radical challenge to the entire concept of an identity based upon sexual orientation or sexual desire because the substitution of a performative, discontinuous Self for one based upon the unique individual actually displaces and voids the concept of sexual orientation itself by removing the bourgeois epistemological frames that stabilize such identifications. Queer sexualities become, then, a series of improvised performances whose threat lies in the denial of any social identity derived from participation in those performances. As a refusal of sexually defined identity, this must also include the denial of the difference upon which such identities have been founded. And it is precisely in the space of this refusal, in the deconstruction of the homo/hetero binary, that the threat and challenge to bourgeois ideology is queerly executed.

As the rejection of a social identity based upon the differentiation of sexual practices, queer identity must be more correctly aligned with various gender, rather than sexual, identities because it is no longer based, and does not have to be, upon material sexual practice. Perhaps emerging as a response to certain unaccountable and uncontainable sexualities – such as celibate gay men and lesbians; heterosexuals who engage in same-sex sexual activity without taking on an identity based on that activity; or even closeted gays who maintain multiple, exclusive, and discrete social identities by switching back and forth between performative signifying codes – queer identity is not just another in an inventory of available sexual identities. Because sexual behavior is clearly not the determining factor in finalizing a self-nomination, even for conventional gays and lesbians, queerness contains the knowledge that social identities, including those of sex, but especially those of gender, are always accompanied by some sort of public signification in the form of specific enactments, embodiments, or speech acts which are nonsexual or, in the very least, extrasexual. Accordingly, Judith Butler has theorized that

> gender is in no way a stable identity or locus of agency from which various acts proceed; rather, it is an identity tenuously constituted in time – an identity instituted through a *stylized repetition of acts*. Further, gender is instituted through the stylization of the body and, hence, must be understood as the mundane way in which bodily gestures, movements, and enactments of various kinds constitute the illusion of an abiding gendered self.
> (270).

Butler's definition of gender can provide an explanation of queer identity that not only locates that identity within a performative nexus, but also solves the problems of identity formation involving celibate gay men, etc., listed above.

Because gender identity is instituted by repetitive acts, then queer performance is not expressive of the social identity but is, rather, the reverse – the identity is self-reflexively constituted by the performances themselves. Whether one subscribes to an essentialist or constructionist theory of gay and lesbian identity, it comes down to the fact that, at some time, the actor must *do* something in order to produce the social visibility by which the identity is manifested. Postures, gestures, costume and dress, and speech acts become the elements that constitute both the identity and the identity performance. When we shift the study of gay and lesbian identity into a performance paradigm, then every enactment of that identity depends, ultimately, upon extrasexual performative gestures. Even the act of "coming out," that is, the public proclamation of one's self-nomination as gay or lesbian, is constituted by an institutionalized speech act. I suggest that queer identity emerges as self-consciousness of one's gay and lesbian performativity sets in.

In the sense that queer identity is performative, it is by the deployment of specific signifying codes that social visibility is produced. Because the function of Camp, as I will argue, is the production of queer social visibility, then the relationship between Camp and queer identity can be posited. Thus I define Camp as the total body of performative practices and strategies used to enact a queer identity, with enactment defined as the production of social visibility. This expanded definition of Camp, one based on identity performance and not solely in some kind of unspecified cognitive identification of an ironic moment, may come as a bit of a jolt to many readers. It means that *all* queer identity performative expressions are circulated within the signifying system that is Camp. In other words, queer identity is inseparable and indistinguishable from its processual enactment, or Camp. The historical and material evidence demonstrates that this was clearly the case until Sontag's 1964 essay, "Notes On Camp," complicated the interpretations by detaching the signifying codes from their queer signified.

This definition of Camp can facilitate a rereading of Sontag and the subsequent appearance of Pop camp that emerged from her interpretation. By holding to a definition of Camp as the total body of queer identity performance practices, then, Sontag's essay does not signal the availability of Camp as an un-queer practice, nor does it signal the birth of multiple forms of Camp. Because the process of Camp has for its purpose the production of queer social visibility, the same performative gestures executed independently of queer self-reflexivity are unavoidably transformed and no longer qualify as Camp. Instead, what emerges from Sontag's essay is the birth of the camp trace, or residual camp, a strategy of un-queer appropriation of queer praxis whose purpose, as I will demonstrate, is the enfusement of the un-queer with the queer aura, acting to stabilize the ontological challenge of Camp through a dominant gesture of reincorporation. Thus there are not different kinds of Camp. There is only one. And it is queer. It can be engaged directly by the queer to produce social visibility in the praxis of everyday life, or it can be manifested as the camp trace by the un-queer in order, as I will argue, to provide queer access to the apparatus of representation.

THE PROBLEM WITH JOAN

There was a new presence in Chicago's last mayoral election. In April 1991, the race for city hall hosted an unexpected surprise in the figure of Joan Jett Blakk, the first official Queer Nation candidate for municipal office in the windy city (Plate 1).[3] Running a drag queen for the office of mayor did not set well with the powers that be. Despite the flurry of activity and grass-roots support, Ms. Blakk's campaign (her slogan was, among others, "putting the Camp into campaign") was ignored by the gay press even though she attracted enough attention to elevate her to international Superqueer status. Assimilationist gays – many in editorial positions – were especially dismayed by Blakk's campaign strategy, one based on the practice of Camp. Taken for granted to be apolitical, Camp was deemed flippant and demeaning as the foundation for a campaign. Many thought that Blakk needed to be silenced, that her Camp strategy was not serious work, and that the Queer Nation candidate would do damage to the gains made by so-called legitimate caucuses. To delineate a basic division in gay politics along the predictable lines of essentialist and constructionist philosophies does not explain the reactions, because the way that Blakk's campaign was evaluated by both of the opposing positions was through an interpretation of Camp. The role of Camp in the formation of these political factions superseded any allegiance to philosophical theories of identity in favor of more immediate issues of praxis, thus identifying this form of parody as a particularly cogent site for an emerging queer critical theory.

The Queer Nation campaign raised some interesting questions. First, if Camp is apolitical why was it appearing in an overtly political and activist situation? Second, if Camp, as generally defined, is merely an aestheticized sensibility characterized by triviality and lack of content, or simply an operation of taste, then why did it so clearly divide gay political opinion, and in such a strongly articulated way? Clearly there was a conflict. And this conflict was between two constructions of Camp. Joan's actions, identified as Camp by all parties, were being interpreted quite differently depending on whether one believed that Camp is political or apolitical.

Are we talking then about the possibility of multiple forms of Camp? The answer is no. In the case of Joan Jett Blakk, each party to the debate identified precisely the same actions as Camp. There was no deviation in formal recognition. Thus the differences of interpretation could be attributed only to variable analyses of content. But this leads to an even more provocative situation. That is, Camp has often been defined as a sensibility devoid of content. The mainstream gay politicos used that definition as the justification for silencing Blakk. In other words, what we heard was the familiar discreditation of Camp using the claim that it has no content. But this was a claim advanced through an analysis *of* the content that isn't supposed to exist.

When Joan decided her primary campaign strategy would be publicized and highly theatrical shopping sprees in the glamor fashion stores of Chicago's wealthy Gold Coast district, everyone recognized the actions as Camp. So the issue was not whether Camp was political, but whether it was appropriate or effective to politic*ize* it. Since the 1980s, when ACT UP consciously and successfully brought Camp to bear on activist politics in its graphics, or now when Queer Nation bases its demonstrations on expressions of Camp executed through street theatre, there has been the need to reevaluate gay and queer parody. What I will advance in this Introduction is a reconceptualization of Camp prompted by its recent political applications.

PROCESSING THE NOTES

In 1964 Camp was propelled into public consciousness via Susan Sontag's now famous essay, "Notes on Camp." With its homosexual connotations downplayed, sanitized, and made safe for public consumption, Sontag's version of Camp was extolled, emulated, and elaborated upon in a flurry of writing on the subject that lasted until the end of the decade. Though the erasure of homosexuality from the subject of Camp encouraged the public's embrace, it also had a mutational consequence. Earlier versions of Camp were part of an unmistakable homosexual discourse bound together by a shared referent (the "Homosexual"-as-Type). By removing, or at least minimizing, the connotations of homosexuality, Sontag killed off the binding referent of Camp – the Homosexual – and the discourse began to unravel as Camp became confused and conflated with rhetorical and performative strategies such as irony, satire, burlesque, and travesty; and with cultural movements such as Pop.

The adoption, in the 1960s, of the term "Camp" to describe so many diverse strategies produced the impression that there were many different kinds of Camp. This unquestioning attitude toward the existence of multiple forms of Camp has provided writers with access to a successful evasive tactic. By conceptualizing Camp as simply a common nomination shared by unrelated cultural phenomena, writers have been spared the task of studying relationships among the total range of expressions that have been labeled as "Camp," or even of defining the object of study. Jonathan Dollimore, for example, writing on Camp in 1990, claims that "The definition of camp is as elusive as the sensibility itself, one reason being that there are different kinds of camp" (310). Dollimore then proceeds with a partial interpretation of Camp justified by the claim that there is simply a surplus of significa- tion.[4] This has been a familiar tactic, one used to support vastly different, often contradictory, interpretations of Camp. While writers on Pop culture simply deny Camp as a homosexual discourse, finding such a construction contradictory to their arguments, gay writers seeking to reclaim the discourse of Camp through a restoration of its homosexual connotations fail to address issues of nongay and Pop culture appropriation.[5] These partial interpretations of Camp derive their authority from Sontag's essay. After all, according to Sontag, Camp is a sensibility and "A sensibility (as distinct from an idea) is one of the hardest things to talk about" (106). She adds that sensibility or taste

> has no system and no proofs. . . . A sensibility is almost, but not quite, ineffable. Any sensibility which can be crammed into the mold of a system, or handled with the rough tools of proof, is no longer a sensibility at all. It has hardened into an idea.
>
> (106).

As long as thinkers, whether gay or nongay, cling to this definition of Camp-as-sensibility, they are invulnerable to critique, forever pro- tected by invoking Sontag's own critical exemption.

In a recent essay, Gregory Bredbeck has tried to dismantle Sontag's defense system by pointing out the evasive strategy employed by defining Camp as a sensibility: "a 'sensibility,' like that Regency term . . . is something understood perfectly until articulated. Sontag's essay demonstrates this slipperiness through its recourse to the most basic theoretical strategy derived from Aristotle, division and classification" (275). The promulgation of various kinds of Camp, argues Bredbeck, effects Camp's transformation into "the nominalists' *flatus vocus*, an empty universal term. It functions as all parts of speech, all parts of a sentence: verb, noun, adjective, adverb; subject, object, modifier" (276), able to become whatever one needs it to be for purposes of argument while simultaneously claiming exemption from criticism. Bredbeck suggests that "A more productive theorization might start by looking not at what the word means, but how it functions . . . [as a] sign" (275).

In order to produce a new reading of Camp, one that can account for its recent politicization, we need to jettison objectivist methodologies. Objectivism, as I am using it here, refers to an empiricist route to knowledge that "posits a real world which is independent of consciousness and theory, and which is accessible through sense-experience" (Lovell 10). This real world can be "discovered" by a knowing subject who is the "source of the sense data which validates knowledge" (Lovell 11). An objectivist methodology becomes extremely problematic in theories of social behavior where the human subjects of study are unavoidably transformed into "objects" of knowledge that are used to generate sense-experience for the observer. As a result, human actors are reduced to "thinglike" status as their own knowledge and experience become rendered as a structure of neutral surfaces readable only by the observer. As a mode for interpretation of queer cultural expressions, the one-way dynamic of objectivism most often results in the erasure of gay and lesbian subjects through an antidialogic turn that fails to acknowledge a possibly different ontology embodied in queer signifying practices. Instead, we need to develop a performance-centered methodology that takes into account and can accommodate the particular experience of the individual social actors under study, one which privileges process, the agency of knowledgeable performers, and the constructed nature of human realities. This approach provides a space for individual authority and experience that, regardless of different perceptions of sexual identity, envisions a power – albeit decentered – that is able to resist, oppose, and subvert. Working with a theory of agency and performance, I will attempt the sacrilegious: to produce a definition of Camp. Such a definition should be stable enough to be of benefit to the reader, yet flexible enough to account for the many actions and objects that have come to be described by the term. Following Bredbeck's cue (that it would be more productive to approach the project through a study of the workings of the Camp sign), I will suggest a definition of Camp based upon the delineation of a praxis formed at the intersection of social agency and postmodern parody.

Broadly defined, Camp refers to strategies and tactics of queer parody. The definition of parody I use is that of Linda Hutcheon. Her postmodern redefinition of parody differs sharply from conventional usages that conflate parody with irony or satire. Rather, as elaborated by Hutcheon, parody is an intertextual manipulation of multiple conventions, "an extended repetition with critical difference" (7) that "has a hermeneutic function with both cultural and even ideological implications" (2). Hutcheon explains that "Parody's overt turning to other art forms" (5), its derivative nature, and its dependence upon an already existing text in order to fulfill itself are the reason for its

9

traditional denigration, a denigration articulated within a dominant discourse that finds value only in an "original." Hutcheon clears a space for a reconsideration of parody through its very contestation of ideas of Romantic singularity because it "forces a reassessment of the process of textual production" (5). At the same time, her redefinition provides the opportunity for a reassessment of Camp, when Camp is conceptualized as parody. Hutcheon's theory of parody is valuable for providing the terms needed to differentiate Camp from satire, irony, and travesty; and to terminate, finally, the conflation of Camp with kitsch and schlock, a confusion that entered the discourse as a result of the heterosexual/Pop colonization of Camp in the 1960s. When subjected to Hutcheon's postmodern redefinition, Camp emerges as specifically queer parody possessing cultural and ideological analytic potential, taking on new meanings with implications for the emergence of a theory that can provide an oppositional queer critique.

While Hutcheon's theory is capable of locating the address of a queer parodic praxis, it still needs to be queerly adjusted in order to plumb its potential for a Camp theory. By employing a performance-oriented methodology that privileges process, we can restore a knowledgeable *queer* social agent to the discourse of Camp parody. While dominant discursive formations of Camp maintain a social agent, that agent is implied, and thus taken for granted to be heterosexual. Camp theorizing has languished since the 1960s when Sontag's appropriation banished the queer from the discourse, substituting instead an un-queer bourgeois subject under the banner of Pop. It is this changeling that transformed Camp into the apolitical badge of the consumer whose status-quo "sensibility" is characterized by the depoliticizing Midas touch, and whose control over the apparatus of representation casts the cloak of invisibility over the queer at the moment it appropriates and utters the C-word. Yet, in order to reclaim Camp-as-critique, the critique silenced in the 1960s, which finds its voice solely when spoken by the queer, we cannot reverse the process of banishment by ejecting the un-queer from the discourse. That kind of power does not belong to the queer. All we can do, perhaps, is to produce intermittent queer visibility in our exile at the margins long enough to reveal a terminus at the end of a pathway of dominant power with the goal of foregrounding the radical politic of parodic intertextuality.

When parody is seen as process, not as form, then the relationship between texts becomes simply an indicator of the power relationships between social agents who wield those texts, one who possesses the "original," the other who possesses the parodic alternative. Anthony

Giddens has argued that structures of signification can only be understood in relation to power and domination. In fact, he defines power and domination as the ability to produce codes of signification (31). Accordingly, value production is the prerogative of the dominant order, dominant precisely because it controls signification and which is represented by the privilege of nominating its own codes as the "original." The "original," then, is the signifier of dominant presence and, because dominance can be defined as such only by exercising control over signification, it is only through the "original" that we can know and touch that power. In that case, parody becomes the process whereby the marginalized and disenfranchised advance their own interests by entering alternative signifying codes into discourse by attaching them to existing structures of signification. Without the process of parody, the marginalized agent has no access to representation, the apparatus of which is controlled by the dominant order (Case 9). Camp, as specifically queer parody, becomes, then, the only process by which the queer is able to enter representation and to produce social visibility.[6]

This piggy-backing upon the dominant order's monopoly on the authority of signification explains why Camp appears, on the one hand, to offer a transgressive vehicle yet, on the other, simultaneously invokes the specter of dominant ideology within its practice, appearing, in many instances, to actually reinforce the dominant order. Gregg Blachford has reminded us that

> the processes at work in the sub-culture are more complicated than might appear at first glance, for there is some evidence that the gay sub-culture negotiates an oppositional challenge to some aspects of the dominant order. The best way to understand this innovatory style is to examine one phenomenon of the gay sub-culture – camp – and to show how it transforms conformity into a challenge.
>
> (193–194).

My goal in the remainder of this Introduction is to explore that Camp challenge, and to investigate precisely the relationship of Camp praxis to the dominant order.

THE QUEER AS HISTORICAL WASTE

The queer's invisibility in representation and his/her dependence upon dominant structures of signification are not so much a negative

11

condition to be overcome, but rather, the very strength to exploit. Michel Foucault, in pointing out that power is not monolithic, but multidimensional, argues that

> there are no relations of power without resistances; the latter are all the more real and effective because they are formed right at the point where relations of power are exercised; resistance to power does not have to come from elsewhere to be real, nor is it inexorably frustrated through being the compatriot of power. It exists all the more by being in the same place as power.
>
> (142)

Working from this premise in order to advance a proposal of Camp-as-critique, I want to explore how this can be deployed to reread the literature on Camp and to explain the role of queer visibility production in subversive transformations of dominant culture.

Terry Lovell has pointed out that

> there are key areas of experience and practical activity which are suppressed, denied, and distorted within dominant ideology. While their suppression makes it difficult to give them a name, and to understand their significance, they are essential to knowledge production and to the critique of ideology.
>
> (50)

The invisible queer subject is an example of such a suppressed and denied area. This suppression and denial are founded on the distortion and discreditation of the language of that subject, the language that carries an oppositional critique and the means by which the subject may be constituted. This discredited language is what I identify as Camp. Often considered frivolous, aestheticized, and apolitical, the discourse of Camp can be reclaimed through a rereading of the phenomenon as a signifying practice that not only processually constitutes the subject, but is actually the vehicle for an already existent – though obscured – cultural critique.

The first move in uncovering and revealing the queer is the removal of the objectivist bias from interpretations of Camp. Sontag and her imitators are quick to define Camp as an attribute of objects. Even when Camp is applied as a description to the actions of persons, that person is described as *a* camp. This objectivist bias that reduces people to thinglike status is used to label Camp as extreme aestheticization and therefore apolitical. The arguments that defuse Camp, that deny it power as a cultural critique, are based, then, on a denial of agency. Yet Sontag herself cannot entirely escape from the human activity that forms the basis of Camp. After giving the reader a list of objects that are considered "Camp," she reminds us that "the Camp eye has the power to transform experience" (107). Therefore Camp cannot be said to reside in objects, but is clearly a way of reading, of writing, and of doing that originates in the "Camp eye," the "eye" being nothing less than the agent of Camp. By this I do not mean to deny the existence of the object of Camp. Instead, by applying a performance paradigm to the study, the visible lines of a ghostlike queer agent manifest themselves in a shift of focus away from the conventional fixation with the object surface to the process with which the object is handled. When a concept of performance is used to establish the existence of a knowledgeable social agent who signifies *through* Camp, then the conventional interpretation of Camp – as a tool used to facilitate the bourgeois appropriation characteristic of consumer culture – can be overturned.

Andrew Ross's extremely influential essay, "Uses of Camp" (1989), is a noteworthy example of the dehumanizing results achieved by applying an objectivist methodology to the study of Camp.[7] Ross brilliantly described the techniques and motives of appropriation that underlie the formation of Pop camp. But when we cease to define queer Camp and Pop camp as two different kinds of Camp, seeing instead two halves of a single phenomenon, then Ross's essay is helpful in explaining the relationship of queer signifying practices to the dominant order. Because objectivist methodologies overwhelm and obscure the processual signifying practices through which the queer articulates the discourse of Camp, the queer is erased in representation at the very moment that Camp is subjected to a dominant interpretation. Pop camp emerges, then, as the product of a visually biased dominant reading of queer praxis interpreted through the object residue that remains after the queer agent has been rendered invisible. Consequently, the bourgeois subject of Pop camp must assume a queer position in order to account for these dispossessed objects and becomes, in fact, queer himself. As I will explain, Pop camp becomes the unwitting vehicle of a subversive operation that introduces queer signifying codes into dominant discourse.

Ross defines the camp effect as created "when the products . . . of a much earlier mode of production, which has lost its power to dominate cultural meanings, become available in the present, for redefinition according to contemporary codes of taste" (139). Subjecting his definition to a theory of queer agency (entailing a focal shift away from the object) reveals a much different narrative. Remembering that Anthony Giddens has defined dominance as the power to control the construction of cultural meanings, then what Ross calls a "mode of production" is actually a mode of *discursive value* production, not *industrial object* production. Accordingly, what he calls "contemporary codes of taste" is nothing less than the dominant ideology that controls the establishment of signifying codes. When Camp is defined as a specifically queer discourse, it follows that what Ross calls the redefinition of meanings is the appropriation, through the application of unequal power, of queer discourse by the dominant order. This appropriation attempts to defuse the Camp critique by redefining the actions of the queer within the nonthreatening context of compulsory reproductive heterosexuality which, because the representational apparatus cannot render a queer subject, constitutes, simply, its erasure. Because the queer has been, as Cynthia Morrill describes, "hurled out of representation" at the impacting moment of appropriation, all that remains is the object of camp which now appears, illusorily, as a fossilized remnant. It is never suspected that the act of appropriation itself has killed off the queer. In order to account for the absence, the conclusion is that the previous owner of the object must long since have passed away. Without a voice to claim possession of the object, the social knowledge of the queer can be ignored because s/he has been relocated to the mists of the bygone past. The perceived threat to dominant ideology by the queer's sexual *non*productivity is then silenced through benign renomination as a *discontinued* productivity. Located in the past, the queer has been assigned to the site of the grave, of death, of nonexistence, of nonpresence, and no longer needs to be taken into account.

Ross's unreflecting use of interpretive codes, by regarding them as simple acts of perception (the trademark of the visual bias of objectivism), masks and obscures the source of value production (Shapiro 5–30). Relocating the queer to a past era by defining him/her as a discontinued mode of production is not the neutral act of identification it is made out to be. Rather, it is a dominant performative gesture of incorporation meant to muzzle an opposing voice by substituting the act of appropriation itself as the referent of camp. Because the act of appropriation includes the erasure of the queer, dominant (read Pop) formations of camp translate this activity into a recognition that Camp *was once* a homosexual discourse, but now refers, more correctly, to the redistribution of objects plundered

14

from the "dead" queer's estate. This technique has been called "the spatialization of time" by Johannes Fabian (25–35). Fabian explained how unequal contemporaneous power relationships between Self and Other become translated into temporal distance by conflating and then substituting the oppositional terms of "now/then" for the directional binary concept of "here/there" (27, 37–69). The "here" and "now" that signifies the praxis of everyday life is replaced by the "there" and "then" signification of the not really real, a substitution of terms that results in a denial of coevalness, or the state of "being-with" the Other (Berger and Luckman 22). Situating the queer's signifying practices in the historical past creates the impression that the objects of camp no longer have owners and are up for grabs. This metaphorical manipulation forms the basis for and justification of heterosexual/Pop colonization of queer discourse and praxis. Thus instead of the harmless reassignment of values to junk store items that Pop theorists have convinced themselves is "camp," the actual maneuver conceals a contemporaneous struggle over meanings and value production by competing discourses.

Importantly, Ross does identify a knowledgeable social agent in his formation of camp. This un-queer agent has some remarkable traits. As he describes: "Camp . . . involves a celebration, on the part of cognoscenti, of the alienation, distance, and incongruity reflected in the very process by which unexpected value can be located in some obscure or exorbitant object" (146). Because the queer is rendered invisible at the moment when values are reassigned in the act of appropriation, it looks as if the objects of Camp have suddenly materialized from nowhere (which is precisely where the queer lives), appearing miraculously as an act of discovery. As if receiving manna in the wilderness, the act of appropriation is perceived as mysterious intervention, a sign of manifest destiny that reinforces the moral authority of the dominant order. Having received the divine dispensation, the bourgeois subject of camp *celebrates* the invisibility of the queer, rejoices in the act of appropriation, and, in effect, derives *pleasure* from the erasure of the queer. Ross indicates that the pleasure derived from the act of appropriation stems from the altogether accidental and "unexpected" quality of the exchange, as if to claim a protected space of moral innocence in the silencing of the queer.

However, the celebratory lynching of the queer cannot take place without knowledge. One does not become a "cognoscente" through celebrating random and "unexpected value." On the contrary, the connoisseur is, by definition, an expert in *establishing* value, not

15

discovering it. The cognoscente is an authority not to be questioned. His is the voice that nominates "the original," who manifests the presence of the dominant order, controls the apparatus of representation by speaking a signifying code into existence, and plays the role of ideological logos (Price 7–22; King in this volume). But then you cannot lynch the "dead," and the appropriation is, of course, benign. Nobody is being hurt. Thus the act of queer erasure becomes a valorized salvage effort on the part of the cognoscente appropriator whom Ross then describes as a "camp liberator," who rediscovers "history's waste [read 'the queer']," a kind of nineteenth-century archaeologist who, by "liberating the objects and discourses of the past from disdain and neglect [read 'by appropriating queer signifying practices']," enfuses himself with "glamor [read 'queer aura']" (151). The whole operation becomes a bizarre love affair with the dead queer who, safely contained within the coffin of a distancing metaphorical historicization, can now be loved and cherished as the source of dominant cultural renewal. The act of appropriation is, after all, a source of pleasure, and Ross describes the activity as a "necrophilic economy that underpins the camp sensibility" (152).

But curiously, Ross goes on to say that

> If the pleasure generated by [camp's] bad taste presents a challenge to the mechanisms of control and containment that operate in the name of good taste, it is often to be enjoyed *only* at the expense of others, and this is largely because camp's excess of pleasure has very little, finally, to do with the (un)controlled hedonism of the consumer; it is the result of the (hard) *work* of a producer of taste, and "taste" is only possible through exclusion *and* depreciation.
>
> (153)

This is a confusing statement. On the one hand, he locates the pleasure of Camp in an act of challenge to the dominant order yet, on the other, this challenge is the result of the hard labor on the part of the producer of taste, the cognoscente, who operates through exclusion. But it is the cognoscente who represents, reinforces, and speaks from the site of power. The production of taste is not a challenge to the dominant order, it *is* the dominant order. Ross's glamorous producer of taste has somehow become both challenger *and* challenged. Without queer visibility, Ross's bourgeois "camp liberator" has not only assumed the role of dominance, but has also assumed the queer subject position which, through the act of appropriation, appears now as vacant property that can be restored to circulation within the economy of properly authorized signification. Ross is correct. This is hard work. And it does operate by exclusion. The bourgeois camp cognoscente "liberates" the queer's oppositional signifying practices from their queer identity and substitutes himself as signified. But because the queer constitutes him-/herself processually, the un-queer is now unwittingly performing the queer. The final effect is the reproduction of the queer's aura by the un-queer camp liberator who has been transformed into a drag queen with no other choice but to lipsynch the discourse of the Other. While Ross's camp cognoscente has successfully appropriated the signifying surface, the lyrics were still written by the queer who has now entered representation by producing his/her visibility on the back of the un-queer bourgeois subject. It may be the bourgeois subject who sings the aria but, like the terrifying phantom of the opera, it is the queer who taught her how, and who still plays the "organ" accompaniment behind the wall of enforced invisibility in the sewer system of "history's waste."

By providing a detailed description of the actions and motives of the un-queer appropriator, Ross has located a position to which the queer agent can read him-/herself back into the discourse by establishing a dialogic relationship. This can be achieved by identifying the social knowledge displayed by Camp agency. As Ross describes: "Pop experience already contains the knowledge that it will soon be outdated, spent, obsolescent, or out of fashion" (151). In other words, the power of Camp lies in its ability to be conscious of its future as an appropriated commodity. Possession of social knowledge is not dependent on access to the apparatus of representation. It is the arrogance of the dominant, derived from ownership of the apparatus of representation, that creates a belief in a monologic construction of social knowledge. When we recognize that the queer is not dead, only rendered invisible by a historicizing metaphor, then we can grant the queer agent the same knowledge as the un-queer appropriator. Operating from under the cloak of invisibility, the queer knows his/her signifying practices will be, *must* be appropriated. As a product of queer agency, it is the process of Camp that selects and chooses which aspects of itself will be subsumed into dominant culture. Queer knowledge can then be introduced and incorporated into the dominant ideology because the blind spot of bourgeois culture is predictable: it *always* appropriates. And it appropriates whatever the agent of Camp chooses to place in its path. The invisible queer is at a certain advantage, because whatever is offered to the un-queer will be unquestioningly received as their own invention, taken as a confirmative sign of their right to possess. Like the little cakes that miraculously appeared to Alice in Lewis Carroll's Wonderland epic, it never occurs to the appropriator to ask who was it that wrote the little tag that says, "Eat Me." And like Alice, the appropriator's body uncontrollably changes its shape at the whim of those unseen hands that place irresistible morsels of discovery before it. By inverting the process of appropriation, Camp can be read as a critique of ideology through a parody that is always already appropriated.

*

The first three essays in this volume explore the discursive formation of Camp before 1900. In "Performing 'Akimbo': Queer Pride and Epistemological Prejudice," Thomas A. King analyzes the gestural codes of the upper classes and the derogatory representations of those codes by the mercantile classes, showing how those same bourgeois interpretations were transferred to the newly visible homosexual subcultures of late-seventeenth- and early-eighteenth-century London. The antagonism of the mercantile classes toward aristocratic strategies for conspicuously displaying the surfaces of their bodies was repeated in their criticism of the constitution of male homosexual subjectivity. King locates this transference as central to the development of the modernist depth model of identity in which the surfaces of the body were interpreted as signifying a consistent and essential subject. Sontag has posited that Camp emphasizes style and surface and slights content, therefore constituting an apolitical action (107). But King sees proto-camp homosexual enactments of frivolity as the embodiment of an alternative politics and an oppositional critique of bourgeois essentialism that offered resistance to the rise of middle-class morality and its new dominant order.

In "Narcissus in the Wilde: Textual Cathexis and the Historical Origins of Queer Camp," Gregory W. Bredbeck explores the political critique offered by Camp textual strategies in an analysis of the works of Oscar Wilde. Bredbeck observes that Wilde's narcissistic collapse of subject and object, in order to effect a play of surfaces, offers a strategy of resistance to the dominant order's heterosexual imperative by displaying hierarchies of value. In this regard, Bredbeck's analysis of Wilde agrees with King's examination of the homosexual gestuary, that is, that the surfaces can be worked as an oppositional politic. Yet, at the same time, Wilde's strategy encodes an alternative. Rather than a substitution of terms of dominance, Wilde's strategy involves the *un*writing of the ontological base of dominance (the heterosexual imperative) by refusing to re-script *any* base as dominant. Camp, then, is a strategy that marks ontology as a cultural process subject to intervention.

In my essay, "Under the Sign of Wilde: An Archaeology of Posing," I have attempted to interweave the textual and gestural strategies of the politics of surfaces analyzed by King and Bredbeck in order to locate a Camp genesis that spirals out from the life and works of Wilde. I maintain that the collapse of subject and object that produces a sign played out solely on the surfaces constituted an act of serious transgression against the depth model of identity and the reification of bourgeois dominance. I see Camp as inseparable from the constitution of a homosexual social identity, and argue that both appeared simultaneously as the result of Wilde's juridico-legal inscription in his 1895 trials. Accordingly, both Camp and the homosexual social identity were the result of the attempt to contain the transgression and threat of Wilde's oppositional political deployment of surfaces.

The four essays that follow deal with issues of contemporary queer Camp and its un-queer appropriations. Drawing upon recent Queer Theory and antecedent poststructuralist and psychoanalytic notions about subjectivity, language, desire, and humor, Cynthia Morrill politicizes Camp as the queer subject's affective discursive response to the perils of compulsory reproductive heterosexuality in her essay, "Revamping the Gay Sensibility: Queer Camp and *Dyke Noir*." In short, Morrill sees Camp as an effect of homophobia. Camp disrupts the dominant order by serving as a marker for the queer subject's uncanny experience of the impossibility of representing his/her desire within the parameters of the essentialized ontology of the un-queer. In order to examine the political dimension of Camp discourse, Morrill turns to an analysis of Sarah Schulman's dyke noir novel *After Delores*, and discusses the particular relationship between Camp and Freud's concept of gallows humor.

Kate Davy's "Fe/male Impersonation: The Discourse of Camp" examines Camp as it is strategically deployed in lesbian theatre produced at the WOW Cafe in New York City. Davy discusses the value of Camp as a strategy for constructing a lesbian spectatorial community in which heterosexuality is dropped from the performative address in order to bypass the erasure of the lesbian in hegemonic representations. Davy's essay investigates the subversive potential of cross-dressing for gay male theatre as it is embedded in the discourse of Camp, and delineates the dangers of the discourse for articulating a feminist subject position vis-à-vis the dynamics of butch–femme gender play in lesbian theatre in relationship to the issue of queer invisibility in representation.

The issue of the camp trace is explored by Margaret Thompson Drewal in "The Camp Trace in Corporate America: Liberace and the Rockettes at Radio City Music Hall." Drewal analyzes what happens to representation when an un-queer signified is attached to a queer signifier in the act of appropriation. In an alternative reading of Liberace, Drewal demonstrates the subtle subversions of which the invisible queer is capable when s/he floods the dominant discourse with camp residues and traces. As Bredbeck identified, the Camp alternative is the erosion of the hierarchy upon which the dominant order bases its power. In that regard, Drewal shows how Liberace, through the camp trace, put dominant codes to work in the service of the queer by harnessing the dominant order itself to do the work of dismantling its own hierarchy of values.

The issue of appropriation is again taken up by Chuck Kleinhans in "Taking Out the Trash: Camp and the Politics of Parody." Through comparative readings of kitsch, trash, and camp films, Kleinhans looks at the ways queer discourse has infiltrated contemporary art production by providing lures for the un-queer spectator to assume queer spectating positions, as well as providing clever spaces for the accommodation of subtextual gay readers. Kleinhans's view of Camp borders on the utopian because of the promise it holds for effecting change and transformation in the dominant discourse. Yet, his is an almost eco-Camp in that the alternative that the queer proposes to consumer culture is a vast representational recycling program. According to Kleinhans, this recycling of representation constitutes the radical politics of Camp: if you cannot invent the game, then you can certainly reshuffle the deck.

NOTES

I wish to thank Terry Kapsalis, Northwestern University, for her many comments on and criticisms of this essay.

1 The writers in this volume alternatively use the terms "queer," "gay," "lesbian," or "homosexual" depending on historical and cultural context, or to achieve particular effects and focus within an individual essay. Some of the examples of Camp discussed are problematic as regards the selection of appropriate labels. For instance, Liberace who, according to the working definition given in this Introduction, might be considered a quintessential queer because of the performative constitution of his identity, has been

described both as "homosexual" and more often as "gay" because of the social contexts in which he worked.

2 In order to distinguish between different constructions of Camp, the following usage has been adopted. When Camp is conceptualized as a politicized, solely queer discourse, an upper-case "C" is used. When an un-queer, apolitical, or Pop culture version of Camp is referred to, a lower-case "c" is used. The only exception to this occurs in cited material where it was mandatory to follow the spelling of the original text. For example, Susan Sontag, in "Notes on Camp," used an upper case "C." But according to the rule of usage employed in this volume, Sontag's version of Camp, because it is an apolitical formation, would be spelt as "camp."

3 My rethinking of Camp was based on observations of Joan Jett Blakk's Chicago mayoral campaign in 1991, before Joan announced her candidacy for the United States presidential election in 1992. My interpretations of the two campaigns are different. Comments about the mayoral campaign do not necessarily reflect my thinking on the presidential campaign.

4 I have cited Jonathan Dollimore in this regard because he is exemplary of the most contemporary writing on Camp.

5 Writers ignore issues of appropriation in different ways. George Melly recognizes the gay origins of Camp, but fails to question just how Pop culture was able to wrest the discourse from this context (161). Andrew Ross's conspicuous erasure of gay identity in his essay, "Uses of Camp," constitutes an active depoliticization of Camp that leads to an articulated denial of Camp as a gay critique (137, 142–144, 162–163). Richard Dyer, on the other hand, identifies Camp as a gay discourse, but then proceeds to define the performances of nongay stars as "Camp." Dyer offers a detailed analysis of Judy Garland as Camp (178ff.), but without addressing the problem of her nongay sexual identity, and without a political analysis of the relationship between gay discourse and nongay producers of Camp.

6 It is not my goal, here, to explain the invisibility of the queer in representation. This has been done admirably in two other essays, Sue-Ellen Case's "Tracking the Vampire," and Cynthia Morrill's "Revamping the Gay Sensibility" (elsewhere in this volume).

7 I use Andrew Ross's essay as the basis for a critique of Pop appropriation of Camp precisely because it has had such a major impact upon Camp theorizing. After Sontag's "Notes," Ross's "Uses of Camp," in my opinion, stands as one of the most significant contemporary documents on the subject. In the current trend to reread Sontag, Ross's essay has been overlooked. Yet, if we are to recover the discourse of Camp from the Sontagian formulation, Ross's essay, grounded as it is on that earlier work, must be included in the ongoing critique of "Notes."

BIBLIOGRAPHY

Berger, Peter L. and Thomas Luckmann. 1966. *The Social Construction of Reality: A Treatise in the Sociology of Knowledge.* New York: Doubleday.
Blachford, Gregg. 1981. "Male Dominance and the Gay World." In Kenneth

Plummer (ed.). *The Making of the Modern Homosexual*. London: Hutchinson, 184–210.

Bredbeck, Gregory W. 1993. "B/O – Barthes's Text/O'Hara's Trick: The Phallus, the Anus, and the Text." *PMLA*.108/2 (March): 268–282.

Butler, Judith. 1990. "Performative Acts and Gender Constitution: An Essay in Phenomenology and Feminist Theory." In Sue-Ellen Case (ed.). *Performing Feminisms: Feminist Critical Theory and Theatre*. Baltimore: Johns Hopkins University Press, 270–282.

Case, Sue-Ellen. 1991. "Tracking the Vampire." *Differences* 3/2: 1–20.

De Lauretis, Teresa. 1991. "Queer Theory: Lesbian and Gay Sexualities/An Introduction." *Differences* 3/2: iii–xvii.

Dollimore, Jonathan. 1991. *Sexual Dissidence: Augustine to Wilde, Freud to Foucault*. Oxford: Clarendon Press.

Dyer, Richard. 1981. "Getting Over the Rainbow: Identity and Pleasure in Gay Cultural Politics." In George Bridges and Rosalind Brunt (eds). *Silver Linings: Some Strategies for the Eighties*. London: Lawrence and Wishart, 53–67.

Giddens, Anthony. 1984. *The Constitution of Society: Outline of the Theory of Structuration*. Berkeley: University of California Press.

Fabian, Johannes. 1983. *Time and the Other: How Anthropology Makes Its Object*. New York: Columbia University Press.

Foucault, Michel. 1980. "Power and Strategies." *Power/Knowledge: Selected Interviews and Other Writings, 1972–1977*. Ed. Colin Gordon. New York: Pantheon, 134–145.

Hutcheon, Linda. 1985. *A Theory of Parody: The Teachings of Twentieth-Century Art Forms*. New York: Methuen.

Lovell, Terry. 1983. *Pictures of Reality: Aesthetics, Politics and Pleasure*. London: British Film Institute.

Melly, George. 1970. *Revolt into Style: The Pop Arts in Britain*. London: Allen Lane.

Price, Sally. 1989. *Primitive Art in Civilized Places*. Chicago: University of Chicago Press.

Ross, Andrew. 1989. "Uses of Camp." *No Respect: Intellectuals and Popular Culture*. London: Routledge, 135–170.

Shapiro, Michael J. 1988. *The Politics of Representation: Writing Practices in Biography, Photography, and Policy Analysis*. Madison: University of Wisconsin Press.

Sontag, Susan. 1964. "Notes on Camp." 1983. *A Susan Sontag Reader*. New York: Vintage Books, 105–119.

Watney, Simon. 1991. "Troubleshooters: Simon Watney on Outing." *Artforum* 30/3: 16–18.

1

PERFORMING "AKIMBO"
Queer pride and epistemological prejudice
Thomas A. King

Aristocracy is a position vis-à-vis culture (as well as vis-à-vis power), and the history of Camp taste is part of the history of snob taste. But since no authentic aristocrats in the old sense exist today to sponsor special tastes, who is the bearer of taste? Answer: an improvised self-elected class, mainly homosexuals, who constitute themselves as aristocrats of taste.

. . . the soundest starting point seems to be the late seventeenth and early eighteenth century, because of that period's extraordinary feeling for artifice, for surface, for symmetry . . .

Susan Sontag (117, 109)

I begin with Susan Sontag's 1964 essay "Notes on Camp," not because Sontag's influential description of Camp as apolitical has not already been sufficiently criticized as inadequate, but because I want to play out the epistemological prejudices upon which her notes depend.[1] In this essay, I situate the development of modern male homosexual identity within early modern debates about the nature of self and the validity of the visual as the basis of knowledge about identity. Sontag placed the origin of Camp in late-seventeenth- and early-eighteenth-century Europe. I will attempt to show, in the case of England, why this might be so. During this period, a model of the self as unique and continuous in the identity of its actions across time and space displaced earlier notions of the self as performative, improvisational, and discontinuous. Residual elements of this performative self were transcoded as markers of homosexuality, making them available for appropriation by an early homosexual subculture like the mollies, which became visible in London around 1700. Sontag took for granted the eighteenth century's polarization of surface and content, artifice and nature, frivolity and sincerity. Her description of the basic Camp maneuver as the blocking out or emptying a thing of its content (110) depends on a differentiation of surface and depth that was subject to a great deal of hostile interrogation in the seventeenth and eighteenth centuries. The proto-camp gestures developed by men like the mollies may have actually worked to displace the epistemological clarity of dominant codes of identity. The early modern origins of English Camp may actually have been well-informed political practices deploying the surfaces of the body oppositionally against the accruing bourgeois capacity for shaping and controlling the subject through his or her interiority.

THE BACKGROUND: REREADING THE ARISTOCRATIC BODY

It was quite correct of Sontag to connect the development of Camp gestures with a shift in the concept of aristocracy from a class difference embodied in the very blood of a specific set of concrete and privileged beings to a stance vis-à-vis "culture" that was not inherited through birth but assumed by certain marginalized subjects. But how are certain gay men – Camp queens – aristocrats of taste? Several sets of ideologically sutured narratives need to be (un)identified here – aristocracy as homosexuality, homosexuality as an aristocracy of taste, and homosexuals as the bearers of gestures once naturally located in the bodies of aristocrats.

As Lawrence Stone has analyzed in detail, the English aristocracy was in "crisis" during the early modern period: the assumed place and privilege of the aristocrats were crumbling under the advent of real political issues demanding substantive actions; aristocratic display was increasingly interrogated according to models of interiority, moderation, and privacy proposed by the Puritans; and the development of new technologies was displacing the center of wealth from land to commerce (1965: 262, 500; 187–188, 331, 584; 185, 259). The aristocracy failed as a ruling class in the seventeenth century through its inability to adapt its concept of nobility to new ideals of social utility. In light of the development of "real" or substantive political issues, the bourgeoisie interpreted the continued promulgation of aristocratic legitimacy through spectacular self-display and conspicuous consumption as empty gesturing, mere appearance with no underlying being.

For example, the upper classes had distinguished themselves by an impassivity or poise like the *sprezzatura* (nonchalance) described in Baldesar Castiglione's *The Book of the Courtier*. Translated into English by Sir Thomas Hoby in 1561, Castiglione's manual advised the courtier "to conceal all art and make whatever is done or said appear to be without effort and almost without any thought about it" (43). As theatre historian Alfred Siemon Golding has noted, the upper classes originally presented themselves as impassive because emotionality was understood as signaling an imbalance of the four humors. The upper classes appeared fit to rule to the degree that they showed themselves to be free of the domination of the humors (Golding 75–76). *Sprezzatura* therefore signaled aristocratic legitimacy through an apparent freedom from excessive bodily movement – not only freedom from external bodily movements like labor, but freedom from internal bodily movements like emotionality and awkwardness. In other words, the upper classes constructed for themselves an aristocratic body purged of those elements it shared in common with other classes. During the eleven-year period of his personal rule (1629–1640), an attempted, revival of monarchial absolutism, Charles I was painted by Sir Anthony Van Dyck after Castiglione's courtier – "celebrated," as Roy Strong has written, "as the perfect *cortegiano*" (56). Plate 2, Van Dyck's *Charles I à la ciasse*, shows the monarch in a moment of (studied) relaxation; and yet the graceful pose, with the left arm set akimbo, or bent from the hip, and the hand turned back, reminds the viewer, as Strong has suggested, that even in repose Charles was essentially a monarch (56). In showing themselves with arms set akimbo, the aristocrats were presenting their difference from other classes as a recreation of body through an act of will(power).

The bourgeoisie saw aristocratic affectation not as self-control, but as a dissembling of nature. As the physiognomical philosopher John Bulwer cautioned the orator in 1644, "Shun affectation; for all affectation is odious; and then others are most moved with our actions when they perceive all things to flow, as it were, out of the liquid current of nature" (244).[2] Defining the aristocratic body as dissimulated, the bourgeoisie constructed themselves oppositionally as "open," as the Abbé du Bos described it in his *Critical Reflections on Poetry and Painting* of 1719. One hundred years later, in his manual for actors and orators, Gilbert Austin quoted du Bos's judgment that "nature, herself sincere and candid, intends that mankind should preserve the same character, by cultivating simplicity and truth, and banishing every sort of dissimulation that tends to mischief" (474). This "real" or "inner" self was not that to be discovered in the formal rhetoric of court portraits, masques, or processions: the "natural" self was that which would be "visible" only when the subject was not "performing." Aristocratic self-display became resistantly represented by the bourgeoisie as empty shows, dissimulations concealing a lack of social being. The bourgeoisie associated aristocratic lack of openness with the arbitrariness characteristic of the period of Charles I's personal rule and for which he lost his head – an arbitrariness associated with Italianate Machiavellianism and popery. The aristocratic adoption of a studied casualness as a way of marking their difference from the social body was reread by bourgeois critics as a kind of perversion, a disjunction of the self and the social body.

The juxtaposition of aristocratic affectation and bourgeois openness followed an already established tenet of the popular science of physiognomy, which held that identifications of gender, class, race, and so on, could be seen in the lines and manners of the body. As early as 1644, Bulwer had insisted that the lines of the body and its movements disclosed "the present humor and state of the mind and will" (5). Bulwer claimed that gestures indicated the interior complexion of the individual and were not dependent on culture or custom (16). This assumption of the purity of the semiotics of gesture had a utilitarian function: it was, as Bulwer wrote, "a great discoverer of dissimulation, and great direction in business" (5).

Against the spectacle of the aristocrats, the bourgeoisie argued that the surfaces of the body were politically meaningful only to the extent that they disclosed an integrity and capacity of self useful to the social majority. Substituting a self (a content) where there had been a body (a surface), bourgeois liberalism held that consciousness was political, while the surfaces of the body were not. This model of the self-as-content favored the rise to ideological dominance and political centrality of the middle classes by insisting on the utility and consistency of the self against a simple privilege of place. It is important to note that what was at stake was not the invention of a model of psychological depth, but the increasing identity (or equivalency) of self-performance and self-originality: the performance of identity increasingly found its necessity in an origin located within the unique subject.

SEEING THE SELF, OR HOMOSEXUAL HERMENEUTICS

The paradigmatic body upon which these models of the self were negotiated was implicitly male.[3] For this reason, the problem of effeminacy frequently served as a test case for the reliability of the semiotics of the body. For John Bulwer, "effeminacy" had several implications. Occasionally, he used this or similar terms misogynistically to describe the presence in men of behaviors that he attributed to women. More frequently, he used the term effeminacy to describe the arrogance, affectation, and sloth of the ruling classes, and what he perceived as their difference from the bourgeois values of dependability and productivity. In his manuals on the gestures of the hands, Bulwer distinguished effeminate gestures by their difference from two normative gestures representative of Protestant bourgeois values – the handshake, by which business partners sealed their negotiations and showed trustworthiness, and the hands raised in prayer or thanksgiving. In Bulwer's "Alphabet of Manual Expressions," the extended, open, or offered hand appeared frequently as a sign of good will. To the open hand, he contrasted excessive gesturing with the hands, which he described as "subtle gesticulation and toying behavior" – terms generally used to describe the actions of courtiers and women. Excessive gesturing was like the "sleight of hand" of magicians, pickpockets, and actors, all of whom "mock the eye" (229–230). Gestural excess, then, was the lowest common denominator of all sorts of effeminacy.

Bourgeois ideology was increasingly concerned with limiting excess through a criticism of its content. Throughout his treatises on gestures, Bulwer seems caught between understanding effeminacy as a sign of excessive or dissimulated interiority (a false use of one's body), or as a new kind of interiority, a new content (a characteristic use of the body by a particular kind of person). At one point, Bulwer argued that wagging the hand in a swinging gesture indicated that "kind of *wantonness* and *effeminacy*" that should disqualify a man from military service (62–63). Moreover, as a habitual mannerism, wagging the hand was not only effeminate as a gesture, it indicated an inherent effeminacy of the subject.

Bulwer's hypothesis that habitual behaviors indicated innate character was part of the accumulating discourse that, by 1700, would produce the knowledge that a man who had sex habitually with other men was innately different from a man who had sex habitually with women. This corresponded with the politically motivated disclosures of the molly subculture in the first two decades of the eighteenth century. The mollies were an underground society of men who met in taverns to have sex with other men and to parody in improvised performances the increasingly normative concept of companionate heterosexual marriage prevalent among the Puritan bourgeoisie.[4] The tendency to treat effeminacy as a test case for the normative definition of the self suggests that the writers of these documents understood the

27

effeminate man as challenging the legitimacy of bourgeois morality. That the bourgeoisie were meeting resistance to their rhetoric of the self as open (self-evident) is suggested by the increasing precision with which their readings of the body were produced.

In 1753 the English painter William Hogarth tackled the problem of the relation of the self to self-presentation, proposing with increased precision that an individual's character could be reduced to a simple line, all contradictions or excesses smoothed away. Just as a sparkler leaves a trace of its movements in the air, wrote Hogarth in *The Analysis of Beauty*, so one could imagine "a line formed in the air by any supposed point at the end of a limb or part that is moved" (140). The body that Hogarth envisioned had a coherent and immediate presence such that each of its surfaces, rather than deferring to a complex history of social negotiations, referred to an original subjectivity. Hogarth's claim that "the motions of one part of the body may serve to explain those of the whole" (141) was more insidious than Bulwer's because its reductiveness supported an increased invasion and objectification of the body.

Hogarth's ascription of the complex semiotics of difference to a mere difference of types of lines enabled moral evaluations based on a reading of the surfaces of the body as degrees of divergence from the "natural." The less the extent of deviance, or the less excessive the line, the more useful the body and, for Hogarth, the more beautiful. It is highly indicative of the mystification of bourgeois ideology that a method of reading the body that Bulwer had explicitly declared necessary to the promotion of business was now, 109 years later, being used to produce an identification of the moral and the beautiful.

But Hogarth's attempt to see psychological difference in the difference of lines foregrounds a paradox within bourgeois ideology: how to make consciousness visible while at the same time denying the performability of the body. On the one hand, the bourgeoisie had set themselves against upper-class spectacularity; on the other, they recognized that interiority had to be made visible if moral judgments made on the basis of character were to be legitimated. This paradox may have been aggravated by the growing awareness that the new molly identity developing after 1700 among lower- and lower-middle-class men was not always immediately recognizable in the surfaces of their bodies. Half a century after Hogarth's *Analysis*, the author of *The Phoenix of Sodom* noted:

It is a generally received opinion, and a very natural one, that the prevalency of this passion has for its object effeminate delicate beings only; but this seems to be . . . a mistaken notion; and the reverse is so palpable in many instances, that the Fanny Murry, Lucy Cooper, and Kitty Fishers, are personified by an athletic Bargeman, an Herculean Coalheaver, and a deaf tyre Smith.

(13)

The answer to this paradox was the development of hermeneutic criticism. Where the aristocrats cast themselves, as I shall show, as virtuosi, the bourgeoisie cast themselves as critics: they would find "content" everywhere; they would be able to read the real truth underlying the performances of others. It was the bourgeois victory that a homosexual content could be disclosed critically even when the Hogarthian difference of surfaces could not be seen. But in attempting to transcode effeminacy from a criticism of the aristocracy to a content of homosexuality, the bourgeoisie had retained the old notion of visual excessiveness as part of its definition. So the paradox remained – homosexuality as excessive line, and homosexuality as critical content. In the rest of this essay, I want to examine how a hermeneutics of homosexuality was created by rereading the aristocratic gesture of the arm set akimbo as signaling both the pride (narcissism) and lack (castration) "characteristic" of sodomites.

SEEING AKIMBO: THE ARISTOCRATIZATION OF HOMOSEXUALITY

While the etymology of the word "akimbo" is uncertain, it seems to have been closely aligned with the Middle English words for a crooked stick or piece of wood (*cammock* or *cambok*). These in turn may be related to the Welsh noun *cambren*, a combination of *cam* (crooked) plus *pren* (wood, stick).[5] A clever queer might know where I am going here; s/he might want to explore the association of crooked sticks with trickster figures,[6] or the English tendency to hear the Welsh "b" as "p," suggesting another hypothetical root for our "Camp." For the purposes of this essay, it is sufficient to note that there was something "bent" about setting the arm akimbo.

In 1644, Bulwer cautioned the speaker against standing with arms akimbo: "To set the arms agambo or aprank, and to rest the turned-in back of the hand upon the side is an action of pride and ostentation, unbeseeming the hand of an orator" (219). Bulwer's invocation of "pride and ostentation" recalled the attribution of the deadliest of the seven deadly sins – pride – to the ruling classes. Consider a caricature of Prince Rupert, nephew of Charles I, from a broadsheet of 1646 in which he is depicted as preying on the British people and is shown with his right arm set akimbo (Plate 3). The caricature is an attempt to discredit the gentry by critiquing their gestural style.

Setting the arm akimbo with the hand turned back was undoubtedly cultivated by the aristocrats: it appeared in many of their portraits during the mannerist and baroque periods. A spectacular example is the anonymous double portrait *Sir Walter Ralegh and His Son*, depicting the transmission of aristocratic privilege through the learned imitation of the gesture (Plate 4). The Restoration and early-eighteenth-century theatres accordingly included this gesture in the proper form for issuing a command; and actors adopted it in their own portraits (Plate 5). It could also be used theatrically to show the various perversions of authority, including raillery, boasting, and most frequently, pride (Plate 6).

But by the mid-eighteenth century, the bourgeois strategy of specifying an affected bodily style as sodomy – a transcoding from the connection of aristocratic spectacularity with sexual excess – had produced a reading of this gesture as characteristic of the effeminate sodomite. In a 1761 satire called *The Fribbleriad*, David Garrick assigned the gesture to two sexually suspect "fribbles," one of whom had "a thumb Stuck to his hips, and jutting bum" (28) while the other had "kimbow'd arm, and tossing head" (30). Hogarth, in his *Analysis of Beauty*, added the gesture to his sketch of a famous Roman statue of Antinous (Plate 7). Hogarth praised the serpentine line embodied by the Antinous: "If uniform objects were agreeable," he wrote, "the Antinous's easy sway, must submit to the stiff and straight figure of the dancing master" (20). But in his accompanying sketch, Hogarth exaggerated the *contrapposto* stance of the Antinous beyond that of the classical sources themselves. In the drawing, Antinous totally depends on the dancing master for support, as if he were a *prima ballerina* being presented to the audience by the *danseur*. Hogarth called attention to the excessivity of their respective lines both by foregrounding Antinous's missing right hand and by linking the line of the drapery around Antinous's right wrist with the cuff of the dancing master's sleeve. Hogarth also gave his Antinous the conventional signs of aristocratic pride, emphasizing the aristocratic profile and setting the left arm – missing or damaged in most of the classical examples – akimbo on the hip with the hand turned back.

It is an open secret among art historians and classical scholars that

Antinous was the lover of the Roman emperor Hadrian. Upon Antinous's unexpected death in the prime of his beauty, Hadrian had the boy deified, established games in his honor, founded an oracle and an entire city in Egypt in his name, and littered his empire with statues and busts of the youth, hundreds of which survive today.[7] The implications of this would have been obvious to an English middle class traditionally resentful of the homosexual favorites of their kings, the example of William III only the most recent in Hogarth's memory. Did Hogarth depict the Antinous's "submission" to the dancing master as a satire on the production of *sprezzatura?* Both the dancing master and the Antinous became, in his sketch, *petits maîtres* (little masters) – the dancing master because he is too affected, the Antinous because he is effeminate, both aristocratic and dependent. Hogarth valorized the serpentine line as the standard of the beautiful, which he defined as the form and proportion necessary to sustain the subject, or the "fitting." But here, that line is made excessive, and we are to read that excess as giving way to a *content.* Hogarth's sketch seems to ask us to see the difference between a "fitting" serpentine line and the illustrated example, and to register that difference as homosexuality.

PRIDE AND NOTHINGNESS

Until the end of the seventeenth century, sodomy was taken to be a symptom of the excessive pride of the aristocrats. As the author of the Preface to the published proceedings of the trial of Mervyn Touchet, Second Earl of Castlehaven, claimed in 1699, "*Pride, Luxury,* and *Irreligion*, were the Infernal Parents of *Sodomy*" (A5). Likewise, in his *Institutes*, Sir Edward Coke had noted, "The sodomites came to the abomination by four means, *viz.* by pride, excesse of diet, idlenesse, and contempt of the poor" (qtd in Smith 166). Pride underlay all the other excessive behaviors of the aristocrats and the upwardly mobile gentry who imitated them.

At least since John Cassian's *De institutis coenobiorum* (c. 420), the capital sin of pride had been described as the originary sin, the cause of all other sins: "How great is the evil of pride, that it rightly has no angel, nor other virtues opposed to it, but God himself as its adversary" (qtd in Bloomfield 69). Pride was the misuse or perversion of free will, the opposition of the self to God (Bloomfield 75; Dollimore 136–137). In turning away from God, the proud man perversely abandoned his proper self; pride was therefore the origin and epitome of the

31

Augustine concept of sin as *privation*. The proud man's excessive concern with himself actually recreated him as *lacking being*:

> And I asked what wickedness was, and I found that it was no substance, but a perversity of will, which turns aside from Thee, O God, the supreme substance, to desire the lowest, flinging away its inner treasure and boasting itself an outcast.
>
> (qtd in Dollimore 133).

According to Augustine, to turn from God to oneself "is to come nearer to nothingness" (qtd in Dollimore 136). The sin of pride was the refusal of divine plan (which interpellated individuals into their proper selves) and the occupation of a stance outside God's order, a place which was *nowhere*. It is this rhetoric of pride as the tendency toward a place that was nowhere, this description of sin as appearance rather than substance, that found its most perfect expression in the concept of sodomy as the sin that could not be named.[8]

As a symptom of pride, sodomy, too, was a misuse or excess of the will: for the aristocrat, as Coke had noted, sodomy was a perverse willfulness toward pleasure. But by the eighteenth century, these traditional representations of the proud aristocrat as homosexual were reversed, and the newly visible sodomite was described in the theological terms of pride, as a self against (his)self. With the increased visibility of the mollies around 1700, there seems to have been a tendency to explain homosexuality by, not the cardinal sin of *fornicatio*, but the cardinal sin of pride. This happened when sodomy was understood, not just as a slippage in "normal" (heterosexual) behavior, but as a consciously willed and repeated set of behaviors that set the self against the normative order. Like the perverse will described by Augustine, the sodomite "turn[ed] aside from . . . substance, . . . boasting [him]self an outcast." It was this *boastfulness* (a specifically queer pride) which most disturbed homophobic critics. From this description of the sodomite as proud and boastful, it is only a short step to Sontag's definition of the homosexual as a new aristocrat.

ARISTOCRATIC EXCESS AND BOURGEOIS CONSCIENCE

Classical statues like those of Antinous became familiar to Englanders around 1614 following the importation of artwork by virtuosi like Thomas Howard, Earl of Arundel, the Duke of Buckingham, and even Charles I himself (Houghton 67). The virtuosi were gentlemen of leisure who compensated for the increasing shortage of royal posts by creating new social roles for themselves as amateur scientists and antiquarians, collectors of natural and artificial rarities, and artistic connoisseurs (Houghton 52ff.; Stone 1965: 715). Through their collections, the virtuosi introduced into England the mannerism characteristic of courtly portraits showing the arm set akimbo.

H. G. Koenigsberger has written that the courtly style of mannerism "could play havoc with that most central of classical Renaissance achievements, the correct use of perspective" (242). I suggest that, by confusing perspective, mannerism displaced the figure from his or her proper place in a mathematically benevolent world "view," substituting virtuosic technique for social alignment. The opposition to pure perspective evident in mannerist art conveyed the same message as *sprezzatura* in the bodily style of aristocrats. Perspective could be learned by any patient craftsman, and classical iconography by any student; as with courtesy, manuals were available for these purposes. But the mannerist gesture – like *sprezzatura*, like akimbo – was at once to invoke perspective and to defer it, foregrounding style over mathematical placement.

Precisely where the virtuosi could have contributed to the revival of aristocratic legitimacy, they were discredited as not useful. Before 1680, Samuel Butler had described the character of an antiquarian: "He values one old invention, that is lost and never to be recovered, before all the new ones in the world, though never so useful" (rpt. in Morley 324). Likewise,

> A Curious Man . . . cares not how unuseful anything be, so it be but unuseful and rare. . . . He admires subtleties about all things, because the more subtle they are the nearer they are to nothing, and values no art but that which is spun so thin that it is of no use at all.
>
> (rpt. in Morley 340)

Finally, Butler's "Virtuoso" was ignorant of himself, and the tasks he set himself were a misuse of his nature (Morley 324ff.). The virtuoso was anti-utilitarian because he did not contribute to the study of "man." He did not contribute to the study of (and construction of) normative human subjectivity. As John Locke had succinctly put it, "Our business here is not to know all things, but those which concern our conduct" (65). This latter criticism was most clearly made by the philosopher Anthony Ashley Cooper, Third Earl of Shaftesbury, a pupil of Locke and the grandson of his patron.

Shaftesbury's criticism of typical virtuosi was based on what he considered to be their lack of depth: the virtuosi were insubstantial because they lacked interiority. In Shaftesbury's system, the ability to define (know) the truth about one's self was primary to, and the origin of, all political, social, ethical, and even aesthetic discourses. Shaftesbury was the philosopher of the bourgeois internalization of the look. To "recognize" oneself, he wrote, was to divide oneself into two: "if the Division were rightly made, all *within* would of course . . . be rightly understood, and prudently manag'd" (1710: 170). Shaftesbury therefore posited "*Two Persons* in one individual *Self*" (1710: 185), the second of which censored the first and secured the continuity of one's actions and identity. Shaftesbury's internalization of the look was a necessary solution to the maintenance of social order through spectatorship once the feudal order of performance had been overturned.

By rereading aristocratic arbitrariness as lacking being, bourgeois consciousness guaranteed identity by securing the consistency and continuity of the subject's actions. Human will was structured by the necessity of identity (equivalency); the threat of nonresolution mandated the will as resolution, as deliberation and discipline, and also in the ocularcentric sense of a clarification of one's impulses. As Shaftesbury put it, the disciplining of the passions was necessary

> to gain him *a Will*, and insure him a *certain Resolution*; by which he shall know where to find himself; be sure of his own Meaning and Design; and as to all his Desires, Opinions, and Inclinations, be warranted *one and the same* Person to day as yesterday, and to morrow as to day.
>
> (1710: 187)

Where John Locke had proved existence by the ability of the subject to find himself thinking, Shaftesbury described in more detail the proper method for that discovery. Shaftesbury declared that artists and philosophers were responsible for inscribing this resolution by providing "looking-glasses" in which subjects might find themselves, so that "by constant and long Inspection, the Partys accustom'd to the Practice, wou'd acquire a peculiar *speculative Habit*; so as virtually to carry about with 'em a sort of *Pocket-Mirrour*, always ready, and in use" (1710: 195). Such self-knowledge, believed Shaftesbury, was prerequisite to three goals of philosophy: "Friendship, Society, and the Commerce of Life" (1710: 286).

THE CLOSETED BODY AND THE BODY SOCIAL

What guaranteed the sociality of this speculative habit was "taste," the sense of the fitting or the becoming. Taste, as a common way of seeing (an interesting displacement of bodily functions), guaranteed the identity of looks, not only within the subject, but also between agents. Taste dictated that, from the study of himself, the [male] philosopher would "*ascend* beyond his own immediate Species, City, or Community, to discover and recognize his *higher Polity*, or *Community*, that *common* and *universal-one*, of which he is born *a Member*" (1714: 158). Thus Shaftesbury criticized the virtuosi's "pretended Knowledg [*sic*] of the Machine of *this World*, and of *their own Frame*," suggesting that "this super-speculative Philosophy" be replaced by "a more practical sort, which relates chiefly to our Acquaintance, Friendship, and good Correspondence with *our-selves*" (1710: 291–292).

Taking it as (self-)evident that "in the very nature of Things there must of necessity be the Foundation of a right and wrong TASTE" (1710: 336), Shaftesbury privileged critics as the arbiters of taste: "Now a TASTE or *Judgment*, 'tis suppos'd, can hardly come ready form'd with us into the World. . . . A legitimate and just TASTE can neither be begotten, made, conceiv'd, or produc'd, without the antecedent *Labor* and *Pains* of CRITICISM" (1714: 164–165). Against the virtuosi, who could be aligned with a revival of aristocratic privilege based on excessive and pleasurable knowledges, Shaftesbury opposed the critic, whose leadership of taste regulated such privileges according to morality and normality (1714: 163). It was only through taste, Shaftesbury asserted, repeating his insistence that manners and morals should be one and the same, that the virtuosi could become virtuous (1710: 338).

Shaftesbury identified the greatest good as those networks of friendship between men that Eve Kosofsky Sedgwick has called homosocialism (1–2). Shaftesbury distinguished this male–male sociality from more "effeminate" intercourses between men and women,[9] and from the suspect sexuality of the more marginal virtuoso. While Sedgwick, in her book *Between Men*, has described the various tropes through which homosociality is played out, she has not described the bodily metaphors through which *homosocialism* marks itself as separate from *homosexuality*. In the late seventeenth and early eighteenth centuries, the virtuoso kept his collection in a cabinet – a special room or closet for the private display of his knacks, rarities, intricate machines, or trivialities. As an externalization of his personal and antisocial taste, the virtuoso's cabinet threatened the homosocialism of philosophy, especially in the Greek model of the public forum or dialogue favored by Shaftesbury and others. Whereas the (homosexual/virtuoso) cabinet was close(te)d, the homosocial body was open, extended, repercussive.

Where English philosophy was knowledge of the useful and the proper, especially regarding the relations among social beings, virtuosity was knowledge in and about itself, and therefore excessive. Where philosophy was public, virtuosity was private. And where philosophy was an art of spectatorship – the individual subject as possessor of a gaze originating inward and turned outward – virtuosity was an art of spectacle, an art of excessive collecting, a narcissistic absorption of the gaze creating the subject as s/he who is seen collecting, knowing, demonstrating. In sum, where philosophy discovered the relations among things and proposed models for proper identifications, virtuosity exploited the differences among things, seeking out the monstrous and the excessive rather than the proper and the decorous.

I will close this section by recalling Susan Sontag's description of male homosexuals as a new aristocracy, the arbiters of taste. From the historical sketch I have made here, the contradiction in Sontag's argument should be apparent. I have tried to show that "taste" was developed as the standard of the bourgeoisie, as that which prevented the excessive performances of the self that we might call Camp today. It was exactly those excesses, which taste was understood as correcting, that could simultaneously signal homosexuality. If taste was homosocial, what taste opposed was homosexual. Thus, by calling homosexual men the bearers of taste, Sontag obscured the difference between a dominant system of homosociality and the "monstrous" men who marked its margins.

VIRTUOSI AND SEXUAL SUSPECTS: OF KNACKS AND THE KNACKERED

Shaftesbury complained that the virtuosi were too interested in the odd and the exceptional:[10]

> In seeking so earnestly for *Raritys*, they fall in love with RARITY *for Rareness-sake*. Now the greatest *Raritys* in the World are MONSTERS. So that the *Study* and *Relish* of these Gentlemen, thus assiduously imploy'd, becomes at last in reality *monstrous*:

And their whole Delight is found to consist in selecting whatever is most *monstrous*, disagreeing, out of the way, and to the least purpose of any thing in Nature.

(1714: 156)

Rather than studying the relations of men (*sic*), the virtuosi investigated only "Nature's remotest Operations, deepest Mysterys, and most difficult *Phaenomena*" which they "discuss'd, and whimsically explain'd . . . as to appear an easy *Knack* or *Secret* to those who have *the Clew*" (1714: 160).

In the very idea of whim was the threat of insubstantiality, nonidentity. As Edward Ward wrote of the virtuosi,

> Thus Vertuoso's make a pother,
> About their Whims, to please each other;
> And wond'rous Maggots will advance-ye,
> That have no Being but in Fancy.

(1710: 18)

This criticism had also been made of the courtier, as sketched by Samuel Butler:

> A Huffing Courtier. Is a cipher, that has no value himself but from the place he stands in. . . . His business is only to be seen. . . . He is a kind of spectrum, and his clothes are the shape he takes to appear and walk in, and when he puts them off he vanishes. . . . His ribbons are of the true complexion of his mind, a kind of painted cloud or gaudy rainbow, that has no colour of itself but what it borrows from reflection.

> (Butler [before 1680], rpt. in Morley 318–320)

This is the language of sin itself – at once only appearance and merely appearance, excess and no-thing. Interestingly, Butler seems to have described the courtier's arms as set akimbo: "He carries his elbows backwards, as if he were pinioned like a trussed-up fowl" (Morley 320). The courtier and the virtuoso shared the same psychic makeup according to their critics; they were at once overly concerned with themselves and unable to know themselves, embodying excess but manifesting emptiness.

Having connected the aristocratic gesture of arms set akimbo to the mannerist art collected by the virtuosi, it is important to note that the country gentry and bourgeoisie found the Italianate taste of the virtuosi highly suspect (Stone 1965: 723). Italy was regarded as the home of both

37

Machiavellian and homosexual subversions of identity, as well as the center of papacy. To the critical eye there was something perverse in the virtuosi's fondness for the nude Greek and Roman statues, an almost palpable homoeroticism that comes through even in defenses of the virtuosi. For instance, Henry Peacham had pointed to "the pleasure of seeing and conversing with these old heroes (whose mere presence, without any further consideration, . . . cannot but take any eye that can but see)" (122). Even more emphatic was John Evelyn's record of a visit to Hippolito Vitellesco, librarian of the Vatican, in 1644: Evelyn was struck by the way Vitellesco talked with his statues "as if they were living, pronouncing now and then orations, sentences, and verses, sometimes kissing and embracing them" (qtd in Houghton 191 n.72).

Was the virtuoso's private intercourse with the antique marbles like the connection of the dancing master and the Antinous in Hogarth's sketch (Plate 7)? Recalling that the virtuosi were responsible for bringing classical iconography to England, it is interesting that Hogarth turned the Antinous against them, reinterpreting the virtuosi as *petits maîtres*. There was something excessively erotic about the rhetoric used by Peacham and Evelyn that, by Hogarth's day, could only be described as homosexuality.

The virtuosi, as I have shown, were collectors of knacks, showy but insubstantial things. That what went on in the virtuoso's cabinet could appear like homosexuality was especially so, given the multiple meanings of knacks (or knick-knacks) as visually engaging but lacking substance. Most often, knacks were mechanical contrivances or toys like the artificial grottoes and speaking statues collected by the virtuosi (Stone 1965: 717); or the "nice" (curious, precise) apparatuses used by the virtuosi in their scientific experiments. ("Gimcrack," the title character in Thomas Shadwell's *Virtuoso*, is a variant of knack.) But a knack could also be an affected person like Butler's "huffing courtier" or Gimcrack's effusive friend Sir Formal Trifle; and, in the latter context, "to knack" could mean to speak affectedly ("knack" 1989).

In Shadwell's comedy, Sir Formal Trifle's verbal excessiveness is punished by the young, normatively heterosexual couples who are Shadwell's protagonists: his excess casts him as dubiously heterosexual, sexually suspect. The young couples trap Formal in a dark vault with another man disguised as a woman; his excessive speech is turned into excessive sexuality as he attempts to rape the other man in a mistakenly homosexual encounter that is presented as sufficient punishment for his verbal offenses.

Similarly, in Edward Ward's satire "Of the Vertuoso's [*sic*] Club"

(1710), the virtuosi are punished by arousing their curiosity about a particular "knack" – antilaxative butt plugs used by "Egyptians," which the virtuosi enthusiastically smell, lick, nibble, and discourse on until the trick (knack) is disclosed:

> With that one began to Spit, another Keck, a third Spew, a fourth, in a Passion, crying, *Z—s, Sir, I hope they did not wear them in their Arses! As sure,* reply'd the Gentleman, *as you have had them in your Mouths.*
>
> (1710: 23).

A homosexual, then, could be a knack or a gimcrack; he could also, like a virtuoso, be a keeper of knacks. Laurence Senelick has suggested that a typical effeminate's occupation was maintaining toy shops, known as knick-knackatories (Senelick 39; "Knick-Knackatory" 1989). Finally, as "knackers" were testicles, the homosexual could be at once a collector of knack(er)s and castrated (knackered). Like the similarly castrated Sir Formal, he could also speak in knacks; which is as much as to say that his speech was knackered.

Likewise, the fribble had been commonly described as incapable of feeling or acting on his feelings. In 1712, Richard Steele wrote in *The Spectator* that the fribble was impotent in mind, so that "those who are guilty of it [are] incapable of pursuing what they themselves approve" (rpt. in Chalmers 4:210). Garrick's *Fribbleriad*, referred to earlier, described them as lacking power, unable to realize pleasure, "[f]or ever wishing, ne'er enjoying" (23). The idea was more fully developed in 1789, when Lavater described the fribble as lacking (bourgeois) sensibility, incapable of either sensing deeply or expressing fully normative human experiences. As Hogarth had done, Lavater assumed that the fribble's "lack" was obvious, as he demonstrated by comparing the "Contrasted attitudes [of] a man and a fribble" (viii) (Plate 8):

> Which of these two attitudes would you prefer? . . . The answer to this question is obvious, and there is no room for hesitation. If I ask farther, which of these figures announces a harebrained coxcomb, a petit maitre – a man whose conversation is equally insipid, tiresome, and teasing – a mind incapable of feeling either the great and beautiful, or the simple and natural . . .? The question, in truth, may still be easily answered, and there will be only one opinion of the matter.[11]
>
> (3:213)

The passage is unusually vituperative, even for Lavater, and therefore highlights the hostile representational tactics whereby increasingly "visible" homosexuals were "recognized" by their excessivity, while simultaneously "seen" critically as lacking psychic substance. In other words, the fribble had come to stand in for, or enclose, the absence of subjectivity (conscience, sincerity, identity, utility, sensibility) once assigned by the bourgeoisie to the aristocrats as a class. It is interesting to note, then, that "fribble" itself meant lacking or incapacitated: "to fribble" was to falter verbally (to stammer) or physically (to totter) ("fribble" 1989).

In creating homosexuality as a nonidentity (as unspeakable, as fribblish, as offstage), the bourgeoisie were casting off onto the concept of homosexuality all the traits associated with the obsolete aristocrats – not only sodomy, but also arbitrariness, excessiveness, and, most emphatically, social impotency. For this reason, what was most bothersome about newly visible sodomites like the mollies was that they occupied this no-place, this lack, mimetically, as the basis of improvisations within an increasingly normative society.

AKIMBO EXPROPRIATED: QUEER PRIDE AND (UN)IDENTIFICATION

If the bourgeois critics had attempted to transfer already existing registers of effeminacy from courtiers to lower-class sodomites, or mollies, in doing so they had helped to create homosexuality as a new content. In other words, where the aristocrats had once been criticized as sodomitical, the hermeneutics of homosexuality had in turn aristocratized sodomy. As bourgeois ideology of the self spread through all segments of society, it became increasingly viable to possess oneself as a homosexual. By 1726, as Alan Bray has shown, it was possible for an Englishman named William Brown to assert under arrest, "I did it because . . . I think there is no crime in making what use I please of my own body" (qtd in Bray 114).

Randolph Trumbach has written of the mollies: "All stood to lose a great deal if their actions were discovered. There was daily contempt for the obvious sodomite, and for all there were the possibilities of ostracism or blackmail, the pillory or hanging" (1977: 15). That the mollies were willing to be visible in the face of raids and prosecutions by the Society for the Reformation of Manners (and despite media attention by hack writers like Ward) indicates that they benefited from the new sodomite identity strongly enough to be willing to risk all to occupy it. But just what sort of identity were the mollies occupying?

Not only was sodomy understood to be a nonidentification, a loss of self; as a symptom of pride like aristocracy, it was also understood to be a willing or excessive flaunting of difference from the social structures of self. Sodomy, that is, had become *an effeminate's occupation*, both a sitting-in a place that was nowhere (knackered) and a trade (knick-knackery). I want to suggest that what the mollies felt was not so much a coming into view of a "new kind of self," but an (un)identification with the normative models of self mandated by the increasingly dominant bourgeoisie, by philosophers like Locke and critics like Shaftesbury, and by political machines like the Society for the Reformation of Manners.

Molly identification happened with entry into certain spaces (molly houses, cruising grounds, and so on) where desire to have sex with other men became simultaneously perceivable as an occupation of a marginal identity. To occupy these spaces was to "be" a molly: these occupations were therefore transitory and enacted at the expense of other identifications. Indeed, as the author of *The Phoenix of Sodom* suggested, the occupation of a molly identity, within the special molly house or meeting place, made it possible to unidentify oneself from all other everyday identifications:

> It seems the greater part of these reptiles assume feigned names, though not very appropriate to their calling in life: for instance, Kitty Cambric is a Coal Merchant; Miss Selina, a Runner at a Police office; Black-eyed Leonora, a Drummer; Pretty Harriet, a Butcher; Lady Godina, a Waiter; the Dutchess of Gloucester, a gentleman's servant; Duchess of Devonshire, a Blacksmith; and Miss Sweet Lips, a Country Grocer.
>
> (12–13)

One of the most threatening aspects of molly (un)identifications was that they collapsed or suspended other social identifications: the *Phoenix of Sodom* recorded that "Men of rank, and respectable situations in life, might be seen wallowing either in or on the beds with wretches of the lowest description" (11). The same complaint had been made by Ward against virtuosi clubs "compos'd of such an odd mixture of Mankind, That, . . . here sat a nice Beau next to a dirty Blacksmith; . . . yonder a half-witted Whim of Quality, next to a ragged Mathematician" and so on (1710: 18). In the molly houses, fumed Ward, men stopped speaking as husbands, fathers, gentlemen, and laborers, and pretended to speak as women: the mollies, he wrote,

41

are so far degenerated from all Masculine Deportment or Manly exercises that they rather fancy themselves Women, imitating all the little Vanities that Custom has reconcil'd to the Female sex, affecting to speak, walk, tattle, curtsy, cry, scold, & mimick all manner of Effeminacy. . . . every one was to talk of their Husbands & Children, one estolling [*sic*] the Virtues of her Husband, another the genius & wit of their Children; whilst a Third would express himself sorrowfully under the character of a Widow.

(c. 1709: 28)

As described by Ward, both the molly houses and the virtuosi clubs were hermaphroditical, obscuring all those social distinctions upon which identifications depend. The molly houses and the virtuosi clubs did not enclose, reflect, or reproduce stable identifications; they were border spaces where the necessity of primary (gender, class, occupational, etc.) identifications was exchanged for improvisation and experimentation. Indeed, as these descriptions of the molly houses as collapsing social distinctions suggest, occupying a nonidentity as a sodomite required a prior un-speaking, or unidentification of "proper" identifications; that is, molly parodies enabled not a *mis*recognition as "womanly," but an unidentification from the self-knowledges mandated by critics like Shaftesbury.

In suggesting above that the mollies were proud, I meant that they had been described, not just as practicing sodomy (the bisexual Restoration rakes had done this), but as occupying a place (the "I" as a place from which to speak) as a sodomite. This, finally, is what bothered the writers who disclosed molly house practices following the prosecutions – not that they took it up the ass, but that they spoke while doing so: "the perpetration of the abominable act, however offensive, was infinitely more tolerable than the shocking conversation that accompanied the perpetration; some of which . . . was so odious, that [his source] could not either write, or verbally relate" (*Phoenix of Sodom* 11).

Ward recorded an example of such shocking conversation:

Not long since they had cushioned up one of their Brethren, or rather Sisters, according to Female Dialect, disguising him in a Woman's Night Gown, Sarsanet Hood, & Night-rail who when the Company were men [met?], was to mimick a woman, produce a jointed Baby they had provided, which wooden Offspring was to be afterwards Christened, whilst one in a High

Crown'd Hat, I am old Beldam's Pinner, representing[ed] a
Country Midwife, & another dizen'd up in a Huswife's Coif for a
Nurse & all the rest of an impertinent *Decorum* of a Christening.

(c. 1709: 28)

The interjected phrase "I am old Beldam's pinner" stands out, as if
Ward was remembering an improvisation by a particular molly. I
cannot fully reconstruct the meaning of the phrase. One thing seems
apparent, however. Despite the politicized rhetoric linking male
homosexuals and obsolete aristocrats, the mollies were not identifying
with the bisexual rakes or the effeminate beaux of the time. Rather,
they were improvising an identification with another group of marginalized agents – country midwives. The scene seems to have been an
improvisation of midwifery in which one molly was dressed as a
country midwife in a high crowned (witch's?) hat. "Old Beldam" was
a hag or a witch, "a furious raging woman; a virago" ("Beldam" 1989);
hags were associated with midwifery before male doctors outlawed
midwives. Was this molly improvising the role of the hag or witch who
oversaw a female homosocial network that had increasingly come
under scrutiny of male homosocialism?[12] The increasing marginaliza-
tion of midwives as prostitutes during the early modern period may
have made them an appealing object for sympathetic imitation by the
mollies, suggesting both deviant sexuality and a residual, nonbourgeois
empowerment of the body. "Pinner" may have meant "one who
fucks." By casting himself as "old Beldam's pinner," the crossdressed
Molly who was the target of Ward's moral outrage may have been
suggesting that the homosocial bonds between these demonized women
had an erotic dimension which could be appropriated as the basis of his
enactment of his own marginalized sexuality. Perhaps the molly
improvisation may have enabled a refusal of the emergent norms of
(heterosexual, conjugal) masculinity: indeed, this is how Ward interpreted the practice, claiming that molly parodies were enacted "on
purpose to extinguish that Natural Affection which is due to the Fair
Sex" (c. 1709: 28–29). It may be necessary to interpret molly parodies
within the context of the simultaneous glorification of marriage and
disempowerment of women by the bourgeoisie during the late
seventeenth and eighteenth centuries.

Ward's memory of his visit to the molly house suggests that it was
precisely the act of mimetically unidentifying with normative masculinity that most infuriated him. Thus, when Ward met hyper-masculine

sodomites elsewhere, he was so unconcerned as to jostle in among them:

> We then proceeded and went on the *Change*, turn'd to the Right, and Jostled in amongst a parcel of *Swarthy Buggerantoes, Preternatural Fornicators*, as my Friend call'd them, who would Ogle a Handsome Young man with as much *Lust*, as a True-bred *English Whoremaster* would gaze upon a *Beautiful Virgin*.

(1703: 68)

During the same walk, the two "had squeezed [them]selves thro' a Crowd of *Bumfirking-Italians*" (69). There was nothing threatening about these sodomites. It was when homosexuality set itself up as resistant masculinity, as in the case of the mollies, that Ward was disturbed.

As crimes against nature, acts of resistant sodomy were not to be spoken, indeed could not be spoken, because to do so threatened the stability of social relations structured as intersecting networks of discourse. The imposition of silence on sodomy preceded and preserved the homosocial speech acts mandated by Shaftesbury. That is, Shaftesbury's philosophical system can be understood as an attempt to reduce speech and gesture to identificatory practices so that it became impossible to use language without speaking or showing the truth about one's self. This is the demand that language (speech, gesture) should lay bare the unique "I" as the most interesting "fact" of the language act. As a way of using language to unidentify from Shaftesbury's "I," molly parodies should have remained unspoken/unrecognized; once recognized, however, they had to be critically reevaluated.

PERFORMING AKIMBO: FINAL NOTES ON CAMP

The development of perspective enabled the assertion of bourgeois subjectivity by re-creating the spectating eye as the origin and owner of the field of vision.[13] The claim of perspective to represent a mathematical order of precisely plotted places depended on an arbitrarily assigned vanishing point. The vanishing point provided an origin for the scene and enactment of perspective; by means of it, all other objects and actions were clarified (resolved). Shaftesbury's philosophical system, in turn, depended on the internalization of that vanishing point as conscience. Against all this, mannerism resisted the vanishing point with a gesture of deflection – the arm set akimbo, the body in *contrapposto*.[14] The mannerist substitution of a gesture of deflection where there should have been a vanishing point attempted to make critical resolution (self-knowledge) unattainable. To be "akimbo" – that proud mannerist gesture – was to be at odds with the normal drive of bourgeois ocularcentrism.

Bourgeois criticism may be understood, then, as that which reinscribed the gesture of deferral back into the social order, rereading the mannerist gesture as not (un)identification but indication. The extravagant gesture, argued its critics, drew the eye inward (hermeneutically) to a unique subjectivity which (and this was the ultimate task of middle-class morality) could then be realigned with the measure of things. The success of bourgeois ocularcentrism is apparent in Hogarth's drawing of Antinous and the dancing master. Hogarth's joke seems to ask us to see beyond deflection, to see critically the arm set akimbo and the body in *contrapposto* as indicative of an unspoken, but open, secret about the nature of their relationship. We are to "see" the comic difference between the illustration and Hogarth's philosophical/ aesthetic system, a difference which Hogarth made visible as homosexuality. Represented as nothing in itself, homosexuality at the same time must register whatever difference the critic wants us to "see" there.

Against this, molly gestures could not have blocked out (bourgeois) content, as Sontag wrote of Camp, or created a new phallic plenitude, as a recent and prominent essay has argued.[15] Rather, these gestures reopened the field of the political in which identifications were embodied and performed. By preserving the complexity of the political references of gestures like setting the arms akimbo, mollies, fribbles, and fops may have foregrounded, contested, and coped with the processes by which the bourgeois ideology invaded and inscribed their bodies.

One twentieth-century meaning of "akimbo" demonstrates the final outcome of the historical struggles surrounding this gesture. In 1943, Ivor Brown noted that "akimbo" could mean either "high horse" or overly theatrical (24). As the former, akimbo connotes a performance exceeding taste. As the latter, it also signals excess; but as an excess of theatricality, it registers the very nothingness underlying performance. This is the curious circle, the knack, I have traced in this essay – in the one direction, excess; in the other, nothingness. And yet in the epistemological prejudices underlying bourgeois psychology, excess and nothingness can *appear* as each other: excess and nothingness pivot around "realness" as two kinds of specters/spectacles. On the one hand, conspicuous display of a gesture like arms akimbo registered the excess that displaced bourgeois identifications; on the other, pride and sodomy coalesced as markers of the status of aristocracy as no-thing in itself, an identity misplaced and misspoken. What was once a gesture registering *sprezzatura*, the inherent legitimacy of the aristocracy, connoted the very (homosexual) instability of self for which they were criticized by the bourgeoisie. Later on, as I have shown, excess and nothingness became opposite ends of a ray curving in and meeting to form the concept of homosexuality as at once offstage and antecedent to normative sociality. Shaftesbury's primary discourse of the self – the occupation of the "I" as the basis of all other knowledges and all epistemological certainty – contributed to a concept of homosexuality as both the excessive (or narcissistic) speaking of the self and the dispossession of self, the speaking of an identity that had no place. The homosexual's flamboyance and narcissism became understood as a compensation for (and, later, a specifically pathological compensation for) the lack of self-knowledge.

To recuperate "akimbo" – to reclaim excessive nothingness through Camp – would be to reassert the primacy of performance beyond the epistemological privileging of the real or the ontological prejudice of identity. To perform akimbo would be to set gestural practices against their final critical rereading as merely/too theatrical. To historicize akimbo would be to refute the naturalness of psychoanalytic discourses which have inscribed excess and nothingness as the content of homosexual psyches. Finally, to reclaim akimbo would be to reopen the space of refusal and (un)identification of the self closed by Locke, Shaftesbury, and other prophets of bourgeois morality at the end of the seventeenth century.

NOTES

Earlier versions of this essay were presented under the title "The Politics of Surfaces: Notes on Eighteenth-Century Camp," at the annual conference of the Association for Theatre in Higher Education, Seattle, Washington, 8 August 1991; and Camp/Out, Symposium on Camp Theory, Center for Interdisciplinary Research in the Arts, Northwestern University, Evanston, Illinois, 10 April 1992. I am indebted to Margaret Thompson Drewal for her comments on early versions of this essay.

1 See, especially, Cynthia Morrill's critique of Sontag elsewhere in this volume.
2 In all quotations from original texts, I have modernized the "s" but have left all other spellings and punctuation as found.
3 Sometimes explicitly: "Our norm will be that of the healthy man in the prime of his life" (Jelgerhuis 264).
4 For background on the mollies see: Trumbach 1977; Trumbach 1989; and Senelick. For the rise of the "companionate marriage," see Stone 1979: 217ff.
5 See "Akimbo" 1989; "Cambrel" 1989; and "Cammock" 1989.
6 See Gifford 18–35. Gifford points out that the costume of the fifteenth-century European fool was associated with that of the courtier – an interesting parallel to the court/homosexual/trickster transcodings I am tracing here.
7 See Lambert (passim).
8 The author of *The Phoenix of Sodom* asserted that the "crime" of sodomy "is so detestable, that the law of England blushes to name it; and in all legal process, treats it as a crime not fit to be named among Christians; a silence, which is also preserved by the edict of Constantius, and others" (24).
9 Shaftesbury suggested that men's effeminate interest in feminine politeness was responsible for the virtuosi's "violent desire at least to know the knack or secret by which Nature does it all" (1709: 8).
10 For a description of some of these oddities see Houghton 193.
11 In this later-eighteenth-century drawing, the arm set akimbo now holds a hat; and the hand, formerly turned back on the hip, has been tucked inside a pocket. The fribble's stylistic excess is thereby contrasted to the "man's" more neutral bodily style.
12 For the historical overtake of midwifery by men, see Ehrenreich and English 34; Fraser 441; and Rich 139. I am indebted to Salome Chasnoff for these sources.
13 This point has been developed at length by Barbara Freedman 7–12, 44–46.
14 Mary Ann Caws has described mannerism as a "style of excess and self-conscious contradiction," and a "composition in contrary motions or *contrapposto*" (37). Caws isolated mannerist art by its frequent pointing at pointing; the mannerist gesture, that is, slowed down the gazing eye, forcing the eye to linger on and move across the surface of things, returning the gaze to the gesture itself.
15 "To emphasize style is to slight content, or to introduce an attitude which is neutral with respect to content. *It goes without saying* that the Camp sensibility is disengaged, depoliticized – or at least apolitical" (Sontag 107, emphasis mine); and:

> It might seem that the man in drag has put his identity in jeopardy by confusing the very oppositions which sustain the gendered difference our symbolic legislates. . . . However, analysts note, he has feminized himself only in order to "masculinize" (phallicize) himself, attempting to better secure a masculine or phallic and "whole" identity through cross-dressing.
>
> (Tyler 42)

BIBLIOGRAPHY

"Akimbo." 1989. *Oxford English Dictionary*. 2nd edn.

Austin, Gilbert. 1806. *Chironomia, or a Treatise on Rhetorical Delivery*. 1966. Eds Mary Margaret Robb and Lester Thonssen. Carbondale: Southern Illinois University Press.

"Beldame." 1989. *Oxford English Dictionary*. 2nd edn.

Bloomfield, Morton W. 1952. *The Seven Deadly Sins: An Introduction to the History of a Religious Concept with Special References to Medieval English Literature*. East Lansing: Michigan State College Press.

Bray, Alan. 1982. *Homosexuality in Renaissance England*. London: Gay Men's Press.

Brown, Ivor. 1943. *Just Another Word*. London: Jonathan Cape.

Bulwer, John. 1644. *Chirologia: or the Natural Language of the Hand* and *Chironomia: or the Art of Manual Rhetoric*. 1974. Ed. James W. Cleary. Carbondale: Southern Illinois University Press.

"Cambrel." 1989. *Oxford English Dictionary*. 2nd edn.

"Cammock." 1989. *Oxford English Dictionary*. 2nd edn.

Castiglione, Baldesar. 1528. *The Book of the Courtier*. 1959. Trans. Charles S. Singleton. Garden City, New Jersey: Doubleday.

Caws, Mary Ann. 1981. *The Eye in the Text: Essays in Perception, Mannerist to Modern*. Princeton: Princeton University Press.

Chalmers, Alexander (ed.). 1806. *The Spectator: A Corrected Edition: With Prefaces Historical and Biographical*. 8 vols. London: T. Bensley.

Dollimore, Jonathan. 1991. *Sexual Dissidence: Augustine to Wilde, Freud to Foucault*. Oxford: Clarendon Press.

Du Bos, Jean-Baptiste. 1719. *Réflexions critiques sur la poésie et sur la peinture*. Paris: J. Mariette.

Ehrenreich, Barbara and Dierdre English. 1979. *For Her Own Good: 150 Years of the Experts' Advice to Women*. New York: Doubleday.

Fraser, Antonia. 1985. *The Weaker Vessel*. New York: Vintage Books.

Freedman, Barbara. 1991. *Staging the Gaze: Postmodernism, Psychoanalysis, and Shakespearean Comedy*. Ithaca: Cornell University Press.

"Fribble." 1989. *Oxford English Dictionary*. 2nd edn.

Garrick, David. 1761. *The Fribbleriad*. *The Poetical Works of David Garrick, Esq.* 1785. 2 vols. London: George Kearsley, 1: 21–34.

Gifford, D. J. 1979. "Iconographical Notes toward a Definition of the Medieval Fool." In Paul V. A. William (ed.). *The Fool and the Trickster: Studies in Honour of Enid Welsford*. Totowa, New Jersey: Rowman and Littlefield, 18–35.

Golding, Alfred Siemon. 1984. *Classicistic Acting: Two Centuries of a Performance Tradition at the Amsterdam Schouwburg*. Lanham, Maryland: University Press of America.

Hogarth, William. 1753. *The Analysis of Beauty*. 1971. Ed. Richard Woodfield. Aldershot: Scolar Press.

Houghton, Walter E., Jr. 1942. "The English Virtuoso in the Seventeenth Century." 2 parts. *Journal of the History of Ideas* 3/1: 51–73; 3/2: 190–219.

Jelgerhuis, Johannes. 1827. *Lessons on the Theory of Gesticulation and Mimic Expression*. Amsterdam: P. Meyer Warners. In Golding 1984.

"Knack." 1989. *Oxford English Dictionary*. 2nd edn.

"Knick-Knackatory." 1989. *Oxford English Dictionary*. 2nd edn.

Koenigsberger, H. G. 1986. *Politicians and Virtuosi: Essays in Early Modern History*. London: Hambledon Press.

Lambert, Royston. 1988. *Beloved and God: The Story of Hadrian and Antinous*. Secaucus, New Jersey: Meadowland Books.

Lavater, John Caspar. 1789. *Essays in Physiognomy*. 3 vols. Trans. Henry Hunter. London: John Murray, H. Hunter, and T. Holloway.

Locke, John. 1690. *An Essay Concerning Human Understanding*. 1971. Ed. A. D. Woozley. New York: Meridian.

Morley, Henry (ed.). 1891. *Character Writings of the Seventeenth Century*. London: George Routledge.

Peacham, Henry. 1622. *The Complete Gentleman*. 1962. Ed. Virgil B. Heltzel. Ithaca: Cornell University Press.

The Phoenix of Sodom, or the Vere Street Coterie. 1813. London: J. Cook. In Trumbach 1986.

Rich, Adrienne. 1986. *Of Woman Born: Motherhood as Experience and Institution*. New York: W. W. Norton.

Sedgwick, Eve Kosofsky. 1985. *Between Men: English Literature and Male Homosocial Desire*. New York: Columbia University Press.

Senelick, Laurence. 1990. "Mollies or Men of Mode?: Sodomy and the Eighteenth-Century London Stage." *Journal of the History of Sexuality* 1/1: 33–67.

Shadwell, Thomas. 1676. *The Virtuoso*. 1966. Eds Marjorie Hope Nicolson and David Stuart Rodes. Lincoln: University of Nebraska Press.

Shaftesbury, Anthony Ashley Cooper, Third Earl of. 1709. *The Moralists, A Philosophical Rhapsody*. In Shaftesbury 1711, 2:3–153.

—— 1710. *Soliloquy: Or, Advice to an Author*. In Shaftesbury 1727, 1:151–364.

—— 1711. *Characteristics of Men, Manners, Opinions, Times*. 1900. 2 vols. Ed. John M. Robertson. London: Grant Richards.

—— 1714. *Miscellaneous Reflections on the preceding Treatises, and Other Critical Subjects*. In Shaftesbury 1727, 3:1–344.

—— 1727. *Characteristicks [sic] of Men, Manners, Opinions, Times*. 4th edn. 3 vols. [London]

Siddons, Henry. 1818. *Practical Illustrations of Rhetorical Gesture and Action*. 2nd edn. London: Sherwood, Neely, and Jones. 1968. New York: Benjamin Blom.

Smith, Bruce R. 1991. *Homosexual Desire in Shakespeare's England: A Cultural Poetics*. Chicago: University of Chicago Press.

Sontag, Susan. 1964. "Notes on Camp." 1983. *A Susan Sontag Reader*. New York: Vintage Books, 105–119.

Stone, Lawrence. 1965. *The Crisis of the Aristocracy, 1558–1641*. Oxford: Clarendon Press.

—— 1979. *The Family, Sex, and Marriage in England, 1500–1800*. New York: Harper and Row.

Strong, Roy. 1972. *Van Dyck: Charles I on Horseback*. New York: Viking Press.

Trumbach, Randolph. 1977. "London's Sodomites: Homosexual Behavior and Western Culture in the Eighteenth Century." *Journal of Social History* 2/1: 15–18.

—— 1986. *Sodomy Trials: Seven Documents*. New York: Garland.

—— 1989. "The Birth of the Queen: Sodomy and the Emergence of Gender Equality in Modern Culture, 1660–1750." In Martin Bauml Duberman,

Martha Vicinus, and George Chauncey, Jr. (eds). *Hidden from History: Reclaiming the Gay and Lesbian Past*. New York: New American Library, 129–140.

The Tryal and Condemnation of Mervin, Lord Audley Earl of Castle-Haven. 1699. In Trumbach 1986, n.p.

Tyler, Carole-Anne. 1991. "Boys Will Be Girls: The Politics of Gay Drag." In Diana Fuss (ed.). *Inside/Out: Lesbian Theories, Gay Theories*. New York: Routledge, 32–70.

Ward, Edward. 1703. *The London-Spy Compleat*. 1924. London: Casanova Society.

—— c. 1709. *The Second Part of the London Clubs; Containing: The No Nose Club, The Beaus Club, The Mollies Club, The Quacks Club*. Facsimile (n.d.). London.

—— 1710. *Satyrical Reflections on Clubs*. London: J. Phillips.

Plate 1 Joan Jett Blakk, "The Mayor of Queer Chicago," 1991, Chicago, by Genyphyr Novak.

Plate 2 *Charles I à la ciasse*, by Sir Anthony van Dyck, 1635.

Plate 3 Prince Rupert, from a broadside entitled *Englands Wolfe with Eagles Clawes* . . . (London: Printed by Matthew Simmons, 1646). Illustration re-engraved by John Ashton, 1883.

Plate 4 Sir Walter Ralegh and His Son.

Plate 5 Actor Robert Wilks, from Colley Cibber's *Apology*, 1740.
Engraving by R. B. Parkes after the portrait by I. Ellys, 1732.

Plate 6 "Pride," from Henry Siddons's *Practical Illustrations of Rhetorical Gesture and Action*, 1822.

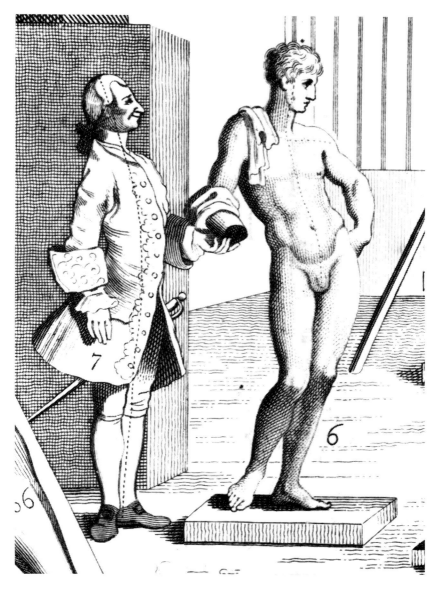

Plate 7 Antinous and Dancing Master, from William Hogarth, *The Analysis of Beauty*, 1753.

Plate 8 "Contrasted attitudes [of] a man and a fribble," from John Caspar Lavater's *Essays on Physiognomy*, 1789. Engraving by Thomas Holloway.

2

NARCISSUS IN THE WILDE

Textual cathexis and the historical origins of queer Camp

Gregory W. Bredbeck

A species comes to be, a type becomes fixed and strong through the long fight with essentially constant unfavorable conditions.

Friedrich Nietzsche, *Beyond Good and Evil*

In the early 1960s, Susan Sontag published her famous "Notes on Camp" and dedicated them to Oscar Wilde. Aside from a few passing comments about Wilde within the essay, there is no explanation of the dedication, as if to imply that the link between Wilde and Camp *should go without saying*. Since that time, Wilde's almost mythical status as the origin of modern gay Camp has been constantly reinscribed. Michael Bronski, for example, in his wonderful act of guerrilla scholarship, *Culture Clash*, honors Wilde as "perhaps the most important figure in the history of gay sensibility" (58), and associates him with several cultural trends leading to modern gay male political Camp. Stephen Gee's history of gay activism suggests both Camp and Wilde as models of how to read moments of gay resistance hidden in history: "gayness might be suggested by the use of Camp as in Oscar Wilde, or in the dark fatalistic metaphors of horror films" (203). Jack Babuscio's pioneering examination of cinematic Camp exhibits Wilde as an example of what is termed the aesthetic mode of Camp (42). Eve Sedgwick has placed Wilde squarely amidst "the intersections of sexual definition with relatively new problematics of kitsch, of camp, and of nationalist and imperialist definition" (132).

At the same time that Wilde has been increasingly written into the history of Camp, Camp has been increasingly written into the history of gay male politics. While contending that much gay male politics simply imitates dominant orders, Gregg Blachford's early theoretical address of the problem also suggests that

the processes at work in the subculture are more complicated

51

than might appear at first glance, for there is some evidence that the gay subculture negotiates an oppositional challenge to some aspects of the dominant order. The best way to understand this innovatory style is to examine one phenomenon of the gay subculture – camp – and to show how it transforms conformity into a challenge.

(193–194)

In 1970, the New York Gay Activists' Alliance coined a strategy of media-oriented demonstration called the "zap," a "unique tactic of confrontation politics, combining the somber principles of *realpolitik* with the theatrics of high camp" (Evans 112). The elements of representation and play that underpin these examples are not without a history. It has been suggested by Bruce Rodgers that the word itself, "camp," is a sixteenth-century derivative from the French word *campagne*, meaning the countryside where transient mime troupes entertained (40).

Why has gay male culture embraced Wilde *as* Camp and Camp *as* political? What might account for these conjunctions? These questions seem to me to be effaced by the more typical questions – what *is* Camp?; *is* Camp gay?; *is* Wilde Camp?; *is* Camp political? – questions that overtly desire a determinism and degree of definition that betray Camp itself.[1] Certainly these latter questions demand attention, and my own Camp response would be: *only her hairdresser knows for sure*. The initial set of questions, I think, offers a more provocative starting place for an examination of the historicity of Camp as it has been perceived as a gay male political strategy. I will begin with three assumptions. First, we can read in Wilde a signifying dynamic that is an ur-form of contemporary gay male political Camp (accepting as an initial premise the current embrace of Wilde *as* Camp). Second, this Camp relates, either in its own time or in its subsequent history, to gay male politics (accepting the embrace of Camp *as* political). Third, this Camp proceeds from and reinforces a strategy of gay male identity (accepting as embraceable the positionality of the gay male). I am not, therefore, proposing a "universalized" Camp, some type of framework that will explain every form of Camp to every person.[2] Rather, I am only concerned with Camp as it meets these three conditions. I am, therefore, speaking as a gay male about gay male Camp, and attempting to do so with some eye toward history and context.

I adopt for this argument Bronski's definition of gay male political Camp:

On some level, it is a way to obtain power in one's own life. On a deeper level, it is the ability to see beyond what is clearly evident; to grasp a reality beneath or totally separate from what is taught.

(43)

I will claim that Wilde's aesthetic maps out this same dynamic, contextualizes it within and against the emerging languages of sexology, and, in the process, reveals the historicity and power of the gay male Camp dynamic. I write as a gay man, I write about a gay man, and I write to reveal the contiguity of these two phenomena. If this process seems a bit self-referential that is all for the best, for my venue into the historical political origins of gay male Camp will be Wilde's intersections with the sexological concept of narcissism.

TEXTUAL INVERSION: POETIC CATHEXIS AND SEXOLOGY

In all unimportant matters, style, not sincerity, is the essential. In all important matters, style, not sincerity, is the essential.

Oscar Wilde,
"Phrases and Philosophies for the Use of the Young"

As one of the six brief parables Oscar Wilde published as *Poems in Prose*, "The Disciple" stands as the most thematically prescient and structurally central for understanding this great critic and artist:

When Narcissus died, the pool of his pleasure changed from a cup of sweet waters into a cup of salt tears, and the Oreads came weeping through the woodland that they might sing to the pool and give it comfort.

And when they saw that the pool had changed from a cup of sweet waters into a cup of salt tears, they loosened the green tresses of their hair, and cried to the pool, and said: "We do not wonder that you should mourn in this manner for Narcissus, so beautiful was he."

"But was Narcissus beautiful?" said the pool.

"Who should know that better than you?" answered the Oreads. "Us did he ever pass by, but you he sought for, and would lie on your banks and look down at you, and in the mirror of your waters he would mirror his own beauty."

And the pool answered: "But I loved Narcissus because, as he
lay on my banks and looked down at me, in the mirror of his eyes
I saw my own beauty mirrored."

(1893: 15–16)

This narrative constructs the sort of paradox that has become the
hallmark of the literary and mythical Wilde. It creates a textual space
that, as Roland Barthes would phrase it, is

> not a line of words releasing a single "theological" meaning . . .
> but . . . a multi-dimensional space in which are married and
> contested several writings, none of them original: the text is a
> fabric of quotations, resulting from a thousand sources of culture
> blend.

(52–53)

The poem issues from the long and convoluted social *pas de deux* Wilde
had been dancing with André Gide, who had just published a book
about the mythological figure (Ellmann 1988: 356–357; Dollimore 3–
20). Moreover, the very choice to write poems in prose demonstrates
the considerable influence of French symbolist poetry. And, of course,
Wilde's own extensive training in the classics undoubtedly shapes the
poem. Yet if we can trace any number of meanings and influences
throughout the brief text, it is also true that we cannot avoid the fact
that the text remakes these meanings, succinctly *inverting* the received
morality of the myth by turning the gazer into the gazed, the subject
into the object. The received moral of Narcissus typically is related to
the dangers of being attracted to oneself. The moral of "The Disciple,"
on the other hand, seems to relate to the dangers of assuming an ability
to know who is attracted to what.

The overt embrace of inversion as a textual principle has been
recognized as an exemplary trait of Wilde's writings. In "A Few
Maxims for the Instruction of the Over-Educated," for example,
Wilde tells us that "Art is the only serious thing in the world, and the
artist is the only person who is never serious" (1989a: 1203). In "Phrases
and Philosophies for the Use of the Young," we are told that "The ages
live in history through their anachronisms" (1894: 434) This type of
inversion, in which dominant relations between certain terms become
flippantly overturned, seemed to signal something far greater than
textual stylistics to Victorian society. An editorial in the London
Evening News written about the announcement of Wilde's sodomy

conviction berates the writer's ability to enact it as a principle of social intercourse:

> To him and such as him we owe the spread of moral degeneration amongst young men with abilities sufficient to make them a credit to their country. At the feet of Wilde they have learned to gain notoriety by blatant conceit, by despising the emotions of healthy humanity and the achievements of wholesome talent.
>
> (qtd in Hyde 12)

What is clearly at stake here is the association between textual inversion and sexual inversion,[3] the "new" invention of *fin-de-siècle* sexology that initiated the construction of the modern "homosexual."[4] Jonathan Dollimore has eloquently summarized this associative pattern:

> One of the many reasons why people were terrified by Wilde was because of a perceived connection between his aesthetic transgression and his sexual transgression. "Inversion" was being used increasingly to define a specific kind of deviant sexuality inseparable from a deviant personality. . . . by the time of Wilde, homosexuality could be regarded as rooted in a person's identity and as pathologically pervading all aspects of his being. As such the expression of homosexuality might be regarded as the more *intentionally* insidious and subversive. Hence in part the animosity and hysteria directed at Wilde during and after his trial.
>
> (67)

"The Disciple" obviously participates in the prolonged program of inversion that typifies Wilde's canon, but it also reinforces the associations between textuality and sexuality in a number of ways that further support and finesse Dollimore's claim. The very choice of rewriting the myth of Narcissus signals an intervention into the psycho-mythology of Victorian sexology. In his massive *Studies in the Psychology of Sex*, Havelock Ellis provides a synopsis of the sexual relevance of Narcissus in the late nineteenth century. He states:

> It has, however, recently been suggested that there really was present in the Greek mind the idea of Narcissus embodying an attitude of mind which would now be termed auto-erotic. In a fragment of a comedy by Kratinos there is an uncertain phrase which Meinecke reads as "the olisbos of Narcissus." The olisbos, as we know, was primarily an instrument for the sexual gratification of women. But there is reason to believe that even

55

> in the days of Greek myth it was recognized that such a device
> could have a masculine use *per anum*, and there is a story of
> Dionysus in point. Kratinos would thus be making fun of a
> Narcissist, though as he wrote in the spirit of caricature and
> parody he was only concerned with a physical manifestation of
> that disposition.
>
> (1900: 3: 348)

I will examine the problematic interplay of narcissism and sexual
inversion marked here at length. For the present it is sufficient to
recognize that the mere invocation of Narcissus suggests the
potentiality of sexual inversion, and that this potentiality is further
activated within Wilde's text by its linkage with a textual inversion.[5]

While there is little within the text of "The Disciple" aside from the
use of the trope of inversion to signal a direct engagement of the images
of the invert carried within Ellis's description, the image of Narcissus
also plays out a complicated web within Wilde's canon and life, a
dispersion of textual images and historical moments that leads us further
into the language of sexology. The house at 16 Tite Street, into which
Wilde moved in January of 1885, sported dark green walls, and "On the
mantelpiece was a small green bronze figure of Narcissus" (Ellmann
1988: 257). The green of the walls might suggest to us the green of the
Oreads' tresses in "The Disciple." It is a color that repeatedly tints
Wilde's writings at crucial and understated moments. "Pen, Pencil and
Poison," for example, is subtitled "A Study in Green" (1889: 320). The
reason for the phrase is only lightly tossed off in the study. In describing
the character of Thomas Griffiths Wainewright, a minor member of the
literati, noted dandy, and notorious murderer, Wilde mentions that "He
had that curious love of green, which in individuals, is always the sign of
a subtle artistic temperament, and in nations is said to denote a laxity, if
not a decadence of morals" (324). Yet this seemingly trivial question of
style is pointedly stressed by the title of the study; and in any event,
Wilde himself has warned us to press such trivial details: "In all
important matters, style, not sincerity, is the essential" (1894: 433). Or,
if we trace not the walls but the bronze itself, we might find this to be
the same Narcissus who resurfaces in "The Critic as Artist," the bronze
Narcissus whose "eyelids . . . are folded in sleep" and who appears
when Gilbert yearns to "play . . . some mad scarlet thing by Dvorak"
(1891: 349).

Frank Harris published "Pen, Pencil and Poison" in *The Fortnightly
Review* in January 1889, and "The Critic as Artist" appeared in Wilde's

essay collection, *Intentions*, in 1891. Given these dates we might safely assume that the text bears at least a possible familiarity with the cultural currents that produced Havelock Ellis's *Sexual Inversion*, which first found publication in 1897.[6] Yet the need for a direct chronology is undermined by Wilde's own inverted advice: "The ages live in history through their anachronisms" (1894: 434). Moreover, the case for an intertext is again supported by the color green, for in a curious moment in Ellis's "scientific" tract, we are presented with a lesson in the history of fashion: "It has also been remarked that inverts exhibit a preference for green garments. In Rome *cinaedi* were for this reason called *galbanati*. Chevalier remarks that some years ago a band of paederasts at Paris wore green cravats as a badge" (1901: 177). This "coloring" of the invert surfaces again in the tract and again draws us back to Wilde, for Ellis suggests a correlation between sexual inversion and synesthesia, the physiological process whereby impressions associated with one sense become translated through a different sense:

> Or we may compare inversion to such a phenomenon as color-hearing, in which there is not so much a defect, as an abnormality of nervous tracks producing new and involuntary combinations. Just as the color-hearer instinctively associates colors with sounds, like the young Japanese lady who remarked when listening to singing, "That boy's voice is red!" so the invert has his sexual sensations brought into relationship with objects that are normally without sexual appeal.
>
> (1901: 186–187)

Wearing green and hearing red become analogies for the invert – and remind us, of course, that the bronze Narcissus against the *green* walls of Wilde's house resurfaces in "The Critic as Artist" at the precise moment that Gilbert yearns to hear "some mad *scarlet* thing by Dvorak."[7] If Wilde's writing seems to lead us toward Ellis, Ellis's writing also leads us back to Wilde. Twice within his essay on Narcissism, Ellis uses Wilde as his grounding example: "Novelists have not only noted the spirit of Narcissus in their creations, they have sometimes demonstrated it in themselves, consciously or unconsciously. This is perhaps true of Oscar Wilde, the author of *Dorian Gray*" (1900: 3:352); "Oscar Wilde's *Dorian Gray* . . . illustrates various aspects of Narcissism, to a greater extent probably than any other imaginative work in English literature, and in it Wilde directly invokes Narcissus" (3:369).

"The Disciple," then, leads us into an examination of sexual representation through two related, but different, courses. There is the direct path into sexology signaled by the content of the poem (the image of Narcissus). Then there are the vague and plural textual cathexes that shoot associations in multiple directions all leading, ironically, to the same point. This second pattern of meaning is the more interesting because it mimetically enacts the psycho-biological problem of synesthesia itself. That is, synesthesia is typically conceived of as an improper cathexis, a bonding of one mode of sensory impression to an object proper to another mode. Synesthesia is, in its broadest sense, a problem of object-choice, an inability to link an internal, subjective process to a normative external manifestation or causality. And this, of course, writes both synesthesia and Wilde's textual dissemination into the general problematics of sexual inversion: all are typified by a "bad" object choice. Sensory perception, sexual desire, and textual influence are all generally thought of in terms of one *straight* line. Synesthesia, sexual inversion, and the poetics of "The Disciple" are all, from this perspective, a bit *queer*.

A BRIEF HISTORY OF NARCISSISM: THE ANACLITIC SELF

It is only the gods who taste of death. Apollo has passed away, but Hyacinth, whom men say he slew, lives on. Nero and Narcissus are always with us.

Oscar Wilde,
"Phrases and Philosophies for the Use of the Young"

I would like to suggest that "The Disciple" enacts a critique of sexology not so much through its direct adoption of inversion and Narcissus, but more through its display of polymorphous textual cathexes. Narcissus and inversion signal an engagement with sexology, but the "queer" poetics of the text signal a resistance. In order to understand this point, it is necessary to take a brief stroll through the "narrativization" of Narcissus that is displayed in the history of sexology – for it is precisely this display that Wilde's poem dis-plays. Initially, Narcissism entered sexology as a discrete topic near the middle of the nineteenth century. Ellis cites three examples of early work with the concept, one from Italy, one from Germany, and one from France. In 1897, Nicefero's *Le psicopatie sessualle* used the term to describe a fifteen-year-old boy who would "derive pleasure from the spectacle of his penis becoming erected, and even the idea of this would give him voluptuous emotions" (1900: 3:354) It further presents the case of another boy who could successfully masturbate only if he could see his own legs while stimulating himself (3:354). Moll's 1898 publication, *Untersuchungen über die Libido Sexualis*, analyzed the case of a 43-year-old man who was attracted to both men and women, but achieved his primary stimulation through gazing in the mirror and comparing his own image to that of other men he had seen (3:354). Féré's contemporaneous studies in France, published under the title *L'Instinct sexual*, presented the case of a girl who stimulated herself by kissing her own hand, and termed the practice "auto-fetichism" (3:354).

What is striking about all three examples is the extent to which they write self-attraction in terms of a self/other or subject/object split. In Nicefero's example, the penis becomes tacitly dismembered from the subject and exists as an external object, a phenomenon outside the subject which then stimulates him. The question that is repressed here is the obvious one: what stimulates the penis to erection in the first place if stimulation is only derived from the erect penis itself? In Moll's example, the issue of self-attraction is preceded by a declaration of the object-attraction of the subject. The self-attraction is further categorized as an engagement of a self/other dynamic – "his *own* image" is simply an intercourse with the images of "*other* men." For the French girl, the hand is not her*self*, but a "fetich," an object which, as Ellis tells us in his essay "Erotic Symbolism," only functions in "the absence of the beloved person" and as the surrogate for the beloved. (1900: 3:18). Desire, it seems, can only manifest itself across the great divide – "/" – and the self cannot exist in any sense that is entirely self-sufficient. Narcissism in these instances seems to hint at a mode of desire that precedes or escapes the divisive binaries of sexual and gender ontology but, at the same time, this possibility also is clearly subordinated to an articulation that privileges this binaristic logic.

Narcissism maps a complicated interplay between the autonomy of the self and the need to tether this autonomy to the dependence of object-choice. These two tensions are best displayed in Freud's summation and refinement of the earlier Victorians' explorations in sexology. In his essay "On Narcissism: An Introduction," Freud provides a vocabulary for expressing the two elements of this tension.

> The first auto-erotic sexual gratifications are experienced in connection with vital functions in the service of self-preservation. The sexual instincts are at the outset supported upon the

ego-instincts; only later do they become independent of these, and even then we have an indication of that original dependence in the fact that those persons who have to do with the feeding, care, and protection of the child become his earliest sexual objects; that is to say, in the first instance the mother or her substitute. Side by side with this type and source of object-choice, which may be called the *anaclitic* type, a second type, the existence of which we had not suspected, has been revealed by psychoanalytic investigation. We have found, especially in persons whose libidinal development has suffered some disturbance, as in perverts and homosexuals, that in the choice of their love-object, they have taken as their model not the mother but their own selves. They are plainly seeking themselves as a love-object and their type of object choice may be termed *narcissistic*.

(1914: 68–69)

The difference marked here is also the difference marked between self-attraction and self/other attraction. The anaclitic relation is a manifestation of cathexis to an other, a dependency on an eroticized or nuturing object-choice. Narcissism, on the other hand, eschews object cathexis, or, in a more proper sense, cathects the self to the self. Moreover, this division between anaclitic and narcissistic types becomes the basis for an implicit hierarchization of cathexes. Narcissistic cathexis becomes associated with "perverts and homosexuals," while the association between anaclitic cathexis and the mother links it to reproductive heterosexuality. Later Freud tells us that "complete object-love of the anaclitic type is, properly speaking, characteristic of the man," while "the maturing of the female sexual organs . . . seems to bring about an intensification of the original narcissism" (1914: 68–69). The anaclitic/narcissistic binary becomes a master trope that replicates and grounds the sexual binary of heterosexual/homosexual and the gender binary of man/woman.[8]

This strategy of intervalidating binaries as expressive of each other is not unusual in Freud. In discussing the dynamics of sadism and masochism, Freud explains that "We should rather be inclined to connect the simultaneous presence of these opposites with the opposing masculinity and femininity which are in bisexuality – a contrast which often has to be replaced in psycho-analysis by that between activity and passivity" (1905: 26). The explanation of the difference between anaclitic and narcissistic desire becomes a mimetic enactment of the primacy of the anaclitic, for narcissistic and anaclitic cathexis are

60

"leaning-up-against"[9] one another and are anaclitically dependent on one another in much the same way that the binaries of man/woman, homo/hetero, and passive/active can only find expression and meaning in anaclitic dependence and contradistinction.

Freud's perhaps unconscious desire to (re)present the anaclitic/ narcissistic difference as a grounding of the anaclitic shows forth strongly in his earliest invocation of the term *narcissism*. In 1910 Freud added a lengthy footnote on sexual inversion to the essay "The Sexual Aberrations" in *Three Essays on the Theory of Sexuality*, originally published in 1905. The note begins with an analysis of narcissism and the invert:

> It is true that psycho-analysis has not yet produced a complete explanation of the origin of inversion; nevertheless, it has discovered the psychical mechanism of its development, and has made essential contributions to the statement of the problems involved. In all cases we have examined we have established the fact that future inverts, in the earliest years of childhood, pass through a phase of very intense but short-lived fixation to a woman (usually their mother), and that, after leaving this behind, they identify themselves with a woman and take *themselves* as their sexual object. That is to say, they proceed from a narcissistic basis, and look for a young man who resembles themselves and whom *they* may love as their mother loved *them*.
>
> (1905: 10 n.1)

In every respect, this formulation casts *in*version as a *re*version of the object relations that typify anaclitic cathexis.[10] The other receives the authority of the self; the self in turn is free to function as the other. The formulation again posits binaristic desire as its subtending narrative, for the difference of narcissism and inversion is presented as a misprision and refiguring of the cross-gendered anaclitic cathexis between son and mother. Narcissistic inversion becomes a sustenance of anaclitic heterosexual object relations for, throughout the life of the male invert, Freud tells us, his motives will still be determined by a cross-gender libido action: "Their compulsive longing for men has turned out to be determined by their ceaseless flight from women" (1905: 10 n.1).

The strategy at work here is at once both subtle and obvious. On the one hand, there is a need to explain the *difference* of the invert, and this need is met through the construction of narcissistic cathexis. On the other hand, this alternate authority becomes prey to what might best be called sexology's fetishization of narrative – its desire to subject its "scientific observations" to an explanatory mimetic principle. Freud succinctly maps and acknowledges this narrative in an addition he made to his essay "Infantile Sexuality" in 1915. As he states:

> The final outcome of sexual development lies in what is known as the normal sexual life of the adult, in which the pursuit of pleasure comes under the sway of the reproductive function and in which the component instincts, under the primacy of a single erotogenic zone, form a firm organization directed towards a sexual aim attached to some extraneous sexual object.
>
> (1905: 63)

Elsewhere and frequently Freud problematizes the authority of this narrative. Discussing the relationship between prostitution and polymorphous perversity, he claims that "it becomes impossible not to recognize that this same disposition to perversions of every kind is a general and fundamental human characteristic" (1905: 57). Examining "the extraordinarily wide dissemination of the perversions," he suggests that

> it must also be considered that an unbroken chain bridges the gap between the neuroses in all their manifestations and normality . . . the disposition to perversions is itself of no great rarity but must form a part of what passes as the normal constitution.
>
> (1905: 37)

While explaining the sexual uses of the mucous membranes, Freud inserts a purely social-constructionist stance into his biologically determined theory: "the limits of . . . disgust are, however, often purely conventional" (1905: 17). Such moments reveal a polymorphous flux at play within Freud's theory;[11] yet this play is also always at odds with a desire to congeal this fluidity into a mimetic hypostatization of the picaresque heterosexual narrative journey from foreplay to pro-creation – a journey that reenacts and is reenacted in the normative developmental model wherein the perverse play of the infantile body slowly but surely contracts over time into one unitary procreative thrust.

The texts from the years surrounding the addition of this master narrative statement to the *Three Essays* witness a refiguring of both narcissism and sexual inversion within Freud's writings, a series of changes that subordinates both to the teleology of procreative heterosexuality. In an addition to the footnote on inversion from 1915, Freud tells us that "it has been found that all human beings are capable of making a homosexual object-choice and have in fact made one in their unconscious," and further adds that

> thus from the point of view of psycho-analysis the exclusive sexual interest felt by men for women is also a problem that needs elucidating and is not a self-evident fact based upon an attraction that is ultimately of a chemical nature.
>
> (1905: 10 n.1)

Yet the "equal abnormality" of both homosexuality and heterosexuality is, again, skewed within the text; for Freud does not further address the "problem" of heterosexuality, but instead explains the misprisions that lead to homosexuality:

> In inverted types, a predominance of archaic constitutions and primitive psychical mechanisms is regularly to be found. Their most essential characteristics seem to be a coming into operation of narcissistic object-choice and a retention of the erotic significance of the anal zone.
>
> (1905: 10 n.1)

This is a statement which characterizes inversion as a pre-civilized impulse, a nonanaclitic choice, and a manifestation of an early phase of infantile sexuality.[12] Through implication, heterosexuality becomes civilized, anaclitic, and mature.

We might think here of Freud's famous letter to an anonymous American mother with a homosexual son, wherein he tells her: "homosexuality is assuredly no advantage, but it is nothing to be ashamed of, no vice, no degradation, it cannot be classified as an illness; we consider it to be a variation of the sexual function produced by a certain arrest of the sexual development" (1935: 419).[13] As with Freud's problematizing of heterosexuality in the 1915 note, the liberal sentiments here appear laudable. However, the statement also privileges the narrative of heterosexual development, assigning homosexuality to the status of an "arrest," an inability to tell the story in its entirety. As these theorizations draw homosexuality into the content of the psychodynamics of the subject, they also implicitly skew the representation in such a way as to privilege heterosexual object-choice. In the process, inversion becomes not a separate dynamic of cathexis with its own authority, but a misplaying of the singularly authorized heterosexual cathexis.

Not surprisingly, narcissism follows a similar course within Freud's refinement of his theory. Initially, Freud accepted the term from the earlier work of Ellis and Rank, and Ellis's own critique of Freud provides an excellent ground against which to view Freud's reconstruction of narcissism. As Ellis states:

> For me Narcissism was the extreme form of auto-eroticism, which, it must be remembered, was a term devised to cover all the spontaneous manifestations of the sexual impulse in the absence of a definite outer object to evoke them, erotic dreams in sleep being the type of auto-erotic activity. Auto-eroticism while thus not properly a perversion . . . might become so deliberately pursued at the expense of the normal objects of sexual attraction. The psycho-analysts in adopting the term "auto-eroticism" have given it a different meaning which I regret, as being both illegitimate and inconvenient. For the psycho-analyst "auto-eroticism" generally means sexual activity directed toward the self as its object. That is illegitimate, for the ordinary rule is that a word compounded with "auto" (like automobile or autonomous) means not *toward* itself but *by* itself. It is inconvenient because if we divert the term "auto-eroticism" to this use we have no term left to cover the objectless spontaneous sexual manifestations for which the term was devised.
>
> (1900: 3:362–363)

That to which Ellis objects – though these precise terms might escape him – is the increasing territorialization of the narcissistic cathexis by the anaclitic framework that dominates the Freudian model.[14]

What Ellis perceives is an increasing effort to erase anything that disrupts the hegemony of the anaclitic subject/object divide. While Freud is not responsible for initiating this strategy – we have already seen it in the earliest theories of the term – his primary engagements of the concept succinctly summarize the problem Ellis pinpoints. In both the *Three Essays* and his essay "On Narcissism: An Introduction," Freud seems to posit a difference and an authority to narcissism and inversion, claiming that homosexuals "have taken as their model not the mother but their own selves. They are plainly seeking themselves as a love-object and their type of object-choice may be termed narcissistic" (1914: 69). Already, as I have suggested, Ellis's objection is verified, for narcissism is figured not as "auto-erotism" – a process of and by the self – but as a mode of anaclitic cathexis *to* the self. Moreover, Freud's 1914 expansion of the concept adds a new twist: "we say that the human being has originally two sexual objects: himself and the woman who tends him, and thereby we postulate a primary narcissism in everyone, which may in the long run manifest itself as dominating his object-choice" (1914: 69). The difference of narcissistic cathexis is effaced. It becomes fully anaclitic and fully present in every subject from birth.

This reconfiguration of the narcissistic cathexis as anaclitic shows forth most strongly in Freud's "short survey of the paths leading to object-choice":

A Person may Love:
(1) According to the narcissistic type:
    (a) What he is himself (actually himself).
    (b) What he once was.
    (c) What he would like to be.
    (d) Someone who was once part of himself.
(2) According to the anaclitic type:
    (a) The woman who tends.
    (b) The man who protects.

(1914: 71)

The subdivision of the narcissistic type fully imitates the divisions of subject and object present in the works of Nicefero, Moll, and Féré; and the specification of the anaclitic type suggests the ways in which the subject/object divide becomes associated with and supportive of a heterosexual narrative: the divide is governed by a nurturing mother figure and an aggressive father figure who play the key roles in the Oedipal narrative of social development.

Examining Freud's curious repression of clitoral orgasm, Thomas Laqueur provides a summary that might also be used to synopsize the theoretical development of narcissism in *fin-de-siècle* sexology. As he states: "Freud's concern . . . is somehow to assure that bodies whose anatomies do not guarantee the dominance of heterosexual procreative sex nevertheless dedicate themselves to their assigned roles" (243). Narcissism and its closely related concept of sexual inversion seem to recognize alternative cathexes that betray the dominance of the heterosexual narrative. They seem to be a token concession to "material reality." But, at the same time, this concession is consistently subjugated. In all the examples included here, both narcissism and inversion become, first, ensnared by an anaclitic division that replicates the *form* of heterosexual union, and thereby both narcissism and inversion seem to make that form inevitable and universal. Second, and particularly in the case of Freud, the *difference* of narcissistic and inverted cathexis is erased by rewriting the potentiality for both as a universal trait of the universalized subject. The traits of objective scientific observation and liberal acceptance that initially seem to mark the emergence of sexology support a mimetic strategy of subjective inscription and liberal accommodation – a strategy that unswervingly maps out differences only as they can serve a socialized and reproductive tale of *indifference*.[15]

DIS-PLAYING THE ANACLITIC: THE ORIGINS OF QUEER CAMP

Even the disciple has his uses. He stands behind one's throne, and at that moment of one's triumph whispers in one's ear that, after all, one is immortal.

Oscar Wilde,
"A Few Maxims for the Instruction of the Over-Educated"

Ironically, Wilde's brief tribute to Narcissus offers an alternative perspective to the historical development of the heterosexual narrative precisely because it acts out the equality of narcissistic and anaclitic cathexes. On one level, Wilde's poem adopts a method of direct allusion that textually imitates the dynamics of anaclitic cathexis. The poem overtly authorizes itself by its direct attachment to the Greek myth, its tropic replication of sexological inversion, and its adoption of a key figure within the sexual mythology of the era. These direct allusions, in which the text reaches out toward and "leans up against" already existing objects and discourses, mark a type of "object-choice," a process wherein the "meaning" of the text it*self* becomes inscribed in the space of the *other* to which it cathects. On another level, the poem also displays a different mode of meaning, one which is entirely independent of the anaclitic allusions and that marks an entirely self-referential discourse. The Narcissus in the poem by Wilde cathects with the Narcissus in the home built by Wilde; the green of the hair depicted by Wilde cathects with the green of Wilde's walls and the green of "Pen, Pencil and Poison," another Wildean text. And if the color green also leads us to Ellis's *Sexual Inversion*, this also leads us back to Wilde who, as the Marquess of Queensberry told the world, posed "as a somdomite [*sic*]" (Hyde 28). If the anaclitic level of the text leads us from point A (Wilde) to point B (traditions), this other level leads us from point A (Wilde) to point A (Wilde). This is, I would claim, a level of narcissistic textual cathexis, a system wherein the self leads to the self or, more properly, the self never leaves the self. In the most proper sense of Ellis, this level of the poem manifests an "auto-eroticism," or at least an "auto-textualism."

The equality of anaclitic and narcissistic cathexis within Wilde's poem compares favorably with Freud's model of cathexis *prior to* the installation of the anaclitic, heterosexual imperative. In his lectures of 1916–17, Freud offered this model of cathexis for the layperson:

> Think of those simplest of living organisms [the amoebas] which consist of a little-differentiated globule of protoplasmic substance. They put out protrusions, known as pseudopodia, into which they cause the substance of their body to flow over. They are able, however, to withdraw the protrusions once more and form themselves again into a globule. We compare the putting out of these protrusions, then, to the emission of libido on to objects while the main mass of the libido can remain in the ego; and we suppose that in normal circumstances ego-libido can be transformed unhindered into object-libido and that this once more be taken back into the ego.
>
> (1916–17: 517–518)

In the simplest form of "nature" (which, as that most civilized missionary Katherine Hepburn tells us in *The African Queen* [1951], "is what we're put in this world to rise above"), the narcissistic ego-libido and the anaclitic object-libido exist in perfect symbiosis. It is only the intervention of the cultural narrative that hierarchizes and thereby "rises above" this play.

Wilde's poem might be thought of as a mimetic dis-play of the cultural supremacy of the anaclitic. "The Disciple," like "those simplest of living organisms," can be read as neither entirely anaclitic nor narcissistic, but at the same time must also be read as both – or, more precisely, as the *difference* of both. Wilde's poem, then, with its complicated structure of allusion and reference, can be read as a metaphor for the polymorphous flux of libido that is the hallmark of the "liberal" Freudian subject, a metaphor that at the same time refuses to accommodate this flux to the freeze-frame that is anaclitic heterosexual object choice. This dis-play is not simply another Wildean inversion, for that dynamic would entail subordinating the anaclitic to the narcissistic. Rather, this strategy involves *un*writing the dominance of the ontological base – the heterosexual narrative – and *refusing to re-script any base as dominant*. In the process, the strategy also marks ontology as a cultural process subject to intervention.

Wilde's poem perhaps runs the risk of seeming hopelessly parasitic or reactionary.[16] The understandable impulse to begin an identity politics on a statement of "who we are" finds no expression in a poetics that simply disarticulates the dominance of other discourses by resisting the totalizing impulse of the anaclitic cathexis. Yet this dis-play also seems to be recognized by Wilde as a potent and political aspect of cultural theory. Early in his Oxford commonplace book, Wilde notes the importance of basing cultural meaning on a multiplicity of cathexes: "The human spirit cannot live right if it lives by one point alone" (1989b: 108). If we return this comment and "The Disciple" to the language of sexology, we might also perceive the possibility of both an identity and a politics.

In the 1916–17 lectures, Freud realigns the narcissistic and anaclitic cathexes with the dynamics of the ego-libido and the object-libido. In so doing, he explains this structure in terms of the diagnosis of dementia praecox:

Already in 1908 Karl Abraham, after an exchange of thoughts with me, pronounced the main characteristics of dementia praecox . . . to be that *in it the libidinal cathexis of objects was lacking.* But the question then arose of what happened to the libido of dementia praecox patients which was turned away from objects. Abraham did not hesitate to give the answer: it is turned back on to the ego and *this reflexive turning-back is the source of the megalomania* in dementia praecox.

(1916–17: 516)

The dis-play of the anaclitic cathexis is perceived within sexology as a source of hyper-subjectivity, the potentiality of the isolated, autonomous, and narcissistic megalomaniac. Freud's lecture seems to signal that this possibility of a subjectivity that privileges the narcissistic cathexes of the ego-libido is a site of some anxiety. Not only does he allow this possibility only within a discussion of dementia praecox ("which is to say," as Katherine Hepburn tells us in *Suddenly, Last Summer* [1959], "she's mad as a hatter, poor child"), but he also uses the occasion to narrow the gap between dementia and normality, suggesting that narcissistic psychoses are congruent with the language of anaclitic subjectivity: "megalomania is in every way comparable to the familiar sexual overvaluation of the object in (normal) erotic life" (1916–17: 516).

By disrupting the continual pressure to subordinate the narcissistic to the anaclitic, Wilde's poem also disrupts sexology's increasingly stringent efforts to reify identity as a universalized and intransigent phenomenon, a "thing" existing in the margins of a teleological narrative of anaclitic dependence and subjection. Lest we think that this strategy has nothing to do with a queer identity politics, we should note one of Freud's earliest statements about the relationship between sexology and homosexuality:

> Homosexual men, who have in our times taken vigorous action against the restrictions imposed by law on their sexual activity, are fond of representing themselves, through their theoretical spokesmen, as being from the outset a distinct sexual species, as an intermediate sexual stage, as a "third sex". They are, they claim, men who are innately compelled by organic determinants to find pleasure in men and have been debarred from obtaining it in women. Much as one would be glad on the grounds of humanity to endorse their claims, one must treat their theories with some reserve, for they have been advanced without regard for the psychical genesis of homosexuality. Psycho-analysis offers the means of filling this gap and of putting the assertions of homosexuals to the test.
>
> (1910: 48–49)

The almost pathological desire to "fill gaps" and build explanatory processes that efface differences emerges clearly here, and makes this "test" – at least to me – seem more like genocide.[17] For what remains unsaid here is, again, what remains empowered: the narrative of teleological, reproductive (hetero)sexuality waits poised to obliterate anything that cannot make the grade. Wilde's plural cathexes erase the dominance of this narrative by producing an equal display of the cathexes that sexology attempts to skew in order to "naturally" replicate the *form* of reproductive sexuality. At the same time, the poem refuses to inscribe the possibility of any *one* dominance. Narcissus in the Wilde, then, seems to display the idea of identity as difference – as subject *to* difference(s) *and* the subject *of* difference(s) – and, in the process, to dis-play the cultural narratives that seek to legislate what this difference should or should not be. It is, to narcissistically cathect to the definition with which I began, "a way to obtain power in one's own life" through "the ability to see beyond what is clearly evident"; it is an effort "to grasp a reality beneath or totally separate from what is taught" (Bronski 43). That this queer dis-play happens around the figure of Narcissus and the concept of narcissism seems only appropriate, for, as Wilde himself has so aptly taught us, "to love oneself is the beginning of a life-long romance" (1894: 434).

NOTES

Completion of this essay was facilitated by a residential fellowship at the Center for Ideas and Society at the University of California, Riverside. I thank the center's director, Bernd Magnus, for the numerous ways in which he and his staff made thought not only possible, but inevitable. I would like also to acknowledge the debt I owe to students in English 148X, "Oscar Wilde: The Tropes of Authority," at the University of California, Riverside; especially Lisa Brechbiel, Maria DeMaci, David Herman, Erik Kruger, and Andrew Rempt. Research for this essay was partially underwritten by grant funds from the Academic Senate at the University of California, Riverside.

1 Some of the most provocative work on Camp tends to avoid this urge toward determinism. Philip Core, for example, tells us, "CAMP is in the eyes of the beholder, especially if the beholder is camp" (7). On this point see also my forthcoming article, "B/O," on Roland Barthes and Frank O'Hara.

2 Those interested in seeing a complementary examination of Camp in the lesbian community should consult Case. I am indebted to Case's strategy, for she posits Camp, drag, and lesbianism as grounding assumptions to her argument, and thereby places herself in a position to demonstrate how the butch–femme roles in lesbian history and culture enable women to "play on the phallic economy rather than to it" (291). By grounding her argument on these terms, rather than creating an argument about what grounds these terms, Case allows herself to escape the deterministic and hierarchized assumptions of phallic, heterosexual ontology. I sense in Case's argument what Stephen Heath would call "the risk of essence" (99), the strategic process whereby the totalizing narratives of heterosexuality are placed in suspension, and my own argument exploits Case's move.

3 In a classic Foucauldian argument about Victorian sexology George Chauncey has noted that "sexual inversion, the term used most commonly in the nineteenth century, did not denote the same conceptual phenomenon as homosexuality" (116). This may be true; but what will come to be the focus of my argument is the way in which the progression of sexology (especially as it culminates in Freudian psychoanalysis) increasingly consolidates inversion, narcissism, and homosexuality. For a full discussion of the vexed status of the term "inversion," see Halperin 15–18.

4 For extensive social and legal discussions of the relationship between the Wilde trial and the development of contemporary gay politics, see Weeks 91–117, 171–181, 265; Marshall; and Lumsden.

5 See also Ed Cohen, "Writing Gone Wilde," for an examination of the ways in which *The Picture of Dorian Gray* intersects with theories of sexual inversion in order to produce a homosexual identity. On this point see also Regenia Gagnier 140.

6 My stress on a chronology based on "cultural currents" rather than direct textual indebtedness is meant to indicate the extent to which both sexology and literature channel dominant cultural motifs that very often find an origin much earlier. See Dijkstra for a convincing documentation of the "reactionary" status of sexology. Dijkstra concluded that "it is thus

clear that the 'discovery' of narcissism and the autoerotic mentality by the psychoanalytic community trailed behind the vogue for the same subject on the part of artists and writers by quite a bit" (147, 144–155 passim).

7 Wayne Koestenbaum also notes a similar iconography of green that involves Wilde. The *fin-de-siècle* Uranian poet Marc-André Raffalovich, it seems, marked all the books in his library written by inverts with "bookplates of a green serpent – suggesting not only a phallus, but Wilde's green carnation" (46).

8 This moment in sexology seems to bear out what Eve Sedgwick means when she says, "The question of how same-sex desire could be interpreted in terms of *gender* was bitterly embattled almost from the beginnings of male homosexual taxonomy" (134).

9 *Anlehnungstypus*, the German word translated by "anaclitic," literally means "leaning-up-against" (Freud 1914: 69 n.13).

10 A complementary argument to this formulation can be found in Judith Butler. Butler posits a stressed reading of Freudian and Lacanian psychoanalytic theory in order to reach the deconstructive stance that "We might then rethink the very notions of masculinity and femininity constructed here as rooted in unresolved homosexual cathexes" (54, 35–78 passim). This is a theoretical inversion perfectly appropriate to a discussion of sexual inversion.

11 All of the quotations here appear in the original 1905 edition of the *Three Essays*. As such, they can be thought of as revealing an originary fluidity that becomes increasingly subjugated as Freud adds to the essays in subsequent editions. The evolution of the *Three Essays* seems to imitate the ultimate model of Freudian development, in which polymorphous fluidity becomes masked and territorialized by the cultural narrative of Oedipal reproduction.

12 Ibid. The second phase of infantile sexual development, following the oral but preceding the genital, is the sadistic anal (1905: 64).

13 For a further examination of this letter, as well as for a cogent political examination and defense of Freud and homosexuality, see Fletcher.

14 While Ellis seems here to maintain narcissism as a purely nonanaclitic activity, in his essay on auto-eroticism he too associates narcissism with femininity, which again grounds the concept on an anaclitic base. For a discussion of the relationship between auto-eroticism, narcissism, and femininity, see Dijkstra 119–159.

15 I use the term *in*difference to signal my indebtedness to Teresa de Lauretis's examination of the difficulty encountered in expressing sexual difference in representational structures dominated by heterosexual technologies in her essay "Sexual Indifference and Lesbian Representation." See also her argument about narrative in "Strategies of Coherence."

16 The parasitic nature of the poetics of "The Disciple" also suggests a link between the poem and contemporary gay political Camp. Andrew Ross has fortuitously labeled Camp a "parasitical practice . . . [that] had become a survivalist way of life for the counterculture" (151).

17 Wayne Koestenbaum uses this passage as the opening to a brilliant extended discussion of Freud's theoretical construction of homosexuality and his ambivalent tension within his masculine partnerships (17–42). I borrow the

term "genocide" from Louis Crompton's courageous and pioneering article, "Gay Genocide from Leviticus to Hitler."

BIBLIOGRAPHY

Babuscio, Jack. 1984. "Camp and the Gay Sensibility." In Richard Dyer (ed.). *Gays and Film*. New York: Zoetrope, 40–57.

Barthes, Roland. 1986. "The Death of the Author." *The Rustle of Language*. Trans. Richard Howard. New York: Hill and Wang, 49–55.

Blachford, Gregg. 1981. "Male Dominance and the Gay World." In Kenneth Plummer (ed.). *The Making of the Modern Homosexual*. London: Hutchinson, 184–210.

Bredbeck, Gregory W. 1993. "B/O – Barthes's Text/O'Hara's Trick: The Phallus, the Anus, and the Text." *PMLA*, 108: 268–282.

Bronski, Michael. 1984. *Culture Clash: The Making of Gay Sensibility*. Boston: South End Press.

Butler, Judith. 1990. *Gender Trouble: Feminism and the Subversion of Identity*. New York: Routledge.

Case, Sue-Ellen. 1989. "Towards a Butch-Femme Aesthetic." In Lynda Hart (ed.). *Making a Spectacle: Feminist Essays on Contemporary Women's Theatre*. Ann Arbor: University of Michigan Press, 282–299.

Chauncey, George, Jr. 1983. "From Sexual Inversion to Homosexuality: Medicine and the Changing Conceptualization of Female Deviance." *Salmagundi* 58–59: 114–146.

Cohen, Ed. 1987. "Writing Gone Wilde: Homoerotic Desire in the Closet of Representation." *PMLA* 102: 801–813.

Core, Philip. 1984. *Camp: The Lie That Tells the Truth*. New York: Delilah.

Crompton, Louis. 1978. "Gay Genocide from Leviticus to Hitler." In Louis Crew (ed.). *The Gay Academic*. Palm Springs, California: ETC Publications, 67–91.

De Lauretis, Teresa. 1987. "Strategies of Coherence: Narrative Cinema, Feminist Poetics, and Yvonne Rainer." *Technologies of Gender: Essays on Theory, Film, and Fiction*. Bloomington: Indiana University Press, 107–126.

—— 1990. "Sexual Indifference and Lesbian Representation." In Sue-Ellen Case (ed.). *Performing Feminisms: Feminist Critical Theory and Theatre*. Baltimore: Johns Hopkins University Press, 17–39.

Dijkstra, Bram. 1986. *Idols of Perversity: Fantasies of Feminine Evil in Fin-de-Siècle Culture*. Oxford: Oxford University Press.

Dollimore, Jonathan. 1991. *Sexual Dissidence: Augustine to Wilde, Freud to Foucault*. Oxford: Clarendon Press.

Ellis, Havelock. 1900. *Studies in the Psychology of Sex*. 1936. 4 vols. New York: Random House.

—— 1901. *Sexual Inversion*. Philadelphia: F. A. Davis.

Ellmann, Richard (ed.). 1982. *The Artist as Critic: The Critical Writings of Oscar Wilde*. Chicago: University of Chicago Press.

—— 1988. *Oscar Wilde*. New York: Alfred A. Knopf.

Evans, Arthur. 1973. "How to Zap Straights." In Len Richmond and Gary

Noguera (eds). *The Gay Liberation Book.* San Francisco: Ramparts Press, 111–115.

Fletcher, John. 1989. "Freud and His Uses: Psychoanalysis and Gay Theory." In Shepherd and Wallis 1989, 90–118.

Freud, Sigmund. 1905. *Three Essays on the Theory of Sexuality.* 1962. Trans. James Strachey. New York: Basic Books.

—— 1910. *Leonardo da Vinci and a Memory of His Childhood.* 1964. Trans. Alan Tyson. New York: W. W. Norton.

—— 1914. "On Narcissism." 1963. Ed. Philip Rieff. *General Psychology Theory: Papers on Metapsychology.* New York: Macmillan, 56–82.

—— 1916–17. *Introductory Lectures on Psycho-Analysis.* 1966. Trans. James Strachey. New York: W. W. Norton.

—— 1935. "A Letter to an American Mother." 1970. *The Letters of Sigmund Freud, 1873–1937.* Ed. Ernest L. Freud. London: Hogarth Press, 418–419.

Gagnier, Regenia. 1986. *Idylls of the Marketplace: Oscar Wilde and the Victorian Public.* Stanford: Stanford University Press.

Gee, Stephen. 1980. "Gay Activism." In Gay Left Collective (ed.). *Homosexuality: Power and Politics.* London: Allison and Busby, 198–204.

Halperin, David M. 1990. *One Hundred Years of Homosexuality and Other Essays on Greek Love.* New York: Routledge.

Heath, Stephen. 1978. "Difference." *Screen* 19/3: 99.

Hyde, H. Montgomery (ed.). 1948. *The Trials of Oscar Wilde.* London: William Hodge.

Koestenbaum, Wayne. 1989. *Double Talk: The Erotics of Male Literary Collaboration.* New York: Routledge.

Lacqueur, Thomas. 1990. *Making Sex: Body and Gender from the Greeks to Freud.* Cambridge: Harvard University Press.

Lumsden, Andrew. 1989. "Westminster Barbarism." In Shepherd and Wallis 1989, 242–257.

Marshall, John. 1981. "Pansies, Perverts, and Macho Men: Changing Conceptions of Male Homosexuality." In Kenneth Plummer (ed.). *The Making of the Modern Homosexual.* London: Hutchinson, 133–154.

Rodgers, Bruce. 1972. *Gay Talk: A (Sometimes Outrageous) Dictionary of Gay Slang.* New York: Paragon Books.

Ross, Andrew. 1989. "Uses of Camp." *No Respect: Intellectuals and Popular Culture.* London: Routledge, 135–170.

Sedgwick, Eve Kosofsky. 1990. *Epistemology of the Closet.* Berkeley: University of California Press.

Shepherd, Simon and Mick Wallis. 1989. *Coming On Strong: Gay Politics and Culture.* London: Unwin Hyman.

Sontag, Susan. 1964. "Notes on Camp." 1966. *Against Interpretation.* New York: Noonday Press, 275–292.

Weeks, Jeffrey. 1981. *Sex, Politics and Society: The Regulation of Sexuality since 1800.* London: Longman.

Wilde, Oscar. 1889. "Pen, Pencil and Poison." In Ellmann 1982, 320–340.

—— 1891. "The Critic as Artist." In Ellmann 1982, 340–408.

—— 1893. "The Disciple." 1980. *The Complete Works of Oscar Wilde.* 15 vols. New York: AMS Press.

—— 1894. "Phrases and Philosophies for the Use of the Young." In Ellmann 1982, 433–434.

—— 1989a. "A Few Maxims for the Instruction of the Over-Educated." *The Complete Works of Oscar Wilde*. New York: Harper and Row, 1203–1204.

—— 1989b. *Oscar Wilde's Oxford Notebooks: A Portrait of the Mind in the Making*. Eds Philip E. Smith II and Michael S. Helfand. Oxford: Oxford University Press.

3

UNDER THE SIGN OF WILDE
An archaeology of posing
Moe Meyer

"Camp" was a new word when it first appeared in J. Redding Ware's 1909 dictionary of Victorian slang, *Passing English of the Victorian Era*. Ware's book, considered extremely competent for its day, was written both as a companion for and an extension of the foremost English slang dictionary of the nineteenth century, John S. Farmer's *Slang and Its Analogues*, published between 1890 and 1904. Ware was concerned with documenting the jargon of his decade. New slang words came and went so fast (he called it "passing English" to describe its fleeting nature) that many had escaped even Farmer's masterwork and were lost forever. Ware's project was to produce a contemporary supplement to *Slang and Its Analogues*, documenting only new slang that had emerged since its publication (Partridge 114). Because the term "Camp" is not found in Farmer's dictionary, a conclusion is that it was a new word that entered the English language only during the first decade of this century.

Ware defined Camp as "Actions and gestures of exaggerated emphasis. Probably from the French. Used chiefly by persons of exceptional want of character" (61). The conventional and accepted interpretation of Ware's definition concludes that the word "Camp" has a French etymology (see for example Booth 33, 39–40; Brien 873–874; Goodwin 39; Rodgers 40; and Ross 145). Against this, I will propose an alternative reading of Ware's definition informed by Thomas A. King's study of the politics of Camp gestures in chapter one of this volume. King has argued that Camp gesture signals an ontological challenge that displaces bourgeois notions of the Self as unique, abiding, and continuous, while substituting instead a concept of the Self as performative, improvisational, discontinuous, and processually constituted by repetitive and stylized acts. He proposes that bourgeois identification of Camp (homosexual) gesture is based upon a

75

logic that is recognizable for its unique contradictions: first, the gesture must be judged as excessive according to the standards of acceptable and conventional bourgeois male deportment; and second, that the gestural excess signifies a lack of Self (and thus lack of membership in the social body).

Accordingly, I read Ware's definition not as suggesting that the word "Camp" is from the French, but that the actual and specific gestures he describes have been imported from France. If, as King proposes, specific gestures identified simultaneously by exterior excess (Ware's "exaggerated emphasis") and interior lack (Ware's "exceptional want of character") are constitutive markers of homosexual identity, then the first text reference to Camp in 1909 already encodes a homosexual subject. This coding is noticeable both by its definition based on excess/lack and through its attribution of these gestures to the French: the discourse of English Francophobia included the assumption that homosexuality was a French import (see Crompton 4–5, 37–38, 52ff.).

My goals in this essay, then, are:

1 to identify a system of gestures, perhaps actually originating in France, which was coherent enough to be stored, transmitted, reproduced, manipulated, and exported, and to suggest that such a gestuary is precisely what Ware was calling "Camp" in 1909. I identify the nineteenth-century French system of actor training, known as Delsarte, as this gesture scheme;

2 to explain why the word "Camp" appeared only in the first decade of this century, and how its appearance signals the successful transcoding of this system of gestures to serve as a constitutive marker of homosexual social identity;

3 and, finally, to explore how the transcoding of this gesture scheme was accomplished. I will argue that it was an applied Delsartean semiotic that Oscar Wilde used to undergird his gradual formulation of homoerotic representational strategies both in text and in the performance of everyday life.

My point of departure will be Oscar Wilde's pedagogical contact with the Delsarte system in 1882. From that contact I will identify the Delsartean method for constructing a performative and discontinuous Self by manipulating the surface codes of gesture, posture, speech, and costume and show how this semiotic was developmentally deployed by Wilde in what appears to be a series of experimental attempts to construct a homosexual social identity. I conclude with an analysis of his sex scandal trials of 1895, arguing that the trials represent the collision of Wilde's experiments in Delsartean identity formation with the State legal apparatus, and how Camp emerges as the result of this head-on ontological crash.

The central organizing image for the Delsarte system – for purposes of both abstraction and physical praxis – was the "pose." My interpretation is based on tracking this concept of the "pose" as it enters and is developed in the life and works of Oscar Wilde. I will offer an archaeology of posing that is, perhaps, more useful than another unsubstantiated etymology of "Camp". I use the term "archaeology" in the Foucaultian sense, that is, not a search for origins, but an investigation of ideas that can provide the descriptive foundation for establishing Camp as a discourse (Foucault 1972: 140).

AESTHETICISM AND ITS DISCONTENTS

Oscar Wilde's American lecture tour of 1882 was a turning point in his life, one that left him greatly changed (Ellmann 1988: 210). Upon his return to England he abandoned the knee breeches, lily, green tie, and velvet jacket that made him famous as "The Great Aesthete" and "The Professor of Aesthetics" and, instead, resurrected the cult of the dandy (which had been dead for several decades), dedicating the effort to Balzac (Moers 295).[1] Wilde's version of dandyism was new. He was not the inheritor of a continuous tradition but was, rather, a dandiacal send-up, an assemblage of dandy poses and sentiments long since passed.

One major departure of Wilde's dandyism from its Regency predecessor was the addition of a homoerotic presence. Previous versions of dandyism often drew suspicion from those who viewed the dandy's sometime effeminacy as peculiar, but these never possessed more than the most unclear and seemingly implausible allusions to the love that dare not speak its name (Pierrot 136–137). Rather, the dandies' effeminacy was attributed to a disinterest in sex, not to an interest in same-sex sexual activity (Moers 36–37). It was Wilde who transformed dandyism into a vehicle for a homoerotic presence and a sexualized symbol of the Decadence, marking his version as radically different from those of the past.

Yet the question remains, why did Wilde abandon his prophetic aestheticism in favor of this dandy revival? In a recent essay, "Writing Gone Wilde," Ed Cohen argued that Wilde, up until his trials of 1895, was experimenting with resistant strategies in his writing that could

77

embody homoerotic desire. These embodiments of desire consisted of transgressive reinscriptions of dominant discourses acting in lieu of a representational praxis with which to render a homosexual social identity at a time when the language for articulating such an identity did not exist. I use Jonathan Dollimore's term "transgressive reinscription" to indicate a subversive, resistant, and destabilizing maneuver in which "identification with, and desire *for*, may coexist with parodic subversion *of*" (321). I suggest that Wilde's enactment of the dandy was yet another instance of this resistant strategy: there was something about the dandy that suggested a venue for this project that was not available in his previous enactments of the aesthete. Although breaking down the boundaries between art and life was his rallying call as an aesthete, it was a call only. Aestheticism was a theory, but dandyism, on the other hand, offered a praxis.

Wilde's choice of a Balzacian dandyism is significant. Balzac himself was no model practitioner: "The great enchanter was one of the oiliest and commonest looking mortals . . . ever beheld; being short and corpulent, with a broad florid face, a cascade of double chins, and straight greasy hair. . . . [D]ressed in the worst possible taste" he would often "roam the streets . . . in ragged, dirty disarray" (Moers 129). It was certainly not Balzac's practice of dandyism that attracted Wilde. Rather, it was Balzac's theory with its dazzlingly pseudo-scientific approach that intrigued him. As Wilde explained,

> Balzac's aim . . . was to do for humanity what [naturalists] had done for animal creation. As the naturalist studied lions and tigers, so [he] studied men and women. . . . He was, in a word, a marvellous combination of artistic temperament with the scientific spirit.
>
> (1886a: 29).

Balzac's method was articulated in his 1830 essay *Traité de la vie élégante*, where he attempted a scientific approach to self-representation. "Scrutinizing the signs transmitted by different kinds of character, profession, habits, and style of life, he formulate[d] the 'laws' which govern . . . the body" (Stanton 154). Balzac identified four signifying practices for an organized system of self-representation – posture, gesture, costume, and speech – "by which every individual can be decoded and classified" (Stanton 155). Through careful observation and reading of bodily inscriptions, Balzac claimed that he could tell anyone exactly who (and what) they were, based upon a belief in a direct correlation between interior essence and exterior signification (Stanton

155). But more importantly, he believed that these codes of signification, if subjected to a self-reflexive and individual practice, would
render one a living work of art (Stanton 155). The logic behind this
conception was both simple and radical: if a specific interiority
produced a single exterior signification, then the reverse would also be
true – a single exteriority would produce a corresponding interiority –
permitting one to compose the self as one composed a painting.

The relationship between Wilde's dandyism and the writings of
Balzac, however, is indirect. I suggest that Wilde was drawn to
Balzac's theory of dandyism because it had such uncanny resonance
with another formal system of signifying practices to which he was
introduced just months before while in America. This was the practice
of Delsarte taught him by Steele Mackaye in the fall of 1882 (Ellmann
1988: 208). Indeed, Wilde was so moved by Mackaye – they became
close friends and collaborators – that he remained in the United States
several months longer than originally planned. And though it might be
claimed that Wilde remained in America solely as a means to career
advancement (Mackaye was to produce Wilde's plays in the U.S.), the
influence of Delsarte in the formation of Wilde's homoerotic strategies
has never been taken into account.

Delsarte, named after its founder François Delsarte, was initially a
system of voice training used by actors and public speakers in France
from 1839 to 1871, and introduced to America in the 1870s by Delsarte's
only American student, Steele Mackaye.[2] Working intensively with
Delsarte during the last years of the French master's life, Mackaye was
as much a collaborator and a partner as he was a student. With François
Delsarte's approval, Mackaye introduced physical movement into the
system, including a technical science of signifying gestures and
postures. The system of training which Mackaye brought back to
America – by this time it was more Mackaye's than Delsarte's –
became a fashion craze in America where it flourished into the early
twentieth century under various gurus. By the time Wilde began his
studies in 1882, Mackaye was one of the foremost acting teachers in
New York whose Delsarte school had dominated the craft for several
years prior.

Despite Mackaye's impressive changes to the Delsarte system
through the addition of gesture and pose, it was, and would remain,
based on François Delsarte's philosophy of art and life. It is this
philosophy, combined with Mackaye's physical practice, that may have
been responsible for Wilde's turn to Balzacian dandyism and his
subsequent development of homoerotic representational strategies.

Delsarte was a semiotician whose science, like Balzac's, consisted of the classification and decoding of bodily inscriptions based on observations of human conduct in order to determine the causal correspondence between exterior signification and essential interiority. Like Balzac, he believed that although the relationship between exteriority and interiority was absolute, total, and universal, it was also a relationship in which the two terms could act as either cause *or* effect. In a radical break with the epistemology of bourgeois liberalism (which restricted interiority to cause and exteriority to exclusive effect), both Balzac and Delsarte believed that a self-reflexive exterior signification could control and produce interior states through composition of gesture, posture, and voice (Stebbins 1899: 12).

Delsarte taught that art-making involved the construction of an exterior surface (the art object) that would signify the artist's interiority. In other words, the purpose of art was the display of the artist's interiority (Stebbins 1902: 26–27). Accordingly, one could create true art through a studied composition of exterior bodily signifying codes whose purpose, like a painting or sculpture, was to communicate the artist's inner state. In this way, one could – based upon a self-aware semiotic manipulation – collapse the distinctions between subject and object thus transforming oneself into a living work of art. Delsarte's articulation of this operation consisted of two parts. First, there was the construction of a sign consisting of an exterior display (art object) that signified a displaced interiority (the artist). Second, composing oneself as a work of art was the result of "the application, knowingly appropriated, of the sign to the thing," that is, the appropriation of the sign to the signifier accomplished by collapsing the signifier and signified so that the entire sign could be played out on the surfaces (Stebbins 1902: 65). The Delsarte system, then, was a systematic approach to body art composition which provided the praxis for a theory shared in common with Balzacian dandyism.

Wilde had just completed his American lecture tour during which he was represented as a master aesthete, the apostle of the art for art's sake movement. Running headlong into Mackaye and the Delsarte system immediately following the tour had an enormous impact upon him. For while Wilde preached aestheticism and advocated turning one's life into art, Delsarte offered a detailed practice for accomplishing that very goal. In fact, Delsarte saw his system as offering a praxis for the aesthetic movement (Stebbins 1902: 34–35, 414–424). Though Delsarte agreed with the goals of the art for art's sake crowd, he thought that their aestheticism was an empty promise until it could be embodied through specific technique. Wilde, who fancied himself the leading aesthete of his day, must have had an enlightening experience with Mackaye upon learning that – according to Delsarte – he was nothing but a rank amateur who lacked the craft necessary to fulfill his aesthetic agenda, for it was only a matter of weeks after his departure from Mackaye and America that he dropped his aesthetic pose and adopted Balzac's version of dandyism.

The relationship of Balzac to Delsarte was certainly recognized by the Delsartists themselves. Mackaye's student Genevieve Stebbins pointed out that Balzac had formulated identical ideas just a decade before Delsarte appeared on the scene (1899: 13). The major difference between the two systems was in the delineation of signifying codes. Delsarte, who based his theories upon the notion of the trinity, restrictively theorized all phenomena in terms of the number three. Thus he identified three signifying codes – speech, gesture, and posture. Balzac, on the other hand, had an additional fourth code – costume – which, when added to the Delsarte trinitarian system, offered Wilde the opportunity to continue his notorious self-promotion (Gagnier 78). Whereas Delsarte offered a technique for turning oneself into a living work of art, it was a private and meditative practice. By adopting Balzacian dandyism, Wilde could explore this process while simultaneously advertising the attempts by publicly signifying his progress through costume display.

The real value of the Delsarte practices for Wilde was that exteriority, while it could reflect an already posited interiority, could also help create a completely new interiority, a new self, and a new identity. Reading from Genevieve Stebbins's notes, sign appropriation resulted in "placing before us the signification of exterior[ity] . . . enabl[ing] us to outwardly express that which is . . . within" (1888: 11). In other words, both the signifier and the signified were located on the surfaces of the body, and interiority existed only as a potential that required an exterior display in order to be activated and read (Stebbins 1902: 26–27). This was, in effect, a recognition of the constructedness of social identity. Wilde's early experiments with dandyism from 1883 to 1885 can be read, then, as an exploration of identity formulation through a signifying practice that was identifiably Delsartean.

Wilde's attempt to formulate a homosexual social identity through dandyism during the first years after his return from America was a project doomed to failure, though. His Delsartean dandy was a masturbatory fantasy that had not taken into account how homosexuality was figured in Victorian culture. There was as yet no cultural conception of a homosexual social identity, only of sodomy, a recognition of a specific sexual activity in which men could engage, but which did not yet grant a discrete social identity to the performers. Because homosexuality was conceptually organized around a partnered act, its desire could only be conceived as relational, publicly expressed in a shared subject position. Without an already established discourse of homosexual social identity to invoke a corresponding "body," that is, without a unified cultural sign of homosexuality to display on the surfaces, Wilde's dandyism was read only as a transgressive reinscription of the bourgeois male. The most he could accomplish was to appear as Not-Masculine, as Other to appropriate male behavior. By appropriating the signs of the bourgeois male, even the dandy's effeminacy was read simply as a disinterest in sex, not even as homoerotic. As Regenia Gagnier put it, Wilde succeeded only in effecting a "crisis of the male" (51), and still lacked the language with which to think a homosexual identity. If he was to institute the signification of a new identity based on the Delsarte method of the appropriation of the sign, he needed first to construct a sign of homoerotic desire that could be appropriated to the surfaces of his body. Because the conceptualization of homosexuality was dependent on interaction with another, this could only be realized by inscribing the object of desire, that is, by establishing his own identity on the surfaces of the body of the sexual partner.

Beginning in 1886, one can trace the development of Wilde's efforts to formulate (at least on paper) a strategy capable of constructing a sign of identity by objectifying homoerotic desire and situating it on the surfaces of the body of the sexual partner conceived as an art object. Constructing a sign by fixing, stabilizing, and giving permanence to desire was a necessary first step in order to prepare for the appropriation of the sign that would render him as a living work of art while simultaneously bestowing a homosexual identity. The way in which this was accomplished was through a concept of "posing," which in the Delsarte system represented the highest form of art because it collapsed the distinctions between subject and object (Stebbins 1902: 444–461). By setting up the partner as posed object and himself as subject, Wilde was attempting to establish a sign whose appropriation would play out both the desiring and the desired on the surfaces of his own body thus freeing him from dependence on the relational sodomitical identity capable of expressing homoeroticism only. If successful, Wilde would be able to produce a homosexual social identity that could exist independently of engaged sexual acts. At the time though, Wilde had no idea of what the outcome of his experiments would be. Rather, it was an exploration of the unknown in search of an identity that could signify his growing awareness of difference.

THE PROFESSOR OF POSING

Many critics have seen Wilde's 1889 short story "The Portrait of Mr. W. H." as his first articulation of homosexuality (W. Cohen 1989: 219). But by working with the concept of "posing," I suggest that Wilde's textual homoerotics can be found emerging at an earlier date. In "The Relation of Dress to Art," a review of James Whistler from 1886, Wilde identifies the locus for his future endeavors and begins to formulate the strategy which underwrites "Mr. W. H.": the signifying pose. While the dandy was viewed as the exemplar of the Decadence (Moers 287–314), Wilde, in this review, seems to have resituated his own signifying project onto the body of the object of desire when he proclaimed the artist's model, not the dandy, "as the sign of the decadence" (18).

The model, to whom he gave the title of "professor of posing," was a primary example of pastiche, a practice of stylistic imitation that, according to Wilde, had the ability to empty art of meaning (1886b: 18). Fredric Jameson has called pastiche "the imitation of . . . style, the wearing of a stylistic mask, speech in a dead language" (1983: 114). This was also how Wilde thought of pastiche when he claimed that the model could only appear "as everything he is not, and as nothing that he is" (1886b: 18). The model as pastiche, divorced from his own interiority, offered up his body surfaces and made them available for inscription by the artist. The artist, in turn, used them to signify his own inner state. In severing the connection between surface and content, the model made a living by skewing the depth model of identity upon which bourgeois notions of the self were based. In his 1889 essay "London Models," Wilde assessed the skill of a model precisely by his ability to produce a usable surface, with use value determined by the degree to which the model was able to put his personal identity under erasure. The effect achieved by the model was the construction of a "neutral" surface, a tabula rasa, acting as an objectified site of the artist's desire.

Conceptualized as a neutral surface, the model's body could be ethically objectified by the artist, for the model's own interiority would be left untouched, forever innocent, even when used to signify the artist's desire, however perverse its physical expression. This neutrality figures prominently in Wilde's 1889 short story "The Model Millionaire," in which the young protagonist feels sorry for a man in rags who is posing in an artist's studio only to find later that the beggar is actually one of the richest men in Europe. The discrepancy between the artist's inscription and the model's "true" identity becomes the justification for manipulation of the model's body because, regardless of what was done to it, the encounter was solely a harmless dialogue between the artist and a neutral surface. Dealing only with a neutral body, Wilde could blindly and naively justify the exploitation. In "London Models," for example, he narrates: "Occasionally . . . an artist catches a couple of gamins in the gutter and asks them to come to his studio. The first time they always appear, but after that they don't keep their appointments" (113). Wilde then describes the boys' extreme discomfort in being forced to pose, but finds such behavior merely charming.

The effect of surface neutralization is the elimination of the model's identity. In "The Portrait of Mr. W. H." this becomes a paradox that drives the narrative. This detective story is an extended meditation on the portrait of a boy thought to be Shakespeare's lover: the plot revolves around the search for the identity of the portrait model in order to establish Shakespeare's homosexuality by proving the boy is the same "W. H." to whom the bard dedicated his sonnets. This search must fail utterly for, in order to posit the model as the object of the playwright's desire, the boy's identity must first be erased. Wilde's rationale for publicly writing the homoerotic was based on purifying desire under the ideal of art. But to justify homoerotic desire as art, the model's identity had to be relinquished in the production of the "pure," immaculate body surface, the only kind of surface that could qualify as an acceptable site of inscription. Therefore, it was only the process of body surface neutralization that permitted him to be read as a signifier of Shakespeare's homosexuality. To solve the mystery of W. H., Wilde would have to surrender his interpretation of the portrait, but to do so would entail a loss of the narrative. Like a dog chasing its own tail, Wilde circles round and round, leading finally to an exhausted abandonment of the search for the boy's identity. As John Berger pointed out: "To be on display is to have the surface of one's own skin . . . turned into a disguise which . . . can *never* be discarded" (54, emphasis mine).

The decision to quit the search represented a conscious choice for Wilde: what was at stake was *his* (the spectator's) identity. In "Mr. W. H.," Wilde was attempting to construct and justify a personal homosexual identity by positing Shakespeare as precedent; thus the search for the model's identity becomes a desperate, frantic, and personally invested exploration of his own. But, as Diana Fuss reminds us, "identity is always purchased at the price of the exclusion of the Other, the repression or repudiation of non-identity" (103). Wilde had created a booby trap by reading the boy's identity as his own, thus deconstructing the dialogic relationship between Self and Other needed to establish the difference upon which to articulate his own identity. The boy in the portrait could either signify the artist's interiority or signify his own, but he could not signify both. The character of Erskine, frustrated by the impossibility of resolving the paradox and refusing to surrender his assertion of the boy model's personal identity, ostensibly commits suicide at the end of the story. In other words, he loses his identity by allowing the model to maintain his, symbolizing the outcome of one of two possible choices. The nameless narrator of the story (Wilde) chooses to relinquish the quest, saves himself, and inherits the portrait from Erskine upon his death: he acquires the homoerotic sign. "The Portrait of Mr. W. H." represents, then, Wilde's first formulation of a homoerotic subjectivity, the outcome of a rather painful choice. As Laura Mulvey has explained:

> an image constitutes the matrix of the imaginary, of recognition/ misrecognition and identification, and hence of the first articulation of the "I" of subjectivity. This is a moment when [a] . . . fascination with looking . . . collides with the initial inklings of self-awareness. Hence it is the birth of the long love affair/ despair between image and self-image.
>
> (365)

The "affair/despair" that runs through "Mr. W. H.," represented by the very different choices made by Erskine and the narrator, is responsible for the text's obtrusive tension. For while Wilde had finally constructed a homoerotic sign, it had yet to be appropriated to the surfaces of his own body, thus simultaneously producing a complacent elation in its construction and a frustrating disappointment in failure to complete the Delsartean operation through appropriation of that sign. Yet, in choosing the model/poser as signifier of his own homoerotic desire, the establishment of the subject–object relationship between the artist and an exterior surface had at least allowed the completion of the first half of the Delsarte semiotic by constructing the portrait-as-sign.

In what became a completion of the Delsartean operation, Wilde took the portrait-as-sign which was constructed in "The Portrait of

Mr. W. H." and (by substituting Dorian for W. H. as boy-surface, and Basil Hallward for the narrator as desiring subject) replicated it in *The Picture of Dorian Gray* (1891). In *Dorian Gray*, the painter Basil Hallward inscribes his desire onto the posed body of the young and beautiful Dorian by painting his portrait, thus activating the sign by using an external gestural display to signify the artist's displaced interiority. Ed Cohen has also identified this sign construction:

> Within the narrative structure, Dorian is an image – a space for the constitution of male desire. From the time he enters the novel as the subject of Basil's portrait . . . Dorian Gray provides the surface on which the characters project their self-representations. His is the body on which Basil's . . . desires are inscribed.
> (806)

The artist's inscription, as it did in "The Model Millionaire" and "Mr. W. H.," displaces and eliminates the model's "true" identity by neutralizing Dorian's body surfaces in order to render him as the object of desire. The discrepancy between the artist's inscription and the model's personal identity, that earlier had provided the means for constructing the portrait as a homoerotic sign, had also produced a paradox that prevented that sign from being appropriated. In "The Portrait of Mr. W. H.," Wilde had trapped himself in the hall of mirrors it created: in order to establish the portrait as homoerotic sign he needed the model's identity, but the model's identity negated the sign through an antidialogic turn. In *Dorian Gray*, he found a way to resolve the paradox through a remarkably simple and creative maneuver that allowed the portrait-as-sign to be appropriated to the surfaces of the model's body.

Dorian, who fears the loss of his beauty and desirability in the process of aging, prays for and receives a magical transference: his portrait is literally appropriated to the surfaces of his body. By appropriating the portrait-as-sign, Dorian's body reflects only the painted image, thus he will no longer age. This is not because the painting frames a moment in time, but because Basil Hallward's desire – as the signified – has also been relocated to the surfaces of Dorian's body as a necessary affect of the appropriation of the sign. With his body surfaces now signifying only *Basil's* interiority, Dorian's own "essence" (personal identity) is put under erasure and transferred. Because Wilde conceptualized the model's bodily inscription as pastiche, the appropriation of the portrait-as-sign to the model's body transforms the material canvas by stripping it of meaning, turning it into an empty frame, a vacuous sign. Thus it becomes available as a site for depositing the model's "true" identity, displaced through a neutralization that emerges along with and because of the appropriation of the sign. As Dorian commits crime after crime, his interiority is reflected by the mutating monster on the canvas, but his body surfaces, because they now signify only Basil's desire purified under the ideal of art, remain unchanging and immortal. So how did Wilde solve the problem of the pesky, paradoxical presence of the model's identity? He simply draped a sheet over it and hid it in the attic.

Situating desire in art, and art on the surfaces of the posed body, was a peculiarly Delsartean maneuver. In the Delsarte philosophy, the pose was considered the highest form of art and, more importantly, art was the expression of desire; therefore, the pose could be interpreted as its highest and noblest representation. Interpreting *Dorian Gray* through the lens of Delsarte not only yields an alternative reading, but provides the logic to explicate the emergence of the portrait model as the represention par excellence of the desired Other: because for Wilde, as for Delsarte, art was the field produced by the intersection of desire and vision. When Wilde asserted that "the basis of life – the energy of life . . . is simply the desire for expression, and Art is always presenting various forms through which this expression can be attained" (1889a: 311), he was rehearsing the Delsartean identification of art as the site in which to inscribe desire (and in which it could be fulfilled). According to Delsarte, only art had practical, beneficial, and, more importantly for Wilde, purificatory results for the expression of desire. Delsarte taught that it was art alone that could fix desire, giving it permanence, thus potentially stabilizing an identity organized around its expression by consolidating the various objects of desire under a single ideal (Stebbins 1902: 27). Accordingly, the Delsartean sign could transcend the physical so that, regardless of its stigmatized grossness, the sexual act could be aligned with the ideal, freeing Wilde from self-definitional dependence on the physical presence of the sexual partner.

In *Dorian Gray*, it is the appropriation of the sign to the surfaces of the model's body that stabilizes desire, and which is represented as Dorian's arrest of the aging process. Because it is Basil's desire, not Dorian's, that is fixed on the surfaces, Dorian's body has become the site of a double identification with both gaze and image, and Dorian's impetus to action is motivated only by Basil's desire. In that case, Dorian's murder of Basil Hallward marks the final success of the appropriation of the sign, a success that frees Basil from dependence upon the Other by literally enacting the collapse of subject and object through a joyous self-immolation, eliminating the need for a shared subject position.

By composing or reading on an exterior surface, Delsarte believed that the artist could animate and transform objects so as to mark them with his own character, to leave behind an imperishable trace of his being on a foreign body: "It is . . . by the subjective virtues of this ineffable power that he fixes fugitive things, gives permanence to what is momentary and actuality to that which is no[t]. . . . Thus he lives on" (qtd in Stebbins 1902: 27). Because Basil's desire was and remains the signified, his murder can be read, not as a tragic termination, but as the unification of the desiring and the desired on a single surface, the stabilization of desire that allows Basil to become the Other through the medium of Dorian's body: not only does Dorian's body surface (exteriority) as signifier achieve immortality through sign appropriation, but so does Basil's desiring essence (interiority) as signified. The apparent murder of Basil by Dorian actually marks the conceptual birth of Wilde's homosexual social identity by freeing the artist from self-definitional dependence upon the posed model.

Utilizing the metaphor of the pose in this body of work, Wilde explored the possibility of initiating a hitherto unavailable discursive formation of a personal homosexual identity. While he had successfully invented a homoerotic sign through application of a Delsartean semiotic applied to the body of the desired Other figured as an artist's model in his construction of the portrait-as-sign in "Mr. W. H.," and though he had conceptualized a way in which the sign could be replicated through an appropriation that skewed the depth model by stabilizing his own desire on the surfaces of the Other's body in *Dorian Gray*, it was confined to the text. To complete the operation, it needed to be reproduced and enacted in the praxis of everyday life. This apparently occurred in 1895, conjunct with Wilde's sex scandal trials. An examination of the activity of "posing" as it impacted with the legal apparatus can elucidate this process.

THE SOMDOMITICAL (*sic*) POSE

The artist's model, as a recurrent and transgressively reinscribed figure in Wilde's work, signals what appears to be his use of the "pose" as an organizing metaphor through which to codify the surfaces of the Other's body. In "London Models" especially, it is clear that Wilde's use of the term "poser" was used to describe a "type," of which the artist's model was only one example: "Besides the professional posers of the studio there are the posers of the Row, the posers at afternoon teas, the posers in politics, and the circus-posers" (113). Wilde goes on to explain that a flawless male physique is his single criterion for typing, and gives the reader a list of locations at which one can find posers to look at: "the running-ground at Eton, the towing-path at Oxford, the Thames swimming baths, and the yearly circuses" (113). Here, the "pose" provided terms under which he could recognize his own desire in any body that became the object of his homoerotic gaze. In other words, when Wilde applied the term "poser" to a body he was engaging in what, in contemporary gay slang, is termed "cruising," that is, objectifying the body of the Other through a delimiting visual inscription within the circuits of homoerotic desire.

This dichotomous artist/model relationship was one of extreme inequality and disparity, organized around polarized distinctions between active and passive and intimately linked to conceptions of the respective sexual roles involved in the practice of sodomy. At the time, and for many decades following, it was only the "passive" partner (insertee) in the sodomitical act who was stigmatized and thought to be perverse. The "active" partner (insertor) in sodomy was thought to be guilty of a criminal act perhaps, but would not take on a social identity based on that sexual expression. In most cases, the active partner would continue to be perceived as heterosexual: "Men with a strong sense of their . . . masculine gender role could easily enter same-sex sexual relations without challenging their heterosexual sense of self" (Marshall 136). That the "passive" partner alone bore the lion's share of the social stigma and became the bearer of a sexually-labeled identity can be clearly proven by the accounts and definitions given by the participants themselves, particularly the "passive" participants who, too, perceived their "active" partners as heterosexual (Chauncey; Crisp 62; Gough 126–127; Marshall 145–153; and Meyer 33).

When the activity of posing is considered within the context of these active/passive distinctions regarding sexual performance, a nexus of power relationships strikingly emerges. As long as one wielded power by dominating the body of the Other, then the social stigma attached to homosexual and homoerotic practices could be, if not bypassed completely, at least politely ignored. Performing the insertor's role in penetrative sex was only one way to align with this idealized domination. It could also be achieved by controlling the model's body through dictation of the pose or even by figuring the Other as the object of the gaze. By "inserting" the poser into this discourse, the two halves of the equation can be drawn out: on the one hand, the sanctioned domination of the artist/spectator/insertor/inscriptor and on the flip side, so to speak, the perverse receptivity of the model/ poser/insertee/inscriptee.[3] Operating within these politics, Wilde felt he could flaunt his homoerotic hi-jinks – whether in text or in everyday life – as a judgment-free prerogative of his social status. Richard Ellmann recognized that Wilde's "attitude towards sexual transactions was the conventional one of his class. He did not think of his behavior with boys as of any consequence" (1988: 436); men of high standing could, and often with impunity, sexually consort with and deploy the bodies of working-class men as they wished (Weeks 1981: 105). I suggest that this understanding of the issues of power and domination in relation to bodily inscriptions of homoerotic desire can clarify the role of the pose in Wilde's trials of 1895.

In February of 1895, the Marquess of Queensberry, furious over his repeated failures to force the termination of Wilde's relationship with his son Alfred Douglas, sent a card to Wilde, addressed: "To Oscar Wilde posing Somdomite [sic]." Wilde's response is history; he was pushed over the edge, and in an emotionally charged state of anger swore out a warrant for Queensberry's arrest on charges of libel. Queensberry's charge that Wilde was a posing sodomite was not at all incidental. He knew Wilde would be outraged. Simply calling him a sodomite would not have worked nearly as well. Wilde loved to flaunt his proclivities and would most likely, as he had done in the past, use the label as a springboard for some dramatic and witty response. But to charge Wilde with "posing" was to reverse the power relationships along the inscriptive axis of the active/passive distinctions of sodomitical practice. By accusing him of being a posing sodomite, not only did Queensberry intimate that it was Wilde who was being inscribed, thus removing the social protections enjoyed by the inscriptor, but it acted as an insult to Wilde's self-defined class standing, reminding him of the more common heritage he had labored to overcome during his rise to the top.

Queensberry knew exactly what he was doing when he charged Wilde with sodomitical posing. In fact, he had begun formulating this strategy as much as two years prior in March of 1893 (Ellmann 1988: 437). Queensberry has usually been depicted as an unthinking, often idiotic bully. Yet his conscious deployment of the concept of the pose indicates a more sophisticated mind. In a letter to his son of April 1894, Queensberry stated that "to pose as a thing is as bad as to be it" (in Ellmann 1988: 417). He proceeded to castigate Alfred Douglas for posing as a sodomite based on an analysis of gestures, bodily attitudes, and proxemics which he observed displayed by Alfred and Oscar in a public place. This was an extremely conscious analysis which he would repeat as evidence against Wilde in court. He was not only aware of the relationship between interiority and its exterior signification, he was also keen enough to understand that Wilde was flaunting his sexual activities under cover of a clever, transgressive reinscription of the bourgeois male. That Wilde responded to the label just as Queensberry had predicted indicates first, that Queensberry had called Wilde's bluff through a successful identification of his reinscriptive strategy and, second, that there was a philosophy of "posing" commonly understood and shared that provided the normative standard against which Queensberry could analyze Wilde's actions. This philosophy can be outlined by looking at the ways in which the word "posing" was deployed in Wilde's libel suit.

Queensberry pleaded that the card was indeed intended to outrage Wilde, but only to goad him into a face-to-face confrontation. A libel suit was unexpected. He claimed that his only miscalculation was in underestimating the degree of anger in Wilde's response. Yet one must wonder at Queensberry's explanation. He knew that the label "posing sodomite" would enrage Wilde. He knew it was a serious charge, serious enough to deploy only as a strategy of last resort, and one that he had held as the trump for over two years. Certainly it was serious enough to disown. For when Queensberry repeated the charge in court, he subjected it to a subtle change. Instead of "posing sodomite," he stated that the scribbled and almost illegible card actually said "posing *as a* sodomite," a different charge altogether (Ellmann 1988: 438). The difference between "posing sodomite" and "posing as a sodomite" is an important one. If Queensberry had maintained the former, he would have been accusing Wilde of an illegal sexual act and would have had to prove that Wilde had played the "passive" role in sodomy. But the latter charge was confined to a signifying practice. He needed prove only that Wilde *signified* the sodomite. No evidence of actual sexual activity would be required. This helps explain the logic behind the use of Wilde's writings, especially *Dorian Gray*, as primary evidence for the defense: what was on trial was Wilde's signifying practices, thus both his everyday life actions *and* his textual strategies were relevant to Queensberry's revised allegation.

It was going to be difficult for Queensberry to justify his pronouncement of Wilde's social behavior. It was certainly true that Wilde was known for daring suggestions of the homoerotic in his signifying practices of speech, dress, gesture, and writing. In fact, he was notorious for subversively manipulating and exploiting the ambiguity surrounding the dandy's effeminacy and then reveling in the shock he could produce amongst gentle company while flaunting the impunity with which he believed he operated. While it would be an easy task to prove that Wilde signified the Not-Masculine, Queensberry needed to prove additionally that the Not-Masculine was actually the clever disguise of the sodomite. As long as no direct link to sexual activity could be proven, Wilde was confident that the gender ambiguity of his reinscription of the bourgeois male would sustain itself, and that he would naturally win the suit. But the trial had taken a dire turn. Queensberry's detectives had come through with proof of sodomitical practice, evidence of actual sexual activity. Signifying the Not-Masculine was not a crime. If Queensberry won the case Wilde would walk away a free man, but the proof of homosexual activity could lead to charges being brought against him in a separate trial. With this new and damning evidence, Wilde's attorney attempted a bargaining strategy. Wilde would admit to posing as a sodomite if, in turn, the defense attorneys would agree to end the proceedings now, with unopposed acquittal for their client. Wilde's attorney needed to end the trial in order to confine the evidence against Wilde to an examination of his signifying practices and to keep the details of his actual sexual activities from being exposed. All agreed. Queensberry was acquitted and Wilde was found guilty of posing.[4]

Analyzing the concept of posing as it was deployed in this first of Wilde's three trials yields some intriguing conclusions. With regard to the homoerotic, the term "posing" had two circulating meanings: the first, as used in the phrase "posing sodomite," referred to the "passive" partner in a sodomitical act; the second, as used in the phrase "posing as a sodomite," referred to significations of the homoerotic. Though there seems to have been a vague knowledge that these were somehow related, a discursive connection between homoerotic desire and the act of sodomy had not yet been made. That this connection had not yet been formed can be witnessed in the defense strategy. Lacking the discourse with which to render a homosexual identity, the defense tried to retrieve one from Wilde by tricking him into admitting that his homoerotic presentation of self actually signified a sexual practice. This was attempted by blurring the distinctions between the two uses of the term "posing" in the hopes of catching him, rhetorically speaking, with his pants down. Regarding a particular short story, the defense tried to force an admission of the text's depraved morality from Wilde, but he evaded the issue by retreating into a formalist critique:

> Defense: Do you think the story blasphemous?
> Wilde: I think it violated every artistic canon of beauty.
> Defense: That is not an answer.
> Wilde: It is the only one I can give.

> (Hyde 1956: 121)

Frustrated by this evasion, the defense continued, revealing the reason for its line of questioning:

> Defense: I want to see the position you pose in.
> Wilde: I do not think you should say that.
> Defense: I have said nothing out of the way.

> (121)

Playing upon the multiple meanings of "posing," the defense had actually asked Wilde whether he assumed the active or the passive role in sodomy, and he responded with indignation to the subtext. The two parties continued this word game, the defense attempting to attach some implied and suspected specificity to the meaning of "pose," Wilde countering by restoring the term to its protective ambiguity:

> Defense: I think you will admit that any one who would approve of such an article would pose as guilty of improper practices?
> Wilde: . . . I do not know whether you use the word "pose" in any particular sense.
> Defense: It is a favourite word of your own?
> Wilde: Is it? I have no pose in this matter.

> (122)

The wordplay, the innuendoes, and the rhetorical trickery of this juridical repartee suggest that there was no connection, other than through suspicion, between Wilde's signifying practices and his sexual activities. This explains the strategy engaged by the defense, that is, a line of questioning regarding the moral virtues of texts, speech acts, gestural displacements, and visual coding. Though these questions seem incomprehensible and almost humorous today, they had a rational aim: the defense needed first to establish sodomy as the signified of Wilde's signifying practices. The defense, even with an innovative and rather sophisticated reading of Wilde's dandyism, simply did not possess a discourse capable of recognizing, let alone interpreting, the homoerotic.

Limited by the understanding of sodomy as a specific act, and lacking a concept of the homoerotic as a state of being that might yield a particular subjectivity, the defense came up against the same wall that hampered Wilde in his own attempts to fashion a social identity out of homoerotic desire: homoeroticism, even at this date, could only be conceived as relational, organized around the performance of a sexual act with a partner. As long as there was no evidence of actual sexual activity, as long as none of the partners could be produced or exposed, then it was unclear as to exactly what Wilde was signifying.

The courtroom dialogue is evidence that a homosexual social identity did not yet exist as of April 1895. Instead, both Queensberry's charge and his defense suggest that the discursive figure of "The Homosexual" was in the process of emerging. There was a partial knowledge of the possibility that such a figure existed, but there was no language with which to articulate that knowledge. While a discursive homosexual figure had begun to appear in nineteenth-century sexological and medical tracts, this figure had not yet been dealt with in terms of social identity. It was still restricted to descriptions of sexual activities accompanied by theorizing the possible motives for individual engagement.[5] The Criminal Law Amendment Act of 1885, the law under which Wilde would eventually be brought to trial, was successful in establishing specific sexual acts within the juridico-legal discourse, but did not specify how one might identify the individual capable of such acts, and thus also failed to produce a homosexual signification. These limitations are clearly seen in the difficulties Queensberry's defense faced in trying to attach Wilde's signifying pose to the practice of sodomy. They could articulate the act, but not the actor.

If the evidence indicates that there was no discursive homosexual social identity at this date, and if Wilde entered and exited the first trial without such an identity, then how could he receive the jail sentence meted out after the third trial, a sentence that could only be meted out to an individual inscribed into the juridico-legal discourse as a homosexual? I suggest that between the close of his libel suit against Queensberry on April 5, 1895 and the close of the State's case against him on May 25, that The Homosexual was discursively produced. Yet how was this possible when Wilde's own willful efforts to establish this discursive figure through the signifying pose had been so unsuccessful up to this date? For an answer, it is necessary to further examine the politics of posing.

SEMIOTIC CRIMES AGAINST NATURE

Because Queensberry had secured detailed evidence of his criminal sexual activity, Wilde had admitted to posing as a sodomite in order to terminate the proceedings before the new evidence could be presented. Wilde's decision to do so was based on the assurance that Queensberry, if he won the libel suit, would remain silent about the details of Wilde's sexual life. But with the aggressive vindictiveness that had become his trademark, Queensberry double-crossed him. After having his way in court, and despite the assurances given Wilde, he delivered the evidence to the police the very next day after the close of the suit. Thus began the State's case against Wilde on charges of sodomy that led, after two more trials, to his imprisonment.

The trials appear to be the pivotal, historical moment that provided the major impetus for the recognition of a homosexual social identity by the nongay public and the adoption of that identity by homosexuals themselves. According to Jeffrey Weeks, "The Wilde trials were not only the most dramatic, but also the most significant events, for they created a public image for the homosexual" (1977: 21). They established a physical site for a labeling process during which Wilde was constructed as the first public embodiment of what, until then, had appeared only in the pages of case histories.

Weeks recognized that Wilde was brought to trial within a context created by the dependence of the legal system upon the model of the Homosexual-as-type which had been established and propagandized in the literature of sexology since the middle of the century (1979: 167). The result of this alliance between sexology and law was one of identity formation. Foucault has explained that "the interplay of all those notions that have circulated between medicine and jurisprudence since the nineteenth century . . . behind the pretext of explaining an action, are ways of defining an individual" (1979: 18). The power of the trials over definition of homosexual social identity came precisely from this fusion of dominant discourses within an institutional setting which, as Havelock Ellis noted shortly afterward, provided the definiteness needed to transform the homosexual type from a theoretical construct into a system of physical inscription (212). Sexology's narrative of the homosexual type, taking place within an institutional discursive praxis, activated a semiosis through a dominant and emergent inscription of Wilde. According to this interpretation, Wilde did not need to have a discursive homosexual social identity before he went into the court; it was supplied to him there. In other words, Wilde entered the court as a run-of-the-mill sodomite, but exited as the first homosexual.

John Marshall has disputed the claims by Weeks and others that the trials created a homosexual identity (140). He insists that Wilde would have to be recognized *as* a "homosexual" with a preexisting social identity in order to validate Weeks's assessment that the trials "created a public image for the homosexual": you cannot make public what does not already exist in private. Marshall's argument is flawed on two counts. First, he ignores the processes by which Wilde, as an individual agent, produced meaning. Second, by ignoring Wilde's particular experience, he has employed a constructionist methodology contradictorily based on a reified concept of homosexual identity that does not allow an interpretation of homosexual identity as processually *emergent* in the trials. Failure to take individual experience into account is an often identified flaw in many social constructionist interpretations (Thomason 92–93). Rather, the power of the trials to construct a homosexual identity can only be understood in relation to the semiotic of the personalized code of homoerotic signification that Wilde had so laboriously established and brought with him into the legal process.

During the first trial (the libel suit against Queensberry) I have argued that the defense efforts to label Wilde were hampered by an understanding of homosexuality as a specific, relationally defined sexual act in which a single subject position was shared by both of the sexual partners. Wilde's homoerotic signifying through a transgressive reinscription of bourgeois masculinity, issuing as it did from an apparently unified subjectivity, evaded the labeling process by skewing the dominant cultural understanding of sodomy. There was no way, given this figuration, to prove substantially or conclusively that Wilde had somehow managed to establish an individual practice for signifying the homoerotic because his accomplishment did not fall within the parameters of the existing discourse. The problem for the court was the same one faced by Wilde. Though he had found a way to collapse subject and object, desiring and desired, spectator and poser, there was as yet no cultural sign of homosexuality that could be appropriated to the surfaces of his body. Such a sign needed not only the concept of the homosexual-as-type, but a defined system of extrasexual signifying practices with which to perform the type.

The ambiguity of Wilde's self-representation would have maintained itself if not for Queensberry's possession of the details of Wilde's sexual activities. Not only did that evidence bring about the State's prosecution of Wilde but, motivated by the fear of just such a reprisal,

Wilde had conceded that he was indeed posing as a sodomite. Where before the State could only suspect him of subversive signifying, it now had, by Wilde's own admission, the confirmation so eagerly and frustratingly sought during the first trial. It had not only a signifying code for The Homosexual delivered readymade, but a code that boggled the imagination in its attention to detail. Since 1883, Wilde's experiments to produce an embodied homoeroticism had yielded a sophisticated and ambitiously far-ranging system of signifying practices that included dress, speech, gesture, and even a mode of text production. This was his contribution to the State's establishment of the homosexual social identity, a contribution that cannot be underestimated because it both initiated and completed his juridical inscription into discourse. In constructing Wilde as The Homosexual in the second and third trials, the State depended as much on Wilde as it did on the literature of sexology.

Wilde's homoerotic signifying, like the Delsarte practices it was based upon, had for its goal the completion of a two-part operation. One part was the construction of a sign consisting of an object surface that signified the interiority of a physically detached subject. The other part was the collapse of signifier and signified meant to produce the appropriation of the sign to a single surface. As Wilde experimented with this technique for the purpose of constructing a unified subjectivity that could dispense with the shared sodomitical subject position, he had experienced recurrent and paradoxical failure. In "The Portrait of Mr. W. H.," the collapse of signified and signifier, of desiring and desired, onto a single surface caused the disappearance of the object. In the attempt to solve this problem in *The Picture of Dorian Gray*, he experienced the disappearance of the subject. Though he was successful both times in achieving the collapse of subject and object, there was as yet no homosexual sign that could be appropriated and displayed on the surfaces of a single body. Instead, the sign appropriation had to be read through existing representational practices, resulting only in a transgressive reinscription of bourgeois masculinity. But why, exactly, was this reinscription transgressive? What rules of behavior were being broken? What conventions of gender were being subverted? Could the dandy's effeminate gestural displacement, by itself, constitute a threat to the status quo, or was there a more complex maneuver embodied in Wilde's posing that incurred the public's wrath?

By itself, sodomy did not constitute a transgressive act. Despite the very different judgements passed on them, both the "active" and "passive" partners played acknowledged roles: the insertor dominated the other by wielding the power of male privilege, the insertee occupied the objectified site of perversion by relinquishing that power. Together they reproduced, and therefore stabilized, dominant cultural relationships of class and gender. If Wilde had properly engaged his class and gender privilege according to prevailing convention, he would have been allowed the exercise of sanctioned, unimpeded, and judgment-free acts of insertion, whether into bodies (regardless of sex) or into discourse. But Wilde's aim was the production of a homosexual social identity, impossible to achieve under these conditions. Codification of the surfaces of the Other's body, as Wilde had already discovered, involved the neutralization of those surfaces under an ideal or type that erased the personal identity of the individual being inscribed. As long as the act of sodomy was defined by a relational, shared subject position based upon an unequal power relationship between insertor and insertee, there could be no dialogue, hence no autonomous subject, no homosexual social identity, no control over self-definition. The shared sodomitical subject position simply did not permit the articulation of difference prerequisite for identity formation.

It is important to remember that Wilde was initially entered into the legal process not for perverse sexual activity (sodomy), but for perverse signifying (*posing* as a sodomite). He was a semiotic criminal, not a sexual one, guilty of improper deployment of the phallus, not the penis. In attempting to construct an autonomous identity through a Delsartean-inspired appropriation of the sign, he had transgressed the conditions under which his masculine privileges of inscription could be discharged. In an inverted and narcissistic turn which he had mapped out in *Dorian Gray*, he had rerouted the inscription onto the surfaces of his own body to effect a collapse of subject and object, desiring and desired – a double identification with both gaze and image that dispensed with the need for the shared subject position dependent on the physical presence of a partner. He had succeeded not only in stabilizing and fixing his homoerotic desire, but in a way that preserved his personal identity. His signifying had become truly perverse, stripping away the power of bourgeois masculinity by turning it back onto itself. As an inscriptor inscribing himself as his own inscriptee, Wilde was now guilty of a heinous subversion – the display of a flaccid transcendental signifier that embarrassingly exposed the reification of masculine authority, a threatening political maneuver that undermined the exercise of the power upon which dominant culture based its ascendancy. Wilde's parodic posing suggested that the order of things was far from inevitable, that the "natural" was, perhaps, the unnatural. By toying with the pathways of power he showed that dominant culture had a life expectancy. It was constructed; it could be altered; and therefore it could die. Oscar Wilde, posing somdomite (*sic*): a black hole in the fabric of the white man's universe.

CONTAINING THE WILD(E) MAN

When Wilde's posing is looked at as a political act that represented an ontological threat, then the motives, techniques, and circuits of the State's interpellation of Wilde as homosexual subject become understandable. By collapsing subject and object onto the surfaces of his own body, Wilde had challenged the natural order (and its reflection in the stability of the State) by sundering the relationship between exteriority and interiority upon which bourgeois epistemology was based. His imprisonment becomes, then, not the finite result of his legal inscription, but the ongoing, performative State gesture of reincorporation signifying the restoration of the fragile unity of the depth model which he had come perilously close to toppling. Wilde's imprisonment, reread as the bourgeois establishment of an interior Homosexual essence meant to sunder his unified play of surfaces, constitutes the first cultural sign of homosexuality called into being through the ideological mechanism of the strategy of containment, without which the juridico-legal labeling process could not complete itself.

The containment process, meant to offset the cultural instability inaugurated by Wilde's transgressive reinscription, consisted of two parts, each drawn from different sources. The first was sexology's model of the homosexual type which provided the frame name needed to initiate the labeling process. As Fredric Jameson has explained:

> To name something is to domesticate it, to refer to it repeatedly is to persuade a fearful and beleaguered middle-class public that all of that is part of a known and catalogued world and thus somehow in order. Such a process would thus be equivalent, in the realm of everyday social life, of that cooptation . . . that exhaustion of the novel raw material, which is one of our principal techniques for deferring threatening and subversive ideas.
>
> (1977: 847)

The second part was supplied by Wilde himself whose transgressive signifying codes of costume, gesture, and speech constituted the "novel raw material" co-opted and placed under the Name-of-the-Homosexual. Without Wilde's posing strategies there could have been no labeling process. The legal apparatus was not capable of such invention. It could only produce an ideological construct, as Louis Althusser has taught, by replacing the signified of an already existent signifier:

> ideology thus recognizes, despite its imaginary distortion, that the "ideas" of a human subject exist in his actions . . . and if that is not the case, it lends him other ideas corresponding to the actions (however perverse) that he does perform.
>
> (168)

Wilde's transgressive reinscription of bourgeois masculinity, perceived as defused by transformation (through the forced mediation of a juridico-legal inscription) into the signifier of the sexological type and believed to be safely contained discursively by the frame of the name and physically by the frame of the prison, uncannily conforms to the process of ideological production outlined by Roland Barthes in his early work *Mythologies*. Barthes's focus there was on the issue of connotation, or second-order signifying systems that are built upon already existing ones, a model which, though negatively critiqued in *S/Z* (6–7), is still one that he was unsure of rejecting completely, seeing in it possible applications for those texts "committed to the closure system" (7). Such a text is Wilde's legal inscription which had for its goal a closure through containment and for which, in my opinion, Barthes's early connotative model is still valid.

Connotation is

> a signifying model within which the denotative signifier and the denotative signified join together to form the connotative signifier. In other words, the denotative sign . . . becomes in its entirety the starting point for the connotative process. The connotative sign consists of both parts of the denotative sign as well as the additional meaning or meanings which they have helped generate.
>
> (Silverman 26–27)

This additional meaning(s) is the site of ideology, which Barthes located as the connotative signified (1973: 111–117). Wilde's trials, when subjected to a connotative analysis, yield the following outline (Figure). The denotative signifier (Wilde's signifying codes of dress, gesture, speech, text) and the denotative signified (homoerotic desire

1 Denotative Signifier [Wilde's signifying codes]	2 Denotative Signified [Wilde's personal social identity]	
3 Denotative Sign I CONNOTATIVE SIGNIFIER [Wilde's transgessive reinscription]		II CONNOTATIVE SIGNIFIED [Name-of-the-Homosexual]
III CONNOTATIVE SIGN [Homosexual social identity]		

Figure Connotative Analysis of Oscar Wilde's legal inscription
Source: After the diagram by Kaja Silverman, *Subject of Semiotics*
(Oxford: Oxford University Press, 1983) 27.

issuing from a named individual) join together to form the connotative signifier. The denotative sign (Wilde's transgressive reinscription of bourgeois masculinity) becomes in its entirety the starting point for the connotative process (the juridico-legal inscription). The connotative sign (the homosexual social identity) consists of both parts of the denotative sign (as connotative signifier) attached through inscription to the connotative signified (the Name-of-the-Homosexual).

Because Wilde had finally succeeded in collapsing the distinctions between desiring and desired, he himself had forced the legal inscription into a second-order signification by providing a readymade connotative signifier. The result was that the newly constructed homosexual sign had to mold itself in the image of Wilde. The only signifier available to the legal apparatus was composed of Wilde's own personal identity and his idiosyncratic Delsartean code of signification. This was inevitable since the sign was constructed for the express purpose of cultural containment of both. It appears that it was Wilde who was still pulling the puppet strings in a bizarre manipulation that mirrored Basil Hallward's self-immolation in *Dorian Gray*, a perverse will to immortality accomplished by transforming himself into a surface available for inscription and sacrificially offered up to the State. As Wayne Koestenbaum put it:

> Wilde discover[ed] the possibility of reading the Law against itself . . . opening up a rift within the Law and finding a sexual surprise. The surprise is Wilde's resurrection: the persistence of his reputation and of the homosexual "type" molded in his image.
>
> (187)

If we read Wilde's containing inscription into discourse and his physical containment behind bars as the successful culmination of his efforts to construct a personal homosexual social identity, then a solution to one of history's most perplexing psycho-mysteries can be offered. Between the close of his libel suit against Queensberry and his unavoidable prosecution by the state in the second trial, Wilde was given the opportunity to leave the country. He did not take it. Friends, relatives, his legal counsel, even Queensberry himself warned him to get out, and efforts were made to assist him (Croft-Cooke 202–203; Ellmann 1988: 455–456, 466–473; Harris 140–141, 163–164; Hyde 1975: 224–225). Instead, he simply waited for the state to begin its inscriptory process. He allowed himself to be martyred. For almost fifteen years he had tried to achieve the construction of a homosexual social identity, and he needed the state to finish the job he had started.

Wilde needed the state's dominance, with its control over signification, in order to complete the project by linking his transgressive reinscription of bourgeois masculinity to sexology's homosexual type. In this regard, Michel de Certeau has propounded that "The name imposed by the other is . . . authorized by nothing, and that is its special trait. . . . The name is not authorized by any meaning; on the contrary, it authorizes signification" (39). This is in agreement with Anthony Giddens when he put it that "Structures of signification always have to be grasped in connection with domination and legitimation" (31). In fact, he defines power and domination as the ability to establish and produce codes of signification. He further stipulates that

> Domination depends on the mobilization of two distinguishable types of resource. Allocative resources refer to capabilities – or, more accurately, to forms of transformative capacity – generat-

ing command over objects, goods or material phenomena. Authoritative resources refer to types of transformative capacity over persons or actors. . . . The transformational character of resources is logically equivalent to, as well as inherently bound up with the instanciation of, that of codes and normative sanctions.

(33)

While Wilde could control authoritative resources in his personal writings by ordering the actions of fictional characters, or even during sexual exchanges which were based upon (as I have discussed earlier and at length) the exercise of gender and class privilege over the objectified body of the Other, he was not able to command the allocative resources within the larger contexts in which dominant culture exercised its control over the construction of everyday social values and meanings. His writings and his sexual acts simply did not construct themselves as a dominant discourse with the power to initiate a new code of signification.

In order to establish a homosexual social identity initiated by a new code, Wilde needed to submit himself as a potential surface of inscription to a power far greater than his own control over text and genitalia. It was the trials that were able to accomplish the transfiguration of the sodomite into the homosexual because they were the first events to meet all the needed conditions: a signifier, provided by Wilde himself, composed of a code (Wilde's gesturary) and an agent (Wilde's social identity); a signified, mandatorily originating in dominant discourse, comprised of a narrative (the homosexual-as-type provided by the juridical activation of the dormant semiosis within sexology); a definite setting of interaction in which to contain the sign (by normatively defining Wilde's signifying as the "expected" mode of conduct for the new identity); and – most importantly – a means of reproduction (a cultural installment of the sign through the mass spectacle of publicity).

AN EVER-OPEN BOOK

Naming Wilde as the first Homosexual is not to say that before him there were no other individuals who had somehow become conscious of their difference, conscious of the interface between their behavior and the homosexual type represented in the literature. Why did his trials, then, create such a rupture in social consciousness? The answer can be stated in one word: publicity.[6] Besides the interplay of sexology and jurisprudence within a definite interactional setting, the trials of Oscar Wilde were the first to be staged as a public spectacle. The recoding and transfiguration of the sodomite into the homosexual accomplished in the trials accompanied a similar transfiguration of the nature of the legal process itself. Both the trials and the sign of homosexual identity took on the nature of an educational exercise, a public moral lesson that differed from the canonical treatment of the sodomite. Foucault sees the role of publicity as making

> The meaning . . . clear to all; each element . . . must speak, repeat the crime, recall the law, show the need for punishment and justify its degree. Posters, placards, signs, symbols must be distributed, so that everyone may learn their significations. The publicity of punishment must not have the physical effect of terror; it must open up a book to be read . . . the punishments must be a school rather than a festival; an ever-open book rather than a ceremony.
>
> (1979: 111)

The publicity upon which the trials depended for their didactic purposes, as Foucault has taught, could not simultaneously be an instrument of terror. The terroristic and prohibitive functions that would have been possible through a display of Wilde's punishment were superseded by the transmission of the narrative upon which cultural education was dependent. In the case of the Wilde trials, the goal was the containment of his transgressive reinscription under the Name-of-the-Homosexual, thus their primary function was to enter the new sign into cultural circulation. That the sign of homosexual identity was a new one, and that it was unavoidably molded in the image of Wilde himself, can be shown by the fact that for the several years after the trials the word "Oscar" was synonymous with "Homosexual" and was the public's first label for the newly constructed sign (Harris 144).

Whereas the press constructed the trials as a lesson in morals for the general public, the events served a different educational purpose for those who were engaging in homosexual behavior. Rather than discouraging same-sex sexual activity, the publicity produced "an ever-open book," a blueprint for signification of a social identity. For sodomites, witnessing the crucifixion of Wilde provided an "acknowledgment of a likeness, that guide[d] them toward that identity" (Koestenbaum 187). As Havelock Ellis uneasily observed:

> The Oscar Wilde trial, with its wide publicity . . . appears to
> have generally contributed to give definiteness and self-
> consciousness to the manifestations of homosexuality, and to have
> aroused inverts to take up a definite attitude. I have been assured
> in several quarters that this is so and that since that case the
> manifestations of homosexuality have become more pronounced.
>
> (212)

It appears that homosexual social identity emerges after the trials as
sodomites and inverts inscribed themselves under the sign of Wilde.[7]
Ellis described them as taking "up a definite attitude" that resulted in
observable and visible manifestations of homosexuality proliferating
throughout the praxis of everyday life. Yet, as I have outlined, the only
visible aspects of the homosexual sign were Wilde's own signifying
codes of dress, gesture, and speech that were built upon and preserved
as the signifier of the new identity. I suggest that the performance of
these codes is what became known as "Camp," a new word that
appeared along with the identity during the years immediately following the trials, a word that was entered into J. Redding Ware's 1909
slang dictionary and defined as "actions and gestures of exaggerated
emphasis." Camp, then, is the term used to describe Wilde's transgressive reinscription of bourgeois masculinity *after* it was transformed,
through the forced ideological mediation of the juridico-legal inscription, into the connotative signifier of the Name-of-the-Homosexual.

The last laugh is Wilde's though, and we can hear him laughing
hysterically from beyond the grave. Because his codes were co-opted
with a built-in and already embodied Delsartean collapse of signifier
and signified, Camp encodes the unmasking of the ideological illusion
even as it speaks The Name: the lie that tells the truth. Peer beneath the
surface and all you find is another surface. The "depth" of the depth
model is only the unspeakable, dark recess of the penetrated body of the
"posing somdomite [*sic*]." If only Oscar could see us now, his legacy of
Self, his body, indelibly imprinted on the surfaces of millions upon
millions.

NOTES

I want to thank all the contributors to this volume for the many ideas they have
contributed to my understanding of Camp.

1 For a history of dandyism see Moers.
2 For a history of the Delsarte system see Ruyter (17–30).

3 This is will be familiar to many readers as an enactment of Hegel's master–slave metaphor (111–119). Within this dialectic, the master "achieves his recognition through another consciousness" (116), by positioning ("camping"?) the slave as the medium of desire. Because the slave (or "passive" sodomite in this case) relinquishes its own being-for-self, "[The master] is the pure, essential action in this relationship, while the action of the [slave] is impure ..." (116).

4 For details of the courtroom drama, see the transcripts in Hyde 1956. I use the legal title "attorney" as a convenience for the American reader.

5 Histories of the sexological and medical construction of The Homosexual are numerous. For an introduction to this literature, known as "the medical model of homosexuality," see Bullough; Gay 198–254; Foucault 1980a; and Weeks 1979.

6 The ability of publicity to create a rupture in social consciousness should not be underrated. A recent example of this phenomenon would be the spectacle of Christine Jorgensen's sex change. When Jorgensen had her surgery in 1953, there had already been twenty-eight such operations performed, the first as early as 1932. Yet it was Jorgensen who activated the transsexual sign, moving the concept of transsexualism from narrative into signification and becoming, in effect, the first transsexual. This was accomplished through the spectacle of publicity. For an analysis of the Jorgensen spectacle see my "I Dream of Jeannie," and Dave King's "Gender Confusions."

7 Michel de Certeau has described this vast transformative power over identity formation effected by spectacular legal inscription:

> Nomination does in effect assign him a place. It is a calling to be what it dictates. . . . The Name performs. . . . And that is only the beginning. He will "incarnate" his name by believing it. . . . He makes himself the body of the signifier. But the word that is heard designates precisely this transformation. It is more than a splinter of meaning embedded in the flesh . . . it also articulates the *operation* of believing, which consists in passing from a nameless . . . [body] to a body "remade" for and by the name: a [body] formed according to the specifications of the signifier. . . . The signified of the word . . . designates the overall functioning of the signifier, or [the] effective relation to the law of the signifier. It expresses the precondition and the result of believing in the word, when this belief operates as identification.
>
> (39)

BIBLIOGRAPHY

Althusser, Louis. 1971. "Ideology and Ideological State Apparatuses (Notes towards an Investigation)." *Lenin and Philosophy and Other Essays*. Trans. Ben Brewster. New York: Monthly Review Press, 127–186.

Balzac, Honoré de. 1830. *Traité de la vie élégante*. 1922. Paris: Bossard.

Barthes, Roland. 1973. *Mythologies*. Trans. Annette Lavers. Frogmore, Herts.: Paladin.

—— 1974. *S/Z*. Trans. Richard Miller. New York: Hill & Wang.

Berger, John. 1972. *Ways of Seeing*. London: BBC.

Booth, Mark. 1983. *Camp*. New York: Quartet.

Brien, Alan. 1967. "Camper's Guide." *New Statesman* 23 June: 873–74.

Bullough, Vern L. 1974. "Homosexuality and the Medical Model." *Journal of Homosexuality* 1/1: 99–110.

Chauncey, George, Jr. 1985. "Christian Brotherhood or Sexual Perversion?: Homosexual Identities and the Construction of Sexual Boundaries in the World War I Era." *Journal of Social History* 19/2: 189–212.

Cohen, Ed. 1987. "Writing Gone Wilde: Homoerotic Desire in the Closet of Representation." *PMLA* 102: 801–813.

Cohen, William A. 1989. "Willie and Wilde: Reading *The Portrait of Mr. W. H.*" In Ronald R. Butters, John M. Clum, and Michael Moon (eds). *Displacing Homophobia: Gay Male Perspectives in Literature and Culture*. Durham: Duke University Press, 207–233.

Crisp, Quentin. 1977. *The Naked Civil Servant*. London: Duckworth.

Croft-Cooke, Rupert. 1972. *The Unrecorded Life of Oscar Wilde*. New York: David McKay.

Crompton, Louis. *Byron and Greek Love: Homophobia in Nineteenth-Century England*. Berkeley: University of California Press, 1985.

De Certeau, Michel. 1986. *Heterologies: Discourse on the Other*. Trans. Brian Massumi. Minneapolis: University of Minnesota Press.

Dollimore, Jonathan. 1991. *Sexual Dissidence: Augustine to Wilde, Freud to Foucault*. Oxford: Clarendon Press.

Ellis, Havelock. 1901. *Sexual Inversion*. Philadelphia: F. A. Davis.

Ellmann, Richard (ed.). 1982. *The Artist as Critic: The Critical Writings of Oscar Wilde*. Chicago: University of Chicago Press.

—— 1988. *Oscar Wilde*. New York: Alfred A. Knopf.

Farmer, John S. 1890–1904. *Slang and Its Analogues*. 7 vols. London.

Foucault, Michel. 1972. *The Archaeology of Knowledge and the Discourse on Language*. Trans. A. M. Sheridan. New York: Pantheon.

—— 1980a. *The History of Sexuality: Volume One: An Introduction*. Trans. Robert Hurley. New York: Vintage Books.

Fuss, Diana. 1989. *Essentially Speaking: Feminism, Nature, and Difference*. London: Routledge.

Gagnier, Regenia. 1986. *Idylls of the Marketplace: Oscar Wilde and the Victorian Public*. Stanford: Stanford University Press.

Gay, Peter. 1986. *The Tender Passion: Volume Two: The Bourgeois Experience: Victoria to Freud*. Oxford: Oxford University Press.

Giddens, Anthony. 1984. *The Constitution of Society: Outline of the Theory of Structuration*. Berkeley: University of California Press.

Goodwin, Joseph P. 1989. *More Man than You'll Ever Be: Gay Folklore and Acculturation in Middle America*. Bloomington: Indiana University Press.

Gough, Jamie. 1989. "Theories of Sexual Identity and the Masculinization of the Gay Man." In Simon Shepherd and Mick Wallis (eds). *Coming On Strong: Gay Politics and Culture*. London: Unwin Hyman, 119–136.

Harris, Frank. 1916. *Oscar Wilde*. 1989. New York: Dorset Press.

Hegel, G. W. F. 1807. *Phenomenology of Spirit*. 1977. Trans. A. V. Miller. Oxford: Oxford University Press.

Hyde, H. Montgomery (ed.). 1956. *The Three Trials of Oscar Wilde*. New York: University Books.

—— 1975. *Oscar Wilde: A Biography*. New York: Farrar, Straus, Giroux.

Jameson, Fredric. 1977. "Class and Allegory in Contemporary Mass Culture: *Dog Day Afternoon* as a Political Film." *College English* 38/8: 843–859.

—— 1983. "Postmodernism and Consumer Society." In Hal Foster (ed.). *The Anti-Aesthetic: Essays on Postmodern Culture*. Seattle: Bay Press, 111–125.

King, Dave. 1981. "Gender Confusions: Psychological and Psychiatric Conceptions of Transvestism and Transsexualism." In Plummer 1981, 155–183.

Koestenbaum, Wayne. 1990. "Wilde's Hard Labor and the Birth of Gay Reading." In Joseph A. Boone and Michael Cadden (eds). *Engendering Men: The Question of Male Feminist Criticism*. London: Routledge, 176–189.

Marshall, John. 1981. "Pansies, Perverts, and Macho Men: Changing Conceptions of Male Homosexuality." In Plummer 1981, 133–154.

Meyer, Morris. 1991. "I Dream of Jeannie: Transsexual Striptease as Scientific Display." *TDR: The Drama Review* 35/1: 25–42.

Moers, Ellen. 1978. *The Dandy: Brummell to Beerbohm*. Lincoln: University of Nebraska Press.

Mulvey, Laura. 1984. "Visual Pleasure and Narrative Cinema." In Brian Wallis (ed.). *Art After Modernism: Rethinking Representation*. New York: New Museum, 361–373.

Partridge, Eric. 1933. *Slang To-Day and Yesterday*. London: Routledge.

Pierrot, Jean. 1981. *The Decadent Imagination, 1880–1900*. Trans. Derek Coltman. Chicago: University of Chicago Press.

Plummer, Kenneth (ed.). 1981. *The Making of the Modern Homosexual*. London: Hutchinson.

Rodgers, Bruce. 1972. *The Queen's Vernacular: A Gay Lexicon*. San Francisco: Straight Arrow.

Ross, Andrew. 1989. "Uses of Camp." *No Respect: Intellectuals and Popular Culture*. London: Routledge, 135–170.

Ruyter, Nancy Lee Chalfa. 1979. *Reformers and Visionaries: The Americanization of the Art of Dance*. New York: Dance Horizons.

Silverman, Kaja. 1983. *The Subject of Semiotics*. New York: Oxford University Press.

Sontag, Susan. 1964. "Notes on Camp." 1983. *A Susan Sontag Reader*. New York: Vintage Books, 105–119.

Stanton, Domna C. 1980. *The Aristocrat as Art: A Study of the Honnête Homme and the Dandy in Seventeenth and Nineteenth Century French Literature*. New York: Columbia University Press.

Stebbins, Genevieve. 1888. *Society Gymnastics and Voice-Culture*. New York: Edgar S. Werner.

—— 1899. *Genevieve Stebbins System of Physical Training*. New York: Edgar S. Werner.

—— 1902. *Delsarte System of Expression*. 1977. New York: Dance Horizons.

Thomason, Burke C. 1982. *Making Sense of Reification: Alfred Schutz and Constructionist Theory*. Atlantic Highlands, New Jersey, Humanities Press.

Ware, J. Redding. 1909. *Passing English of the Victorian Era*. New York: Dutton.

Weeks, Jeffrey. 1977. *Coming Out: Homosexual Politics in Britain from the Nineteenth Century to the Present*. London: Quartet.

—— 1979. "Movements of Affirmation: Sexual Meanings and Homosexual Identities." *Radical History Review* 20: 164–179.

—— 1981. "Discourse, Desire and Sexual Deviance: Some Problems in a History of Homosexuality." In Plummer 1981, 76–111.

Wilde, Oscar. 1886a. "Balzac in English." In Ellmann 1982, 29–32.

—— 1886b. "The Relation of Dress to Art: A Note in Black and White on Mr. Whistler's Lecture." In Ellman 1982, 17–20.

—— 1889a. "The Decay of Lying." In Ellmann 1982, 290–320.

—— 1889b. "London Models." In Ellman 1982, 109–115.

—— 1889c. "The Model Millionaire." *The Works of Oscar Wilde.* 1980. 15 vols. New York: AMS Press, 4:155–165.

—— 1889d. "The Portrait of Mr. W. H." In Ellman 1982, 152–220.

—— 1891. *The Picture of Dorian Gray.* 1991. Oxford: Oxford University Press.

4

REVAMPING THE GAY SENSIBILITY

Queer Camp and *dyke noir*

Cynthia Morrill

THE TROUBLE WITH MASQUERADE

Some recent postmodernist cultural theories have claimed subcultural lesbian and gay Camp as a model for a particular type of gender performance analyzed through the tropics of masquerade theory.[1] Critics link the material performative practices of lesbian and gay "role playing" (i.e. lesbian butch–femme relations, gay leathermen and drag queens) with the feminist description of psychoanalytic theories about female masquerade and its twisted sister, female mimicry.[2] This effort to circumscribe Camp as a type of masquerade has elided earlier critiques which sought to define Camp as a particular activity or strategy that signaled the material form of a twentieth-century "gay sensibility."[3] To some extent, these earlier discussions were intended to mark the specificity of lesbian and gay identity for the purposes of unifying the then emergent lesbian and gay civil rights movement. By contrast, the current discussion tends to focus upon Camp as a type of performance. Questions about what defines Camp have been reformulated into questions regarding the execution of Camp. In large part, the feminist critique of Camp has answered the question of "how Camp is done" through an analysis that combines psychoanalytic theory with a discussion of the operations of parody, pastiche, and irony.[4] As a consequence of similar discussions about the operations of postmodernism, Camp has become appreciated as an eminently postmodern form. Indeed, Camp has become recognized as an example par excellence of a postmodern denaturalization of gender categories.

The apprehension of a confluence of interests between "camp-as-masquerade" and postmodernism, and the current critical perception of a seeming "triumph of image and spectacle over meaning and 'the real' " (Modleski 101), appears to mark the victory of Camp and postmodernism alike. To a limited extent, the feminist application of psychoanalytic masquerade and mimicry theory can be seen as an interrogation of the "successful" battle strategy of Camp. However, while some critics have celebrated "camp-as-masquerade" as a limited victory over the restrictions of naturalized gender categories made visible through lesbian and gay male role playing, other critics have expressed reservations.[5] But what has largely remained uncritiqued in this discussion is the bringing to bear of psychoanalytic theory upon lesbian and gay subcultures. Given the historically contentious relationship between psychoanalytic theory and the material lives of lesbians and gay men, the current acquiescence to the model of "camp-as-masquerade" is surprising.

The dilemma inherent in the discussion of Camp in this particular psychoanalytic context is its debt to the specific sexual symbolic posited by psychoanalysis. Feminist masquerade and mimicry theory share with "orthodox" psychoanalytic inquiry the reduction of same-sex eroticism to an order delimited by structures pertaining to heterosexual desire.[6] The common argument follows from the presumption that all desire organizes itself around a single signifier that psychoanalytic theory identifies as the phallus. The homology drawn between Joan Riviere's 1929 theory about womanly masquerade, as read through the Lacanian theory of the phallus, combined with the material practice of late-twentieth-century gay male drag (and occasionally lesbian butch-femme performance), springs from feminist critics' perception of gay men and (heterosexual) women's similar stakes against the heterosexual male hegemony.[7] Unfortunately, defining Camp as a type of ironic gender play through notions about mimicry and masquerade, and aligning its performance with a political critique of phallocentric ideology, often displaces the specificity of the queer subject, for this feminist operation requires the queer to desire phallocentrically.

In contrast, radical poststructuralists Guy Hocquenghem and Luce Irigaray have reconfigured the symbolic order to account for other sites of desire and other signifiers.[8] Hocquenghem's theorization of the anus and Irigaray's theorization of the plurality of women's (both lesbian and heterosexual women's) "lips" demonstrate an alternative order for the symbolic. Their ideas regarding non-heterosexual-specific structures of desire complicate the Freudian–Lacanian paradigm of desire and sexual difference that is restricted to concerns about "being" or "having" the phallus.[9] However, with few exceptions, the contemporary psychoanalytic critique of Camp generally ignores these alternative theories and overlooks the possibility that the development of a theory of the phallus might retard a theorization of a lesbian and gay subcultural practice.[10] Indeed, the continuing perception of homosexuality itself as a variant or arrest in a normalizing system of heterosexual development displays an amazing persistence of (mis)vision.

In order to constitute a sense of Camp from the perspective of the queer subject, the historical construction of Camp as ironic masquerade needs to be reconfigured, and the specific conditions of homosexual subjectivity need to be addressed. For that purpose, I envision Camp as the aftermath of the discursive experience of the shattering of representation that occurs when the queer subject encounters his or her contradiction to the dominant order, that is, when the queer discerns the impossibility of representing his or her desire in a discourse predicated upon compulsory reproductive heterosexuality, the enunciative ties of dominant-order discourse collapse, and the queer is conditionally hurled out of representation. In other words, the relations of "difference" that inscribe and produce subjects of discourse and allow for the performance of language in the dominant order are shattered.[11] However, since expression can only occur in representation, the "articulation" of this blissful moment sutures the queer subject back into the enunciative ties of the dominant order. This secondary discursive phenomenon, this reinscription of the queer subject back into enunciation, is what I will identify as "Camp." Later in this essay I will situate a particular example of lesbian Camp through a discussion of a lesbian subcultural form I will call *dyke noir*, but first I must provide an explanation of the queer subject, dismantle notions of Camp as ironic, and describe in more detail the occasion which generates Camp discourse.

LACKING PRESENCE

As my brief discussion of "camp-as-masquerade" demonstrates, and as certain queer theorists have shown, bringing queer subcultural discourses into debates constructed within an economy informed by heterosexual investment in sexual difference serves to untie these discourses from their homosexual contexts by subjecting them to an un-queer ontology that characterizes itself as inevitable and natural.[12] Indeed, the appropriation of Camp as a theoretical strategy for the interests of postmodern and/or feminist deconstruction follows a troublesome critical tradition of refashioning queer subculture into dominant culture's discursive metaphors.[13] In exiting the closet, all too often the queer discovers herself to be wearing the inappropriate clothes of the heterosexual. As Sue-Ellen Case notes:

> Contemporary theory seems to open the closet door to invite the queer to come out, transformed as a new, postmodern subject, or even to invite the straights to come into the closet, out of the roar of dominant discourse. The danger incurred in moving gay politics into such heterosexual contexts is in slowly discovering that the strategies and perspectives of homosexual realities and discourse may be locked inside a homophobic "concentration camp."
>
> (1989: 288)

Eschewing psychoanalytic sexual formation models altogether through a discussion about lesbian vampires, Case accounts for the lack of specificity to the conditions of homosexual discourse by observing that, while the "apparatus of representation . . . belongs to the un-queer" (1991: 9), the framework of dominant representation prohibits the presence of queer desire. Accordingly, queer desire can only become perceptible by recognizing its proscription, since its only representation is through transgression against the essentialized ontology of the dominant, the un-queer. In short, the vampire-like queer casts no reflection because the mirror of dominant representation cannot reflect the presence of same-sex eroticism. By this logic, queer desire is always already absent from an apparatus served by and through compulsory heterosexuality and its claims upon the natural. Case's argument about vampires shifts from the traditional approach of investigating queer desire through a lens focused upon relations between homosexuality and heterosexuality and tropics of sexual difference to an approach that centers upon questions of ontology. She questions the Platonic interests in the "parameters of Being – the borders of life and death," and more specifically, the divisions between the reproductive as sign of the natural and the "non-reproductive" as sign of the unnatural, the uncanny, and the undead (1991: 3).

Her argument razes the hierarchy of Western culture binarisms which work to align Being, the organic, living flesh, reproduction, and heterosexuality on one side (the side that reflects) and non-Being, the inorganic, dead flesh, sterility, and homosexuality on the other (the uncanny side of nonreflectiveness). She writes:

> The lethal offshoot of Plato's organicism has been its association

with the natural. Life/death becomes the binary of the "natural" limits of Being: the organic is natural. In contrast, the queer has been historically constituted as unnatural. Queer desire, as unnatural, breaks with this life/death binary of Being through same-sex desire.

(1991: 9)

Compulsory heterosexuality claims the category of the natural and relegates homosexuality to the sterile category of the nonreproductive, nongenerational undead – that which cannot reflect itself in un-queer mirrors or find its reflection in representation. In short, the queer cannot enter into the generational or (sexually) differentiated economy of Platonic Being. Nevertheless, the queer seemingly reproduces itself; there always seems to be a steady supply. This uncanny reproduction, in a sense, "proves" the existence of queer desire, while at the same time it necessitates its proscription insofar as such "reproduction" transgresses against the "natural." Given the prohibitions of the un-queer ontology, the queer's only representation in this particular framework can be the trace of its proscription. Case's argument ultimately works to shift the ground for discussions about homosexuality from issues about (hetero)sexual difference to questions about presence and absence in un-queer, dominant ideology. What the queer "lacks," then, is not access to a sexual symbolic, as psychoanalytic theory would have it, but "presence" in the essentialized ontology of the un-queer which insists upon *its* specific sexual symbolic as the locus for *all* meaning.[14]

This queer inability to demonstrate "presence" also problematizes the representational machinery of Camp when Camp is envisioned as ironic. Insofar as an ironic voice or writing dissembles in discourse as a means to reveal a "true" meaning, the operations of irony can be seen to fix meaning in a binary system of difference. By speaking the opposite in order to expose an asserted standard, irony relies upon establishing a critical distance (and therefore a critical difference) between an ostensible standard and a point of commentary. Through this constitution of difference, irony erects an inflexible "presence."

The stabilizing quality of irony, then, contradicts the destabilizing effect ascribed to "camp-as-masquerade." The use and deployment of irony in "camp role playing" can only produce a reification of (hetero)sexual difference since irony cements difference into a binary set of standards and commentaries. The ironic role playing of "camp-as-masquerade" requires an *a priori*, present standard to juxtapose

114

against its point of commentary. Clearly, the notion of Camp as ironic role playing falls short of any destabilizing function. If indeed the subcultural queer discourse of Camp unfixes categories asserted as right, inevitable, and natural, then irony, with its ties to discursive presence through its investment in ostensible binary standards, is at odds with the queer operations of Camp, creating a need to propose an alternative understanding of the operation of Camp. This notion would, furthermore, need to respond to the peculiar constitution of the desiring queer subject, as an absence known only by the trace of its proscription.

GAY SENSIBILITIES: A REPLY TO SONTAG

Staging this alternative requires a move away from the tropics of masquerade (that have nonetheless produced some of the most cogent work on Camp) and necessitates a brief return to Susan Sontag's thoroughly overrehearsed "Notes on Camp." As Gregory W. Bredbeck points out, Sontag's "Notes" concede the "slipperiness" of Camp through the articulation of an Aristotelian interest in "division and classification" (275). The fifty-eight notes seek to identify, investigate, and analyze the mysterious origins and inner workings of Camp. A central point of interest for Sontag is the means whereby Camp *simultaneously* asserts contradictory messages: the Camp object is *so* good, beautiful, and/or wonderful, while and because it is also *so* bad, ugly, and/or awful. Unhappily, Sontag's entry into Camp discourse manifests itself in an effort to resolve the discursive contradictions of Camp, a tactic which has burdened subsequent critical discussions. On the other hand, Sontag's efforts to achieve such resolution fail. It is through Sontag's demand for a stabilized definition of Camp that its *destabilizing* function can be seen.

In trying to divide and conquer Camp, Sontag unwittingly describes Camp's disinterest in difference; Camp resists establishing the critical distance necessary for separating statements, objects, and behaviors. But her Aristotelian methodology seeks to *produce* such critical difference through its creation of a classificatory scheme wherein something becomes present because it is not something else, and conversely, something which cannot be differentiated cannot "be." This is not to say that Camp envisions all objects as homogenous, that all things are the same; rather, Sontag's essay correctly (if unknowingly) reveals the "trouble" with Camp as a destabilization of the relations between things. In other words, Sontag's description of Camp symptomatically recognizes the investment of Camp in the disorganization or collapse of the commonly purported differences that separate and thereby define and delimit things, ideas, behaviors, and so forth. Camp disturbs the binary logic of Western culture. Interestingly, the term "homophobia," which combines the prefix "homo" (meaning "same") with the suffix "phobia" (meaning an "irrational or illogical fear"), names a fear of sameness, a fear of that which undermines difference. Thus the term both names and describes the prejudice frequently held against the practice and practitioners of Camp.

Following Sontag's model, "gay sensibility" theories of Camp tend to fix upon projects that would either bolster Sontag's notion of "camp-as-sensibility" (while simultaneously countering Sontag by insisting upon its "gayness") and/or work to establish a definition along an aesthetic continuum including Camp, kitsch, and high art (another Sontagian strategy). The common objective for both of these projects is an interest in situating Camp within gay (and sometimes lesbians') subculture.[15] Significantly, both the "sensibility" argument that attempts to position Camp as a historical category (differentiating it from, for example, nineteenth-century dandyism), and the "aesthetic" argument that works to separate Camp from kitsch and high art, operate within logics that seek to stabilize, and thus reveal, the "presence" of Camp in the representational field. Given my earlier arguments about irony and queer subjectivity, the notion of Camp as a queer strategy or activity in the production of "presence" is highly problematic.

The tension from which the "gay sensibility" debate seems to have emerged, the historical moment when lesbians and gay men began to assert themselves in post-McCarthy America, remains highly significant.[16] For what is at stake in this debate is more than a problem with discourse. The "gay sensibility" debate emerged during the 1960s and 1970s, before and after Stonewall, reflecting the lesbian and gay political movement's claim for cultural, political, discursive, and legislative representation. Interestingly, Sontag's "Notes" make evident, in part, the political stakes addressed by the "gay sensibility" debate.

While on the one hand discounting a totalizing homosexual claim to Camp, Sontag also observes that "Homosexuals have pinned their integration into society on promoting the aesthetic sense" (118). She imagines that this claim results from the use of Camp as "a solvent of morality. It neutralizes moral indignation, sponsors playfulness" (118). Central to Sontag's claim is the presumption that Camp is a discursive

116

mode offered to heterosexuals as a means for homosexuals to gain acceptance. What is entirely excluded from her analysis is the possibility that Camp might be a discursive mode which enables homosexuals to adapt to the conditions of heterosexual homophobia. By discounting a specific homosexual claim upon Camp, Sontag avoids exploring in depth what she terms "the peculiar relation between Camp taste and homosexuality" (117). Indeed, by calling Camp a "taste," she makes Camp into a "preference." This suggests that personal volition determines one's choice to engage Camp. The danger of the concept of "preference" for lesbians and gay men (i.e. the attendant implication that preferences can be corrected or cured) is well known in the current political moment. More to the point, Jack Babuscio's and other critics' steadfast and exclusive claim on Camp as a homosexual practice – a "gay sensibility" – that marks a specific political identity should not be elided from the current reformulation of Camp. Instead, in addition to rejecting the Sontagian critical ambition toward stabilizing a definition of Camp, what needs to be jettisoned is the ahistoric "gay sensibility" notion of an essentialized gay individual. Case's argument about nonreflecting vampires provides a means to avoid essentialism while at the same time allowing for a critique of homophobia. Moreover, her discussion about uncanny queer subjects and the ontology of the un-queer presents a "campy" opportunity for thinking about why homosexuals camp.

THE CAMP CONDITION

In place of perceiving Camp as a "sensibility" or a masquerade, I identify Camp as a discourse that follows from a condition akin to Barthesian *jouissance*. In *The Pleasure of the Text*, Roland Barthes works to delineate the difference between the pleasurable text and the text of bliss (the translator's term for *jouissance*). In one of the more transparent passages in his highly fragmentary discussion, he asserts:

> Text of pleasure: the text that contents, fills, grants euphoria; the text that comes from culture and does not break with it, is linked to a *comfortable* practice of reading. Text of bliss: the text that imposes a stage of loss, the text that discomforts (perhaps to the point of boredom), unsettles the reader's historical, cultural, psychological assumptions, the consistency of his tastes, values, memories, brings to crisis his relation with language.
>
> (14)

Barthes associates the blissful text with cutting, seams, and sutures; it marks the trace of the cut, the laceration. Unlike pleasure, bliss cannot be spoken in words; it exceeds representation; it "brings to crisis [the reader's] relation with language." The text of bliss, then, is not a specific set of representations. Rather, it is a condition of representation that hurls the subject outside of the limits of pleasure (the dominant order) into the midst of bliss (*jouissance*). Bliss is achieved at the moment when the subject of representation ceases to be sutured into meaning. Barthes describes this moment as "like that untenable, impossible, purely *novelistic* instant so relished by Sade's libertine when he manages to cut the rope at the very moment of his orgasm, his bliss" (7).

Barthes's notion of bliss develops in metaphorical relation to male sexual orgasm; accordingly, it has been critiqued for its androcentrism.[17] Further, Bredbeck has argued, "Barthes's *jouissance* is marked by a will to *limited* play"; it maintains an investment (and appears to seek validation) in a discourse predicated upon heterosexuality (271). As a result, the "truth" discovered through the "absolute bliss" of Barthes's *jouissance* is really only "coitus interruptus"; meaning is produced by the frustration of pleasure. Bredbeck's critique of Barthes rises from his efforts to theorize the "absolute play" of homosexual signification; Bredbeck seeks a homosexual language of desire. Yet the prejudices implicit in Barthes's theory may prove helpful to the objectives of this essay. If indeed Camp causes a disruption of dominant-order discourse through a destabilization of un-queer relations of "difference," it is only through an argument that acknowledges the logic of the dominant order that such a disruption can be rendered visible.

Ironically, Barthes writes his text of "*jouissance*-interruptus" prior to his "coming out of the closet" as a homosexual. Therefore, to the extent that his debates defer to phallogocentrism and answer to dominant representation, *The Pleasure of the Text* can be read as a closet text. To some degree, the heterosexism and homophobia Bredbeck finds in Barthes's text may be attributed to the effects of the closet. Yet, despite its phallocentric connotations, Barthes's description of *jouissance* – as a condition of representation that hurls the subject outside of the ties of dominant discourse by unsettling, among other things, his or her historical, cultural, and psychological assumptions – appears to be remarkably consonant with Case's description of the unsettling of the queer subject when he or she encounters the uncanny proscription of his or her desire.

Barthes's model of *jouissance* explains a representational breakdown that is similar to the disruption seen as a symptom in Sontag's description of Camp. *Jouissance* identifies an imposed "stage of loss" that "brings to crisis [the reader's] relation to language"; Camp marks the destabilization of commonly assumed relations between statements, objects, and behaviors, thus razing the hierarchy of Western culture binary logic. Most importantly, Barthes's thoughts on *jouissance* can be redeployed to elucidate the discussion of Camp as an *affective* response – a *jouissance*-interruptus – of the queer subject that results from the homophobic effects of an un-queer ontology. Camp discourse is the epiphenomenon of the queer subject's proscription in the dominant order; it is an effect of homophobia. Through its resistance against definition and its unfixing of relations of "difference," Camp denotes and confronts queer crises in meaning. Notwithstanding its investment in dominant representation (indeed, informed by its phallocentrism), Barthes's "theory from the closet" illuminates the closet discourse of Camp.

What becomes manifest, what initiates the Camp condition, is the queer's position in a representational economy invested in the Platonic parameters of Being. Camp results from the uncanny experience of looking into a nonreflective mirror and falling outside of the essentialized ontology of heterosexuality, a queer experience indeed. By this logic, Camp can be seen to be the aftermath of a shattering of representation, a queer discourse that results from un-queer proscriptions of same-sex desire. Mirroring Barthesian *jouissance*, or by way of another metaphor resembling the "jump cut" experience of losing one's place in the cinematic enunciation of realism,[18] this queer shattering marks a disruption in the dominant order. But, like the momentary interruption of the "jump cut" in realist films, the "Camp condition" is only a momentary suspension, a provisional breach of un-queer logic. Since expression can only occur in representation, the subsequent articulation of the condition which produces Camp sutures the queer subject back into the enunciative ties of the dominant order. Through Camp, the queer subject is reassigned his or her "place."

As the secondary and discursive response following the queer's reinscription into language, the material expression of Camp must accede to the demands, conditions, and prohibitions of un-queer representation, thus Camp may sometimes perform the logics of phallogocentric identities and desires.[19] However, Camp participation in such un-queer logics must be understood as part of a reaction-formation occasioned by homophobia. Indeed, when informed of its ties to homophobia, Camp discourse may enact interrogations of dominant representation and thereby provide significant critiques of the un-queer hegemony.

In conclusion, I would like to propose *dyke noir* as a form of lesbian Camp and briefly discuss a representative text.

DYKE NOIR

C. Carr, a theatre critic for the *Village Voice*, coined the term "dyke noir" in a review essay on works by playwright Holly Hughes. Carr writes about Hughes's development of a "timeless, tasteless world of dyke noir," featuring the "tough-guy talk, the low-life mood [and] the shady shifty operators" (32) usually associated with hard-boiled pulp-fiction authors James M. Cain, Mickey Spillane, and Jim Thompson. Unfortunately, by restricting her analysis of dyke noir to comparisons with dominant cultural forms, Carr obscures, somewhat, dyke noir's consideration as a type of lesbian representation. Its echoing of earlier mass entertainments notwithstanding, dyke noir finds its primary *modus operandi* in lesbian subculture. Eschewing the assimilationism often seen in pre-Stonewall lesbian representation, dyke noir offers no apologies to dominant culture assumptions and traditions. Instead, through its depictions of street dyke walks on the wild side, dyke noir interrogates homophobia, navigates the proscription of lesbian desire, and destabilizes the essentialized ontology of the un-queer as right, inevitable, and natural. By means of the "dark, obsessive, often deliriously over-written" language of the 1950s hard-boiled novel (Jenkins 82), dyke noir renders lesbian ghettos in their 1980s contexts. But all is not so grim as it may seem; dyke noir is also funny. More to my point, by recognizing its particular investment in "gallows humor," dyke noir can be understood as a Camp discourse.

Although Carr's description of dyke noir concentrates on Hughes's plays and performances, the distinguishing features of dyke noir can be found in other artists' works. Sheila McLaughlin's 1987 film *She Must Be Seeing Things* and Jane De Lynn's 1990 novel *Don Juan in the Village* also unfold in the "timeless and tasteless world of dyke noir." But, for the purposes of this discussion, I will focus on Sarah Schulman's 1988 novel, *After Delores*.

In keeping with her earlier work, Schulman sets her third novel (and first publication by a mainstream press) in the lesbian subcultural milieu of New York's Lower East Side. Its narrative chronicles four months in the life of an unnamed narrator, a nihilistic, working class, coffee shop waitress whose life has been unbearable since the title character abandoned her for another woman. Haunted by her unresolved feelings, and fearful of the consequences which might result from a direct confrontation with Delores, the narrator attempts to escape depression over her situation by conducting an investigation into the murder of a recent acquaintance – a teenage runaway go-go dancer whom she calls Punkette. Within the larger narrative context of a crime story, *After Delores* examines the narrator's unsuccessful attempts to assert "justice" for herself by seeking revenge against Delores for the betrayal of their relationship.

Like the antiheroes of men's hard-boiled fiction, the narrator's interest in solving Punkette's murder has little to do with a desire to preserve the State's law and order. Instead, she begins her pursuit of vigilante street justice because "No one [else] was going to take the time to find out what really happened" (30). The narrator's investigation of the murder is aided by an "old-time femme," a woman who prefers to live her life as a 1950s lesbian version of Priscilla Presley. After assisting Priscilla in achieving her "perfect moment" of revenge (Priscilla "tells off" a former lover at a public dance), the narrator realizes that "If you waited for the right moment you could eventually get revenge" (4). More importantly, the narrator is also left with Priscilla's gun, "it was tiny, with a pearl handle, deadly, sleek and feminine" (10). Noting that possession of the gun frees her from worry, "because the next time somebody went too far, [she] had the power to go farther" (27), the narrator begins her pursuit of Punkette's killer while she simultaneously imagines new ways to "even the score" with her ex-lover, chiefly by murdering Delores's new girl friend, Mary Sunshine:

> I could blow Sunshine's brains right out of her head. I'd splatter them all over Franklin Street. I'd have to kill myself too, of course, since the world doesn't understand moments when there are no alternatives but murder. People don't see your pain when you are the killer. So I'd blow away my insides and Delores would have to live with that for the rest of her life. There was something so attractive in that picture that I decided it would be better to give Priscilla back her gun as soon as possible.
>
> (12)

Despite her second thoughts, the narrator decides to keep the gun while she tries to bear in mind that Priscilla's gun is "a trump [she] could only play once" (27). Through a series of chance encounters and accidental discoveries of evidence, the narrator unravels the mystery of Punkette's death and kills her murderer, a psychotic male taxi driver. However, the narrator's anger at Delores remains unabated and unresolved.

In contrast with the novel's grim narrative is its employment of gallows humor. As heard in the above quotations, Schulman's narrator speaks (as do the other lesbian characters) in a world-weary, sardonic tone that, in some measure, shields her from the emotional pain and stress of her everyday life. By way of another example, the narrator justifies her propensity for continually engaging with those people who she knows in advance will harm her by dryly observing:

> I've trained myself to avoid all potentially unpleasant situations with men even though I walk into them constantly with women. Once I realized women could be pretty nasty I actually considered boys for about five minutes until I remembered that they bored me very quickly, and if someone you love is going to bring tragedy into your life, you should at least be interested in them.
>
> (35)

Through these humorous commentaries the narrator accounts for her relationship to both Delores and the hegemonic forces of homophobia, as well as classism, ethnocentrism, racism, and so forth, while she simultaneously expresses her disdain via her humorous attitude. Significantly, in a 1928 essay, Freud celebrates humor in general, and gallows humor in particular, as a psychic mechanism that "saves" the humorist's ego from unpleasant confrontations with the material world by means of "a saving in expenditure of affect" (1963: 263). Freud views humor as a noble "triumph of narcissism, the ego's victorious assertion of its own invulnerability" (265). He further suggests that "Humor is not resigned; it is rebellious. It signifies the triumph of not only the ego, but also of the pleasure principle, which is strong enough to assert itself . . . in the face of the adverse real circumstances" (265). Through "repudiating reality and serving an illusion" (268), humorous pleasure allows for the psychic refusal of material vulnerability of everything from hegemonic power structures to neighborhood bullies; thus enabling the humorist to deny or ignore his or her own subjection. Freud observes, "By its repudiation of the possibility of suffering, it [humor] takes its place in the great series of methods devised by the mind of man [sic] for evading the compulsion to suffer" (265).[20]

To the extent that Freud posits humor as an *affective* response (the humorist responds to specific material circumstances), humor can be differentiated from abstract, rhetorical devices such as irony, parody, or satire. More importantly, if indeed the queer discourse of Camp develops from the material effects of homophobia (the proscription of the queer subject), and brings to bear queer logics upon the un-queer hegemony by destabilizing binary relations of "difference," then Camp analysis requires a model that can account for its deployment and its enunciative form. Freud's theory offers a means to identify and interrogate how the discourse of Camp may humorously mark and communicate the queer subject's *affective* response to the material effects of homophobia. To that end, Freud's theory about humor provides a useful model for investigating examples of Camp discourse which employ humor (e.g. dyke noir) in the service of critiquing the material circumstances of the queer subject of Camp.

On the other hand, Freud's theory also points to a limitation of the usefulness of Camp to gay and lesbian political struggle. Freud notes that, unlike the comic and the wit, who are more dependent on their material form than humor, and who afford a more intense psychic release through "the vent of hearty laughter,"

> the jest made in humour is not the essential [thing]; it has *only the value of a demonstration*. The principal thing is the intention which humour fulfills, whether it concerns the subject's self or other people. Its meaning is: "Look here! This is all that this seemingly dangerous world amounts to. Child's play – the very thing to jest about!"
>
> (268, emphasis mine)

If indeed humor "has only the value of a demonstration," its particular form of "rebelliousness" would appear to be somewhat limited. For example, as seen in Schulman's novel, the narrator's performance of Camp concurrently marks and rejects her proscribed relationship to the essentialized ontology of the un-queer; however, her expression of gallows humor only serves to *demonstrate* her "psychic" or internal response to homophobic oppression and to Delores.

Although her involvement in Punkette's murder preoccupies much of the novel, the narrator's foremost concern is to force Delores to acknowledge and accept responsibility for the betrayal of their relationship. Even though she is successful at solving the crime and avenging Punkette's death by killing her murderer, the narrator remains entirely unsuccessful in her attempts at finding "justice" for herself. At the novel's end, the narrator observes that she "still misses Delores." This inability to find a suitable revenge for herself results from her continuing fear of having to face the consequences of taking action. Near the end of *After Delores*, the narrator asserts that

> The basic obstacle to getting justice is that everything in life has its consequences. Of course, you could argue that *they* hurt *you* and *your* revenge is *their* consequence. But bullies see themselves as the status quo, and when a person is a reactive type, like myself, what you consider "getting even," they call "provocation.". . . For each pleasure I've enjoyed, I've had to pay it back in sorrow.
>
> (133)

Yet the narrator suffers no repercussions for her "pleasure" in responding to or, as she puts it, "neutralizing" Punkette's murder (154). Significantly, despite her success at "delivering justice" for Punkette, the narrator continues to fear the consequences of a confrontation with Delores, a situation that parallels the narrator's relationship to the dominant order. By means of gallows humor, the narrator precludes herself from *acting* in anger toward Delores or the cultural economy of the un-queer. Instead, she "saves" herself by "repudiating reality and serving illusion."

Interestingly, the narrator's pursuit of vengeance for Punkette is played entirely outside of the purview of the state. The narrator is not required to face the consequences for engaging in vigilante justice because the state is not interested in either Punkette's murder or the welfare of her murderer (the taxi driver). *After Delores* presents a social apparatus that endeavors to maintain a climate of homophobia while it simultaneously works to deny the existence of an economically depressed and violent urban underclass. Without advocating the narrator's alternative response of homicidal violence, the narrator's Camp performance of gallows humor provides a containment mechanism for her anger, serving to inhibit an active response.

Andrew Ross's description of the 1969 Stonewall Rebellion provides an interesting case in point. Although Ross defines the "uses of Camp" within an argument that accommodates Sontag's notion of Camp as a "taste" and denies the homosexual specificity of Camp (Ross argues that Camp is a "cultural economy" that overturns the hegemony of dominant culture), he situates his discussion through four key historical events, including the beginning of the current lesbian and gay liberation movement. Ross describes:

1969: The evening of the funeral of Judy Garland (a long time gay icon), members of the New York City Vice Squad come under fire, from beer cans, bottles, coins, and cobblestones, as they try to arrest some of the regulars at the Stonewall Inn in Christopher Street. The mood of the protesters, many of them street queens in full drag, had changed from that of reveling in the spectacle of the arrest, even posing for it, to one of anger and rage, as one of the detainees, a lesbian, struggled to resist her arrest. Some of those present thought they heard the chant "Gay Power," while others only saw a more defiant than usual show of posing; it wasn't clear whether this confrontation was "the Hairpin Drop Heard Around the World" or the "Boston Tea Party" of a new social movement.

(135–136)

Regardless of the "intentions" of the unknown lesbian who resisted, of the protesters who supported her resistance, Ross's description of a change in "mood" would appear to mark the transformation of Camp humor into a riot. Regardless of the conservative effects of Camp, the expression of the queer subject's proscription from dominant culture need not be foreclosed by Camp humor. Indeed, alternative responses remain possible and, to some degree, Camp discourse registers their likely probability.

NOTES

The ideas expressed in this essay were first developed in Sue-Ellen Case's seminar, "Seduction/Performance," University of California, Riverside, Fall 1991. I am deeply grateful to her for her criticism and comments. This essay is dedicated to Townsend McDill Carr in recognition of her invaluable support and assistance.

1 For example, see Case 1989; and Tyler 1991.
2 For an overview of the significant issues and problems central to this theoretical model, see discussions of mimicry and masquerade theory in Tyler 1990: 191–201; and Case 1989: 290–294.
3 For an outline of the gay sensibility debate see Babuscio. Under the term "gay culture," similar ideas are discussed in Cohen and Dyer.
4 See, for example, Bersani 206–208; Case 1989: 286–289; Tyler 1991: 32–34, 53–58. For a discussion of postmodernism, parody, pastiche, and irony see Jameson 113–115.
5 Strong reservations are expressed throughout Tyler 1991.
6 At issue here is the Lacanian theory of the phallus. A helpful introduction to this theoretical argument is provided in Rose and Mitchell.
7 See Riviere. Riviere's work entered into certain feminist film theory

debates in the early 1980s. A "campy" and contentious account of these debates can be found in Case 1989: 292–293.

8 See Irigaray; and Hocquenghem.

9 For a discussion and refutation of charges against Hocquenghem and Irigaray's work as essentialist, see Gregory W. Bredbeck, "B/O – Barthes's Text/O'Hara's Trick: The Phallus, the Anus, and the Text." Ironically, Irigaray's work on mimicry plays a substantial role in the discussion of feminist masquerade and mimicry theory. Regarding Irigaray's discussion of mimicry, see Irigaray 76. Regarding women's same-sex desire see Irigaray 205–218. For a brief critique of Irigaray's theory about homoeroticism, see De Lauretis 1991a: 233.

10 This is not to say, however, that psychoanalytic theory is entirely without application to discussions regarding gay and lesbian issues. Indeed, Freudian theory will return unrepressed later in this essay. My point is that psychoanalytic theory has been unable to offer an account for homosexual desire that is not heterocentric.

11 For a discussion regarding the inscription of the subject in language, see Benveniste.

12 See Bredbeck "B/O" [1993]; Case 1989; and de Lauretis 1988 for discussions of this problem. Regarding my use of the term "queer": in her introduction to the "Queer Theory: Lesbian and Gay Sexualities," issue of *Differences* (1991b), guest editor Teresa de Lauretis identifies, explains, and analyzes the significance of this term amid the emergent field of gay and lesbian studies. She writes:

> The term "queer," juxtaposed to the "lesbian and gay" of the [issue's] subtitle, is intended to mark a critical difference from the latter. . . . For the phrase "lesbian and gay" or "gay and lesbian" has become the standard way of referring to what only a few years ago used to be simply "gay" . . . or, just a few years earlier still, "homosexual."
>
> (iv)

The political struggle reflected in this careful development of names and protocols, historical and present-day struggles with homophobia, misogyny, and separatism cannot and should not be forgotten. However, as de Lauretis points out, the ascendance of the politically correct twin terms, gay and lesbian or lesbian and gay, while reflective of the need for solidarity between lesbians and gay men, can also encourage taking "differences" (i.e. gender, race, class, ethnicity) for granted among lesbians and gay men, and between queers and heterosexuals. The term queer allows for a greater register of difference (there seems to be no limit to the expression of queerness) while at the same time it resists the sanitizing effects of status quo politics.

13 See, for example, the use of the term "cross-dressing" in Showalter.

14 I am using the term "presence" to mark the opposition against queer "absence" in un-queer, dominant representation. This usage does not correspond with Derrida's idea of presence as a transcendental signified that acts as the ultimate point of reference in Derrida 49.

15 See Babuscio.

16 The beginnings of the gay and lesbian civil rights struggle are described in Faderman.

17 Bredbeck observes in "B/O" how Barthes's hermeneutic presents the text as feminine and in the service of heterosexual masculine needs, wants, and desires; he writes: "Like woman in western culture, the text [for Barthes] remains an inert *tabula rasa* waiting to be given significance by the acts of others" (269).

18 The presentation of realist film narratives follows strict cinematic rules with regard to editing and camera work. One of these prohibitions is the thirty degree rule that works to avoid presenting jump cuts, causing the spectator to experience the unpleasant sensation of a jerk or hiccup in the unfolding of narrative space. Each time the camera is moved, the angle of movement must not exceed thirty degrees so that the spectator's experience of the unfolding of the *mise-en-scène* maintains its coherence. A jump cut causes the spectator to lose her place in the shot-to-shot progression of the film's narrative. In other words, she suddenly and momentarily drops out of the film's mapping of narrative space. The employment of jump cuts in the service of destabilizing the film spectator has a long tradition in independent cinema and has been occasionally employed in dominant cinema when it searches for a "non-Hollywood" style or ambience.

19 But this is not to say that queer desire is performed phallogocentrically.

20 Unfortunately, Freud's explication of humor depends, in part, upon his notion of the super-ego. Given that Freud argues elsewhere that those individuals who cannot "satisfactorily" resolve their Oedipal complexes suffer the consequences of underdeveloped or undeveloped super-egos – an inability found in lesbians, gay men, and heterosexual women – it would seem that only a very few have access to humor. On the other hand, Freud avoids specifying humor as a particularly androcentric or heterosexual type of expression. Moreover, Freud incorporates the notion of the super-ego only for the purposes of accounting for the "divided" nature of self-directed humor, wherein the humorous subject concurrently assumes an adult position of superiority and a childlike position of inferiority. To the extent that queer subjectivity is always already a contradictory subjectivity that is constituted by, and anathema to, the dominant order, the queer would appear to have access to self-directed humor by other means. In short, the queer's access to the closet makes possible queer performances of humor.

BIBLIOGRAPHY

Babuscio, Jack. 1980. "Camp and the Gay Sensibility." In Richard Dyer (ed.). *Gays and Film*. London: British Film Institute, 40–57.

Barthes, Roland. 1975. *The Pleasure of the Text*. Trans. Richard Miller. New York: Hill and Wang.

Benveniste, Emile. 1971. *Problems in General Linguistics*. Trans. Mary Elizabeth Meek. Coral Gables, Florida: University of Miami Press.

Bersani, Leo. 1988. "Is the Rectum a Grave?" In Douglas Crimp (ed.). *AIDS: Cultural Analysis/Cultural Activism*. Cambridge, Mass.: MIT Press, 197–222.

Bredbeck, Gregory A. 1993. "B/O – Barthes's Text/O'Hara's Trick. *PMLA*. 108/2 (March): 268–282.

Carr, C. 1987. "The Lady Is a Dick." *The Village Voice* 12 May: 32.

Case, Sue-Ellen. 1989. "Towards a Butch-Femme Aesthetic." In Lynda Hart (ed.). *Making a Spectacle: Feminist Essays on Contemporary Women's Theatre*. Ann Arbor: University of Michigan Press, 282–299.

—— 1991. "Tracking the Vampire." *Differences* 3/2: 1–20.

Cohen, Derek and Richard Dyer. 1980. "The Politics of Gay Culture." In Gay Left Collective (ed.). *Homosexuality: Power and Politics*. London: Allison and Busby, 172–186.

De Lauretis, Teresa. 1988. "Sexual Indifference and Lesbian Representation." *Theatre Journal* 40/2: 155–177.

—— 1991a. "Film and the Visible." In Bad Object Choices (ed.). *How Do I Look?* Seattle: Bay Press, 223–265.

—— 1991b. "Queer Theory: Lesbian and Gay Sexualities/An Introduction." *Differences* 3/2: iii–xvii.

De Lynn, Jane. 1990. *Don Juan in the Village*. New York: Ballantine.

Derrida, Jacques. 1976. *Of Grammatology*. Trans. Gayatri Chakravoraty Spivak. Baltimore: Johns Hopkins University Press.

Faderman, Lillian. 1991. *Odd Girls and Twilight Lovers: A History of Lesbian Life in Twentieth Century America*. New York: Columbia University Press.

Freud, Sigmund. 1963. "Humor." *Character and Culture*. Trans. Joan Riviere. New York: Collier, 263–269.

Hocquenghem, Guy. 1978. *Homosexual Desire*. Trans. Daniella Dangoor. London: Allison and Busby.

Irigaray, Luce. 1985. *This Sex Which Is Not One*. Trans. Catherine Porter. Ithaca: Cornell University Press.

Jameson, Fredric. 1982. "Postmodernism and Consumer Society." In Hal Foster (ed.). *The Anti-Aesthetic: Essays on Postmodern Culture*. Port Townsend, Washington: Bay Press, 111–125.

Jenkins, Steve. 1982. "James M. Cain and Film Noir: A Reply to Frank Krutnik." *Screen* 23/5: 80–82.

Modleski, Tania. 1991. *Feminism without Women: Culture and Criticism in a "Postfeminist" Age*. New York: Routledge.

Riviere, Joan. 1929. "Womanliness as Masquerade." In Victor Burgin, James Donald, and Cora Kaplan (eds). 1986. *Formations of Fantasy*. New York: Methuen, 35–61.

Rose, Jacqueline and Juliet Mitchell (eds). 1982. *Feminine Sexuality: Jacques Lacan and the Ecole Freudienne*. New York: Norton.

Ross, Andrew. 1989. "Uses of Camp." *No Respect: Intellectuals and Popular Culture*. New York: Routledge, 135–170.

Schulman, Sarah. 1988. *After Delores*. New York: New American Library.

Showalter, Elaine. 1983. "Critical Cross-Dressing: Male Feminists and the Woman of the Year." *Raritan* 3/2: 130–149.

Sontag, Susan. 1964. "Notes on Camp." 1983. *A Susan Sontag Reader*. New York: Vintage Books, 105–119.

Tyler, Carole-Anne. 1990. "The Feminine Look." In Martin Kreiswirth and Mark A. Cheetham (eds). *Theory between the Disciplines*. Ann Arbor: University of Michigan Press, 191–201.

—— 1991. "Boys Will Be Girls: The Politics of Gay Drag." In Diana Fuss (ed.). *Inside/Out: Lesbian Theories, Gay Theories*. New York: Routledge, 32–70.

5

FE/MALE IMPERSONATION
The discourse of Camp
Kate Davy

In the course of what is still a relatively brief history of feminist criticism in theatre, much has been written about work that originated in a woman-run performance space in New York called the WOW Cafe.[1] As a collective endeavor, WOW (Women's One World) has no single artistic vision guiding its productions; at base it is a producing organization that allows members of its collective to showcase work. The result is a wide range of offerings each season representing enormously disparate production types and performance styles. WOW is as much a community as it is a theatre and because any member of the collective can produce and perform – including women with no previous training or experience in theatre – shows at WOW vary as much in quality as they do in approach. WOW might be considered a kind of preeminent community theatre, which is not to suggest that its importance lies primarily in its sociology. Some of the most significant feminist theatre of the last decade was created by women who started at WOW and most of these women continue to work there.

Despite vastly different artistic abilities and sensibilities, however, a common and compelling feature of WOW performances can be identified, one that distinguishes WOW work from that of other theatres. WOW productions represent lesbian sexualities on the stage and presume lesbians as the audience. Lisa Kron, a professionally trained actress and long-time WOW director and performer, admits, "Sometimes our theatre is really rough. But the audience we play for needs us. Lesbians never see themselves represented. And seeing yourself represented is what makes you feel you have a place in the world" (qtd in Chansky 39–41).

The world as constituted by lesbians and inhabited by lesbians is the premise from which most WOW productions proceed, a premise whose consequences radically shift the nature of the performative

130

address. These are not "coming-out" plays addressed to straight audiences in a bid for understanding and acceptance. Nor are they plays about lesbian relationships within separatist communities. Instead, parody is the staple of WOW productions, parodies that take on a wide range of forms, from reworkings of classical texts, to spoofs on genres such as the detective film, the romance novel, and the television talk show, soap opera, or sitcom. Some WOW artists employ avant-garde strategies to make essentially non-narrative work, pieces structured more like a poem than a plot. Performance pieces that construct lesbian spectatorial communities tend to drop from the performative address the heterosexuality that underpins hegemonic representations, or what Monique Wittig might describe as the cultural products of "the straight mind" (1980: 103–111). For spectators whose sole experience with dominant culture is one of being either erased entirely or foregrounded as tragically "other" against a (hetero)sexuality inscribed as fiercely normative, the experience of being addressed as if inhabiting a discursive space, an elsewhere eked out in the gaps of hegemonic representations, is both profound and exhilarating.

Traditionally, regardless of genre, what has marked WOW productions is that they are peopled entirely with lesbian characters. For instance, in *Heart of Scorpion*, Alice Forrester's 1984 parody of the romance novel – a form that can scarcely be imagined outside of heterosexual dating and mating – all the couples were lesbian couples. There was only one man in the play and "he" was represented by a life-size, homemade-looking, stuffed dummy with a somewhat piglike face. He had no lines. Using a television talk-show format for her nightclub act entitled *Carmelita Tropicana Chats*, Carmelita addressed her "studio audience" and, by extension, her entire television viewing audience as if all were lesbians.[2] The cast of Lisa Kron's 1988 production, *Paradykes Lost*, which loosely followed a conventional murder-mystery formula, included a detective, an ingénue and her grande dame aunt, a couple (one of whom had a history, in the form a liaison, with the detective), a butler, and an assortment of eccentric singles. Kron used butch–femme as a cultural paradigm for lesbian sexuality to build a play in which all the characters had women's names, all were played by women, and all were explicitly identified as lesbian in the dialogue. None of these productions constructs a world "out there" of heterosexual culture that the world of the play and its characters are up against. As a result, the operations of heterosexuality as an institution are made visible by the unrelenting and rather jolting presumption that heterosexuals do not exist.

Configuring plays peopled almost exclusively with lesbian characters represents one strategy for making work that insists on a lesbian worldview. Of course it is not the only way to create a theatre *for* lesbians, a theatre that responds to lesbian subjectivities. But, until recently, it has been a central and crucial strategy for WOW, one that has distinguished it from its gay male counterpart, that is, Camp or Ridiculous Theatre in which men impersonate women in narratives peopled for the most part by heterosexual characters. In 1988 a group of WOW artists began to experiment with representing heterosexual couples during their improvisational rehearsal process. Although the idea was abandoned before the piece opened, the notion of cross-dressing was in the air and hotly debated among WOW practitioners.

Within the year, the idea was played out in a production of Sheridan's *School for Scandal*, directed by Alice Forrester and Heidi Griffiths (Plate 9). All the roles were played by women including the male characters, which were played by women in drag. In his review of the production for *The Village Voice*, Robert Massa bemoaned the fact that the production inadequately commented on the play's sexism "as if the point of women's theater were simply to cast, not to recast" (97). He said that as a spectator "you soon forget all the roles are played by women." And in the final line of the review he maintained that "Even the ones playing female characters appear to be in drag." In other words, it was possible to read this *School for Scandal* as cast entirely with men. How can agency for women be realized representationally in a theatrical configuration that once again, like all hegemonic discourses, privileges the male voice and erases women as speaking subjects?

Massa's gloss on *School for Scandal* is, of course, particular and as such a matter of reception. Like all spectators, Massa brings to every encounter with any performance his own relationships with discourses and practices in society, relationships that influence in significant ways how meaning is produced and how a performance is read. It is through institutions and their attendant discourses and practices that readers learn how to read cultural artifacts. Spectators who believe that lesbian women are gender-reversed inverts, for example, might read WOW's *School for Scandal* as exemplary lesbian theatre in which the female characters are played by mannish lesbians in drag. But I think not. Women are effaced in *School for Scandal* because there is no institutionalized paradigm for reading male impersonation. Female impersonation, on the other hand, has a long, rich history from classical theatre and film to television (Jack Benny, Milton Berle, Jamie Farr, Red Skelton, Flip Wilson, Jonathan Winters) in which men are not subsumed. On the contrary, female impersonation, while it certainly says something about women, is primarily about men, addressed to men, and for men.[3] Male impersonation has no such familiar institutionalized history in which women impersonating men say something about women.[4] Both female and male impersonation foreground the male voice and, either way, women are erased. Moreover, it is in the discourse of Camp humor that female impersonation is firmly embedded.

"Camp" has been a central descriptor of Theatre of the Ridiculous since its beginnings in the work of John Vaccaro, Ronald Tavel, and Charles Ludlam in the mid-1960s. The same has not been true for lesbian theatre. While reviewers might deem a particular piece "campy," Camp has not been a central identifying feature of WOW work, nor has it been a standard part of the collective's rhetoric. WOW performances have been compared to Theatre of the Ridiculous as having a certain affinity in their farcical style and the use of irony and double-entendre, two core characteristics of Camp. Like Theatre of the Ridiculous, WOW artists borrow scenarios from classical and popular performance forms as sources for their work. But until 1988, WOW performers did not adopt the heterosexual imperative that drives these narratives. They did not impersonate women and men in heterosexual couplings. Impersonation is the arena in which Camp falls short as a definitive characteristic of most WOW work. The butch of butch–femme gender play is engaged in lesbian representation, not male impersonation. I contend that as the notion of Camp has circulated among WOW practitioners in recent years it has garnered a certain currency that has noticeably influenced the work.

As 1990 began, *Anniversary Waltz*, a production by WOW's co-founders Lois Weaver and Peggy Shaw, used a wedding conceit as the frame of reference for a piece about their ten-year relationship as theatre artists and lovers. Weaver donned a traditional white wedding dress and veil, and clutched a bridal bouquet for the opening scene of the piece during which they talked about being "married" without really foregrounding the fact that, as lesbians, this is not one of their civil rights. As 1990 came to a close, the Five Lesbian Brothers (Maureen Angelos, Babs Davy, Dominique Dibbell, Peg Healey, and Lisa Kron) staged *Voyage to Lesbos (II)*, a narrative that focused on the wedding day of an on-again-off-again lesbian. While her future husband remained in the wings, his "dick" and its pleasures were pivotal.[5]

The reasons why WOW work is changing are many, and not all have to do with the issues surrounding impersonation. From an economic perspective, the desire to move out of the fourth-floor walk-up loft space that currently houses WOW and seats only fifty spectators is understandable. Some WOW artists are weary of scratching out an existence in what they think is becoming a ghetto for lesbian theatre. Shaw once commented with pointed irony that "When lesbians make it to Off Broadway, it's the boys who are doing it" (Shaw and Weaver n.p.). She was referring to drag performer Charles Busch's long-running off-Broadway show *Lesbian Vampires of Sodom*. In emulating "'the boys'" success at moving into mainstream venues there is, perhaps, the inclination to think that one must adopt the boys' performative strategies. *Lesbian Vampires of Sodom* is generally heralded as the epitome of Camp.

In her ground-breaking book, *Mother Camp: Female Impersonators in America*, Esther Newton defines Camp as a system of humor, stating that "the drag queen is its natural exponent" (xx). Explicating this assertion is, in essence, the project of her book, a work that includes, as a footnote, the following: "There are also women who perform as men; male impersonators ('drag butches'). They are a recognized part of the profession, but there are very few of them. . . . The relative scarcity of male impersonation presents important theoretical problems" (5 n.13). My argument focuses on the fact of this "scarcity of male impersonation" and posits that it has something to do with the inability of Camp to serve lesbian women engaged in theatrical endeavors in the same way it serves gay men. In her definition of Camp, Newton states that it "depends on the perception or creation of *incongruous juxtapositions*" (106). She explains that while any very incongruous contrast can be campy, "Masculine–feminine juxtapositions are, of course, the most characteristic kind of camp" (107). It could be said that WOW's project has been to sidestep the fierce binarism that drives masculine–feminine heterogendering, a binarism that, by its very nature, subsumes and erases women. My project is twofold: 1) to investigate the subversive potential of cross-dressing for gay male theatre as it is embedded in the discourse of Camp; and, 2) to delineate the dangers of this same discourse for articulating a feminist subject position vis-à-vis the dynamics of butch–femme gender play in lesbian theatre.

When asked to explain the significance of the title of her book, Newton writes: " 'Mother Camp' as an honorific implies something about the relationship of the female impersonator to his gay audience. A female impersonator will sometimes refer to himself as 'mother', as in 'Your mother's gonna explain all these dirty words to you' " (xx). She then describes the drag queen as "a magical dream figure: the fusion of mother and son" (xx). Here Newton makes a gesture toward reception, that is, the hold and effect the drag queen has on his audience. The preponderance of female impersonation – across representational forms and addressed to very different spectatorial communities – suggests that in the intersection of representation and response, there is something both magical and compelling about a cross-dressed male.

Of the cross-dressed female's relationship to her counterpart in popular nineteenth-century theatre, Peter Ackroyd writes:

> The male impersonator, the actress in trousers, seems . . . to lack depth and resonance . . . [and] is never anything more than what she pretends to be: a feminine, noble mind in a boy's body. It is a peculiarly sentimental and therefore harmless reversal. The female impersonator, on the other hand, has more dramatic presence – the idea of a male mind and body underneath a female costume evokes memories and fears to which laughter is perhaps the best reaction.
>
> (102)

In 1928 Cocteau wrote an essay on "a magical dream figure," an American acrobat named Vander Clyde who performed an enormously effective and popular drag act in Parisian music halls under the name "Barbette." Ostensibly writing about the virtues of skill and concentration using Barbette as a model of professionalism, Cocteau produced instead a brief treatise on reception vis-à-vis female impersonation. What Cocteau finds so compelling about Barbette's turn is his ability to seduce the eye of the beholder into believing he is a woman when the empirical evidence suggests otherwise. He describes how Barbette's gown with its tulle shoulder-straps does not conceal the absence of breasts and how his acrobatic act demands he use his body and muscles in such a way that "he doesn't look very feminine" (in Crosland 224).

Cocteau invites the reader to join him in the audience and then explains that:

> When Barbette comes on, he throws dust in our eyes. He throws it all at once, so violently that he can then concentrate only on his work as an acrobat. From then on his male movements will serve him instead of giving him away.
>
> (in Crosland 223)

This metaphor of dust blinding the audience to the "truth" about Barbette suggests that it is not only what Barbette himself does to enact

135

the gender role of the "other," but that the mystifications of the entire
theatrical apparatus support the illusion as well. It is also clear from
Cocteau's description of his own spectatorial response that the
duplicitous nature of this "illusion of woman," this absent presence, is
the source of his fascination. He writes:

> Barbette moves in silence. In spite of the orchestra which
> accompanies his act, his graceful poses and perilous exploits, his
> turn seems to be far away, taking place in the streets of dream, in
> a place where sounds cannot be heard, it seems to be summoned
> by the telescope or by sleep.
>
> (in Crosland 224)

Here Cocteau describes his spectatorial intervention in terms of
fantasy, a fantasy evoked by the distance between himself and Barbette
whom he describes as being far away, unreachable, dreamlike, unavailable to consciousness. Fantasy is also evoked by the condition of
absence constitutive of the experience of watching film. Indeed,
Cocteau relates the effect of Barbette's turn to film:

> The cinema has supplanted realistic sculpture. Its marble figures,
> its large pallid heads, its shapes and shadows with splendid
> lighting replace what the eye previously demanded from statues.
> Barbette derives from these moving statues. Even when one
> knows him, he cannot lose his mystery.
>
> (in Crosland 224)

Cocteau is not so much blinded by the dust Barbette throws in his
eyes as he is transfixed by it, suspended by the duplicity of the image
Barbette constructs. Cocteau contends that Barbette retains his status
as enigma even for spectators who have already witnessed his turn and
know he will pull off his wig at the finish of his act to reveal his
masculine self. Cocteau would attribute Barbette's mystery to his
ability to send mixed, incongruous signals of masculine and feminine in
the guise of a single gender, seducing even those spectators who know
better into, once again, believing he is a woman.

But I think it also has to do with the ways in which the image of
woman circulates in the representational economies of dominant
culture, especially since Cocteau identifies the experience of watching
film as the source from which Barbette's sense of mystery is derived.
The absence of live objects and bodies constitutive of film resonates
profoundly with the absence of woman as speaking subject in the
construction of woman as presence, as body. The appropriation of this

construction by male performers marks a kind of cultural neologism in the form of an image that resists definition and at the same time generates an excess of meanings. The strict polarization of man/ woman in heterogendering precludes the possibility of reading men in drag "wholistically." Female impersonation provides, in short, a seemingly endless source of fascination because, unlike male imperso- nation, the man who appropriates his "opposite" is not simultaneously effaced by it.

The intensely felt sense of mystery Cocteau describes as invoked by Barbette's act is an apt description of the effect Charles Ludlam creates when he plays women's roles in his Ridiculous Theatrical Company productions, an effect he places in the service of very different ends. In his extraordinary 1973 production of *Camille* Ludlam played Alexandre Dumas fils's Marguerite, the Lady of the Camellias, as well as Greta Garbo's version of the character from the 1937 film, to Bill Vehr's Armand Duval in full period costume (Plate 10).[6] Unlike the narrative construction of Barbette's act – his supposed simulation of a woman and subsequent transformation into a man – Ludlam's hairy chest was clearly visible above the cut of his gown, signaling his status as male from his first entrance. Hence, in the process of enacting the passionate and doomed love affair between Marguerite and Armand that domi- nates the *Camille* narrative, Ludlam and Vehr made manifest the desire of two men for each other. At the same time, like Barbette, Ludlam conjured a credible representation of a woman despite clearly visible evidence to the contrary. In his review for *Women's Wear Daily*, Martin Gottfried wrote that "Ludlam becomes quite believable as Camille." Writing for *The New York Times*, Clive Barnes called Ludlam "a completely convincing Camille."[7]

In playing Marguerite, Ludlam negotiated a position somewhere between a Brechtian presentation of the character and an illusionistic portrayal, a position somewhere between the parameters Barthes articulated when he wrote that "The Oriental transvestite [actor] does not copy Woman but signifies her: not bogged down in the model, but detached from its signified; Femininity is presented to read, not to see: translation, not transgression" (53).[8] Although Ludlam mostly played the role for comic effect, he also played it earnestly in moments where he milked the pathos of a scene, hushing the audience, to seduce them into "seeing" a woman as a kind of "set-up" for moments when he dropped the character altogether to deliver a line or two as his actor- playwright-gay-male self.

In the final act, for instance, Marguerite on her death bed – her penniless, consumptive state played earnestly by Ludlam – calls to her faithful maid, "I'm cold. Nanine, throw another faggot on the fire!" Nanine replies, "There are no more faggots in the house." Dropping the character, Ludlam sits bolt upright, surveys the audience skeptically, and says plaintively, "No faggots in the house?" Then throws his dust, returns the character to her death bed and says, "Open the window, Nanine. See if there are any in the street" (in Samuels and Quinton 246).

In a piece entitled "Reading Past the Heterosexual Imperative," I argued that male drag emphasizes the illusionistic qualities of impersonation in that the actor attempts to simulate that which he is not, the "other." Instead of foregrounding dominant culture's fiercely polarized gender roles, men's Camp tends to reinscribe, rather than undermine, the dominant culture paradigms it appropriates for its parody.[9] In this characterization of gay male theatre I was thinking specifically of Ludlam's Ridiculous Theatrical Company on the west side of Greenwich Village, using it as a means for clarifying what lesbian performance at WOW in the East Village is not. Since then, the tortuous experience of the Milwaukee Repertory Theatre's heterosexist production of Ludlam's play *Irma Vep* has jolted me into a reconsideration of what Ludlam's theatre is not.

Subtitled "A Penny Dreadful," Ludlam's *The Mystery of Irma Vep* is a pastiche of popular, sensationalistic Victorian plots to which he adds recognizable touches from *Dracula*, the Sherlock Holmes tale *Hound of the Baskervilles*, and Hollywood films. The action takes place at Mandacrest, a mansion on the English Moors, where a new wife has come to replace the enigmatic and recently deceased woman whose portrait dominates the living room – clearly a reference to Hitchcock's *Rebecca*. The play's four male characters and four female characters are all played by the same two male actors in a tour de force of disguise, impersonation, and breathtakingly rapid costume changes (Plate 11).

The palpable desire of two men for each other that permeated *Camille*, and drove the original production of *Irma Vep* in which Ludlam played Lady Enid to Everett Quinton's Lord Edgar, was utterly absent from the Milwaukee Repertory Theatre's production.[10] Instead, the actors maintained their status as traditionally masculine men foregrounding their ability as actors in a kind of competitive duel of caricature constructions. They never touched at all suggestively and the stage kiss called for in the script was not executed. The intelligent, lovelorn Lady Enid came across as a dithering frump. The touch of disdain these manly men projected at having to play women's parts (a touch required in order to maintain enough distance from gay male performance) cast a misogynous pall over the entire event. In the production's final gesture, one meant to confirm and punctuate the heterosexuality that inscribed this homophobic rendering of Ludlam's work, the actors took their bows then turned squarely to each other and shook hands.

Ironically, but accurately, two of the four reviews of the production use the word "straight" to describe the acting style. The critic for Milwaukee's major morning newspaper wrote, "They play their absolutely ridiculous (that is, in the famed Ridiculous Theatrical Company sense of the word) roles absolutely straight."[11]

The homoerotic potential of the script – after all, the roles could have been cast with a woman and a man – was manifest through the performative strategies of Camp in the performance text of the original production. Wayne R. Dynes writes in the *Encyclopedia of Homosexuality* that "Camp is not grounded in speech or writing as much as it is in gesture, performance, and public display. When it is verbal, it is expressed less through . . . direct statement than through implication, innuendo, and intonation" (189). Gay audiences for Ludlam's production of *Irma Vep* laughed delightedly at double-entendres such as the line "How do you take it?", delivered pointedly by the maid (Everett Quinton) as "she" served tea to Lady Enid (Ludlam). Taken aback, Lady Enid replies, "I beg your pardon?" The maid, tongue in cheek, explains, "Your tea, miss." When Lady Enid insists that she takes it plain, the maid says both caustically and knowingly, "That's queer." To which Lady Enid replies, in a moment of camaraderie and with a conspiratorial tone, "Queer?" (in Samuels and Quinton 770). Even in the absence of such innuendo it is possible for particular readers to understand the text as homoerotic. For instance, following the publication of Ludlam's collected works, Neil Bartlett – who had never seen an original Ridiculous Theatrical Company production – wrote in his review of the collected plays that *Irma Vep* is "an alarmingly true metaphor of the love between two men" (50–51).

Ludlam does not represent homosexuality by writing plays about gay couples. Ludlam's male actors flaunt their sexuality and their desire for each other in texts he constructs out of pieces of classical and popular narratives. They play the heterosexual couples that people these scenarios, flaunting and thereby presenting the gay male under, alongside, and outside of the straight male and female characters valorized in these canonized texts. Ludlam opens a window in representation, takes the faggots he sees in the street, and puts them on the stage making their desire for each other visible.

More importantly, perhaps, homosexual practice is implicit in this presentation of homoerotic desire. Earl Jackson, Jr. argues that male homosexuality both promises and threatens to disestablish "the transcendence of the phallus from the penis, disinvesting male genitalia (and hence biological identity) of their former privilege to universal principles of order and signification" (470). In a cogent explication of the ways in which male homosexuality opposes, by not participating in, the Oedipal triangle, Jackson states, "Male homosexual desire for the penis does not require the penis to be hypostatized into a universal principle, embracing female subjectivity and sexuality as well" (471). Ludlam's making-visible of homoerotic desire signals homosexual practice, the subversive site of all that phallocratic culture attempts to suppress, contain, and eradicate.

That a dominant culture venue such as a regional theatre could so effortlessly erase, render invisible in its (re)production, any representation of the marginalized group that generated the original cultural product, raises a plethora of thorny issues related to appropriation, context, and address. But it also raises questions about the nature of Ludlam's texts as destabilizing forces, questions about his theatre's potential to subvert and disrupt dominant culture's system of representation.

In an interview I conducted with Ludlam during a subsequent run of *Camille* in 1974, he argued emphatically two seemingly contradictory positions for his production. He maintained that his rendering of *Camille* is not an expression of homosexuality and, at the same time, that it represents a form of coming out. In the space of these contradictions lies the operating principle of Camp. In his comedies, Ludlam adheres to a set of aesthetic universals, one of which he identifies as the theatrical convention of men impersonating women both historically and across cultures. Ludlam casts his portrayals of women in the great tradition of transvestism in the classical theatres of the Greeks, Elizabethans, and Japanese. Of his form of impersonation, he says:

> This is nothing new. It has nothing to do with homosexuality. I use it as a theatrical device. It distances the performer from the role. It takes more art to play a role that is very unlike yourself. You must use everything; you must use your imagination to the utmost to create the impression.[12]

140

And the impression he creates undeniably works for "mixed audiences." "It is not a gay audience," he explains. "Although a lot of gay people do see it, an enormous number of straight people also come – couples clutching each other and weeping at the death scene, hugging each other all the closer." He thinks this is true because *Camille* "transcends gay. It's a love story. It's a story of Adam and Eve. It's the romantic ideal questioned and rethought."

Ludlam locates the "homosexual overtones" of his *Camille* in the narrative's dynamics of forbidden love. But his rethinking of the romantic ideal is manifest in his (re)casting; if *Camille* is the story of Adam and Eve, Ludlam's version has two Adams. Of his casting choices, he says:

> I think it's presenting a positive image. I think it's coming out on a certain level. But I don't think it's gay. It's a matter of being able to see the story freshly, without prejudice. It's a matter of giving the audience a new vision instead of reinforcing fixed habits of thought.

In other words, the play is not gay inasmuch as its address is not exclusively homosexual, but within the dynamics of the production the machinations of homosexuality surface, "come out," and are rendered visible in the pockets, gaps, and fissures of an ultimately less-than-monolithic heterosexual configuration. This is Ludlam's way of dismantling prejudice, of gesturing toward a new vision, of negotiating a partially closeted, partially out-of-the-closet artistic and political stance, a stance played out in the contradiction of Camp.

Dynes writes: "Undeniably, camp is subversive, but not too much so, for it depends for its survival on the patronage of high society, the entertainment world, advertising, and the media" (189). This may help to explain why lesbian theatre work produced on the other side of the Village has not moved, as Ludlam's work has, into mainstream venues. The Milwaukee Repertory Theatre is unlikely to present plays with titles like *The Lady Dick*, *The Well of Horniness*, or *Paradykes Lost*.

In her essay "Toward a Butch-Femme Aesthetic," Sue-Ellen Case delineates a strategy within lesbian discourse and performance practice aimed precisely at challenging dominant culture and the violence of its attendant discourses. Camp is a central player in an argument that picks up where Teresa de Lauretis ends in her essay entitled "The Technology of Gender." In this essay, De Lauretis makes an important critical move in distinguishing and moving away from the ideologically bound female subject position to a more promising and, therefore, more encouraging feminist subject. She locates the subject of feminism in the micro-political practices and cultural productions of feminism, characterizing it as existing both inside and outside of gender as ideological representation in that this subject moves between two contradictory spaces. De Lauretis explains:

> It is a movement between the (represented) discursive space of the positions made available by hegemonic discourses and the space-off, the elsewhere, of those discourses: those other spaces both discursive and social that exist, since feminist practices have (re)constructed them, in the margins (or "between the lines," or "against the grain") of hegemonic discourses and in the interstices of institutions, in counter-practices and new forms of community.
>
> (1987: 26)

De Lauretis locates the feminist subject in this "elsewhere," engendered there in the tension created by the condition of inhabiting the two kinds of spaces at once, conscious of the pull in contrary directions.

The female subject, on the other hand, is trapped in hegemonic discourses as "woman," the always already spoken-for construction that replaces women as speaking subjects in representation. This construction is anathema to women as historical beings and social subjects because it signifies a (feminine) essence intrinsic to all women, thereby reducing them to "nature," "mother," and ultimately, the object of (male) desire. "Woman" replaces women and marks their absence. In this configuration, the lesbian is doubly missing in that even her absence is not inscribed. This is both her oppression and her promise as a destabilizing force.

De Lauretis not only distinguishes between the female subject and the subject of feminism. She identifies the female subject position as inescapably trapped in the phallocentric contract of heterosexuality. Borrowing Irigaray's notion of hom(m)osexuality as the term of sexual (in)difference, that is, the term that signifies a single practice and representation of the sexual as male, De Lauretis identifies hom(m)osexuality as, in fact, the term of heterosexuality (1988: 156). So that when she states that in order to begin the process of change "we must walk out of the male-centered frame of reference in which gender and sexuality are (re)produced by the discourse of male sexuality," she means that, at the level of discourse, we must walk out of the hom(m)osexual frame and its phallocratic contract, the heterosexual contract (1987: 17).

In a brilliant theoretical maneuver, Case recuperates the lesbian butch suppressed historically by the feminist movement, reassimilates recent feminist theoretical strategies, and maps the butch–femme subject position – one that provides, in her words, "a ground that could resolve the project of constructing the feminist subject position" (1989: 289). In other words, a position outside the heterosexual contract.

In her project Case employs Camp as a strategy in combination with the discourse of the butch–femme couple to "provide the liberation of the feminist subject" (1989: 286). My only quarrel with her project, a project that has been enormously influential in constructing an alternative to the female subject, is her use of Camp. Because she invokes Camp as a "discourse," instead of merely using its salient elements, the baggage of Camp discourse is imbricated in her argument. The result is that the subject position she constructs does not walk out of the hom(m)osexual frame of reference as effectively as it could, for Camp as a discourse is both ironically and paradoxically the discourse of hom(m)osexuality, that is, male sexuality.

In Case's scheme, Camp is a neutral, nonideologically bound discourse in that it is produced by both gay men and lesbians out of the condition of being closeted. Furthermore, it is available as a strategy for other marginalized groups in much the same way that "coming out" is available for assimilation as a euphemism for heterosexuals coming out of whatever it is they come out of except, of course, the closet of homosexuality. In using Camp generically, Case falls into the same trap De Lauretis identifies when the word homosexual is used to refer to both gay men and lesbians "sliding inexorably, it seems, into its uncanny hommo-sexual double" (1988: 163). The tools that Camp provides – artifice, wit, irony, exaggeration – are available to butch–femme gender play separate from the ways in which they are inscribed by Camp as an historically marked phenomenon.

Equally significant to Camp as a discourse, as a system of signs, is the cross-dressed male who is not merely an element or an instance, but a central figure. Cocteau's Barbette and Ludlam's Marguerite are figures that incorporate and subsume the sexuality of the "other," of woman. Like the construction "woman," the cross-dressed male specularizes the phallus providing a screen on which anxieties of castration and loss of the privileged phallus are projected and compensated for through the dynamics of fantasy. The cross-dressed male plays the absence of women from phallocratic discourse – woman as signifier is profoundly empty.

In theorizing the subversive potential of gay male discourses and practices, Jackson notes:

> Throughout history, for various reasons, male homoerotic practices have been supportive of, rather than subversive to, hegemonic conceptions of masculinity. Even in the postmodern, late capitalist societies of the twentieth century, male homoerotic discourses are often reinscribed within the very patriarchy they would seem to countermand.

(459)

As a discourse with an historical specificity, Camp undermines the attempt to construct a subject position that hopes to resonate with what Audre Lorde describes as a "house of difference." Lorde's house filled with difference(s) suggests for De Lauretis "a more complex image of the psycho-socio-sexual subject . . . which does not deny gender or sex but transcends them" (1988: 164). This is the challenge Case takes on and meets in theorizing her "dynamic duo," as she refers to the butch–femme couple, out of and within recent feminist theories of the psychoanalytic notion of "womanliness as masquerade." Case's dynamic duo "play on the phallic economy rather than to it" (1989: 291), foregrounding its fictions as fiction by negotiating its "realities" between two lesbian women.

I have argued that the iconography of butch–femme culture present in performances at WOW is not about cross-dressing (1989: 156). Wearing the gender of the "other" sex is not the point. Nor is it about drag in the sense of simulation. No attempt is made to hide the lesbian beneath a mask of male or female gender identity; to fool the audience, even momentarily, is not the objective. As a dimension of erotic identity, butch–femme is about sexuality and its myriad nuances. It is also about gender in that it appropriates gender in its social articulation and representational construction. In butch–femme inconography, attributes which in dominant culture are associated with strict gender roles are not sex-class specific. Worn by lesbians, these attributes have meanings for lesbians in a same-sex lesbian culture that do not necessarily symbolize conformity to rules of gender behavior and the oppositional dynamics of polarized gender roles.

The articulation of desire in the dynamics of butch–femme gender play in lesbian performance positions this performance outside heterosexuality both as a social institution and representational model, by realigning what Jill Dolan describes as the "dynamics of desire" between a performance and its spectators. Dolan writes: "When the locus of desire changes, the demonstration of sexuality and gender roles also changes" (1987: 173). Butch-femme as a signifying practice in lesbian theatre differs from male drag performance in that it dismantles the construction "woman" and challenges male sexuality as the universal norm. It challenges the heterosexual contract that De Lauretis identifies as "the site in which the social relations of gender and thus gender ideology are re-produced in everyday life" (1987: 17).

Case's butch–femme subject position is successfully articulated outside the hom(m)osexual frame of reference, where it could have broader play if it were not encumbered by Camp. Positioned inside a lesbian discourse that is every bit as artificial as Camp in its gender play of phallocratic fictions, the butch–femme subject position, like its original referent in the butch–femme couple, is more lethal to hegemonic discourses than Charles Ludlam's Marguerite and Charles Busch's "lesbians of Sodom."

Butch-femme gender roles played in the streets and on the stage signify, through lesbian desire, Irigaray's "goods that refuse to go to market" (110) and Wittig's lesbian subject who is not man/not woman (1981: 47–50). As such, butch–femme artifice is so much more a part of lesbian discourse than Camp discourse that it not only resists assimilation, because it is too dangerous, but it allows for the play of other differences as well.

Dynes emphasizes that "Camp is always presented with an invisible wink" (190). But instead of realizing the promise and threat of its subversive potential for imagining and inscribing an "elsewhere" for alternative social and sexual realities, the wink of Camp (re)assures its audience of the ultimate harmlessness of its play, its palatability for bourgeois sensibilities. When the butch–femme subject winks, phallocratic culture is not reassured.

Camp is neither good nor bad, it is just more or less effectively deployed. In the context of gay male theatre and its venues, Camp is indeed a means of signaling through the flames, while in lesbian performance it tends to fuel and fan the fire. How gay and lesbian theatre as cultural production might effect social change outside of gay and lesbian contexts demands an examination of how its subversive meanings can be articulated and sustained in a hegemonic culture "bent" on benign assimilation or discursive and political eradication.[13] This seems to me the most crucial project for the future if change is the goal. Change is not possible, as De Lauretis so graphically puts it, "without altering the existing social relations and the heterosexual structures to which our society, and most others, are securely screwed" (1987: 21).

NOTES

1 See, among others, Solomon; Dolan 1988; and Davy 1985, 1986, 1989.
2 See Davy 1985; and Dolan 1985.
3 In the chapter entitled "Lesbian Feminism and the Gay Rights Movement: Another View of Male Supremacy, Another Separatism," in her book *The Politics of Reality: Essays in Feminist Theory* (128–151), Marilyn Frye links effeminacy, as a style, with what she calls the "gay institution of the impersonation of women" and writes:

> What gay male affectation of femininity seems to me to be is a kind of serious sport in which men may exercise their power and control over the feminine. . . . Some gay men achieve, indeed, prodigious mastery of the feminine. . . . But the mastery of the feminine is not feminine. It is masculine.
>
> (137)

While in the text she asserts that female impersonation is a "mockery of women," in a footnote she amends her position with "the realization that gay effeminacy has so little to do with women that it is not even primarily the mockery of women I had thought it was" (151 n.3).

4 This is not to suggest that male impersonation was uncommon in certain periods. In this regard see Senelick. See also Sue-Ellen Case's discussion of the salon of Natalie Barney as a form of "personal theatre" in which women performed for all-women audiences (1988: 50–53).
5 While I juxtapose these two productions to indicate a certain shift in perspective, the differences betwen them are paramount. *Anniversary Waltz* employs a number of heterosexual tropes but is not subsumed by them; it maintains its lesbian stance. Shaw and Weaver work through some extraordinary nonheterogendered postitionalities within a butch–femme representational economy. *Voyage to Lesbos*, on the other hand, is obsessively concerned with heterosexuality in a failed attempt to critique it. Without much of a leap, it could be read as a play about lesbian "penis envy."
6 I saw the original production in the Spring of 1973 at the 13th Street Theatre in New York City, as well as every subsequent revival of it. Readers familiar with the experimental theatre scene in those days will appreciate the following anecdote: When I interviewed Ludlam in the Fall of 1974, I mentioned to him that the Living Theatre's Julian Beck and Judith Malina were in the audience the first time I saw *Camille* and that I was struck by their stoicism in the face of such high comedy. Ludlam responded, "Oh, but they came backstage afterward and said that they *loved* it; they just thought it was irrelevant, that it had nothing to do with reality." For a reading of Ludlam's *Camille* that is quite different from mine see Brecht 88–93.
7 Gottfried 1974; and Barnes 1974. These reviews are from the first revival of *Camille* in the Spring of 1974. The original production opened in the Spring

of 1973. Both reviews were obtained from the files of the Ridiculous Theatrical Company.

8 I am grateful to Laurence Senelick for bringing this citation to my attention.

9 See Davy 1989.

10 I saw the Milwaukee Repertory Theatre's production in the Stiemke Theatre in September 1989, as well as Ludlam's original production in his theatre at One Sheridan Square in New York in November 1984.

11 See Joslyn. A review also appeared on the same day in the evening paper: Jacques. In this review, Jacques conflated Camp with drag and then used "camp," "campiness," and "high camp" to describe what he saw.

12 Personal interview with Charles Ludlam, New York City, 13 October 1974. Before beginning the interview, I asked Ludlam to say something to be sure the recorder was picking up his voice. Hence, the first words on the tape are "This is Charles Ludlam speaking for posterity." He died of AIDS on 28 May 1987. All subsequent quotations are from this interview and do not carry page number references.

13 Susan Sontag's enormously influential "Notes on Camp" (1964) strikes me as exemplary of benign assimilation. She nearly edits homosexuals out of Camp and deems it a fundamentally apolitical phenomenon.

BIBLIOGRAPHY

Ackroyd, Peter. 1979. *Dressing Up: Transvestism and Drag: The History of an Obsession.* New York: Simon and Schuster.

Barnes, Clive. 1974. "Stage: An Oddly Touching 'Camille'." *The New York Times* 14 May: 31.

Barthes, Roland. 1982. *Empire of Signs.* Trans. Richard Howard. New York: Hill and Wang.

Bartlett, Neil. 1990. "Just Ridiculous." *American Theatre* 7/1: 50–51.

Brecht, Stefan. 1978. *Queer Theatre.* Frankfurt: Suhrkamp.

Case, Sue-Ellen. 1988. *Feminism and Theatre.* New York: Methuen.

—— 1989. "Towards a Butch-Femme Aesthetic." In Lynda Hart (ed.). *Making a Spectacle: Feminist Essays on Contemporary Women's Theatre.* Ann Arbor: University of Michigan Press, 282–299.

Chansky, Dorothy. 1990. "WOW Cafe: A Stage of Their Own." *Theatre Week* 24–30 September: 39–41.

Crosland, Margaret (ed.). 1972. *Cocteau's World: An Anthology of Writings by Jean Cocteau.* London: Peter Owen.

Davy, Kate. 1985. "*Heart of the Scorpion* at the WOW Cafe." *TDR: The Drama Review* 29/1: 52–56.

—— 1986. "Constructing the Spectator: Reception, Context, and Address in Lesbian Performance." *Performing Arts Journal* 10/2: 43–52.

—— 1989. "Reading past the Heterosexual Imperative: *Dress Suits to Hire.*" *TDR: The Drama Review* 33/1: 153–170.

De Lauretis, Teresa. 1987. *Technologies of Gender: Essays on Theory, Film, and Fiction.* Bloomington: Indiana University Press.

—— 1988. "Sexual Indifference and Lesbian Representation." *Theatre Journal* 40/2: 155–177.

Dolan, Jill. 1985. "*Carmelita Tropicana Chats* at the Club Chandalier." *TDR: The Drama Review* 29/1: 26–32.

—— 1987. "The Dynamics of Desire: Sexuality and Gender in Pornography and Performance." *Theatre Journal* 39/2: 156–174.

—— 1988. *The Feminist Spectator as Critic*. Ann Arbor: UMI Research Press.

Dynes, Wayne (ed.). 1990. *Encyclopedia of Homosexuality*. New York: Garland Press.

Frye, Marilyn. 1983. *The Politics of Reality: Essays in Feminist Theory*. Trumansburg, New York: Crossing Press.

Gottfried, Martin. 1974. "The Theater: Camille." *Women's Wear Daily* 15 May: n.p.

Irigaray, Luce. 1981. "When the Goods Get Together." In Elaine Marks and Isabelle de Courtivron (eds). *New French Feminisms: An Anthology*. Amherst: University of Massachusetts Press, 107–110.

Jackson, Earl, Jr. 1989. "Kabuki Narratives of Male Homoerotic Desire in Saikaku and Mishima." *Theatre Journal* 41/4: 459–477.

Jacques, Damien. 1989. " 'Irma Vep' Succeeds with Silly Spoof." *Milwaukee Journal* 18 September: 4B.

Joslyn, Jay. 1989. "Rep's Spoof 'Irma Vep' smashingly successful." *Milwaukee Sentinel* 18 September: 10.

Ludlam, Charles. 1974. Unpublished interview. New York, 13 October.

Massa, Robert. 1989. "Comedy of Womanners." *The Village Voice* 33 (10 Jan): 97.

Newton, Esther. 1972. *Mother Camp: Female Impersonators in America*. Chicago: University of Chicago Press.

Samuels, Steven and Everett Quinton (eds). 1989. *The Complete Plays of Charles Ludlam*. New York: Harper and Row.

Senelick, Laurence. 1982. "The Evolution of the Male Impersonator on the Nineteenth-Century Popular Stage." *Essays in Theatre* 1/1: 29–44.

Shaw, Peggy and Lois Weaver. 1985. Unpublished interview. New York.

Solomon, Alisa. 1985. "The WOW Cafe." *TDR: The Drama Review* 29/1: 92–101.

Sontag, Susan. 1964. "Notes On Camp." 1966. *Against Interpretation*. New York: Noonday Press, 275–292.

Wittig, Monique. 1980. "The Straight Mind." *Feminist Issues* 1/1: 103–111.

—— 1981. "One Is Not Born a Woman." *Feminist Issues* 1/2: 47–54.

Plate 9 Claire Moed as Sir Oliver Surface and Babs Davy as Sir Peter Teazle in *School for Scandal*, by Donna Ann McAdams.

Plate 10 Charles Ludlam as Marguerite and Bill Vehr as Armand Duval in *Camille*, by John Stern.

Plate 11 Richard Halverson as Lady Enid and Jim Cunningham as her maid in *The Mystery of Irma Vep*, the Milwaukee Repertory Theatre, by Mark Avery.

Plate 12 Liberace with Mom.

Plate 13 Liberace's 1984 souvenir program cover with all the key symbols: Liberace in flashy suit, fingers loaded with diamonds; long flowing keyboard; Rockefeller Center's Prometheus statue; the Rockettes in a precision line; a "classic" car; the dancing waters; the New York skyline; and the proscenium stage with the rainbow effect at center back.

Plate 14 Liberace in long cape with high-standing collar.

Plate 15 Liberace spreading his cape, invoking Bela Lugosi as Dracula.

Plate 16 Liberace was Count Dracula aglitter, America's blue-collar royalty, a kitsch Rockefeller, and a high priest all rolled into one.

6

THE CAMP TRACE IN CORPORATE AMERICA

Liberace and the Rockettes at Radio City Music Hall

Margaret Thompson Drewal

To be natural, as Wilde observed, is such a very difficult pose to keep up. The result is camp: the whole gay masquerade of men and women who self-consciously act; who flaunt incongruous allusions, parodies, transvestite travesties; who are still sanely aware of the gap between their feelings and their roles; who continue to proliferate a protean, and never normative, range of fantasies in social dramas of their own choosing.

Harold Beaver (106)

But what happens when Camp performance is detached from its gay identity and that identity is displaced or put under erasure?[1] Or, from another angle, if gay signifying practices serve to critique dominant heterosexist and patriarchal ideology through inversion, parody, travesty, and the displacement of binary gender codes, then what happens when those practices are severed from their gay signifier and put into the service of the very patriarchal and heterosexist ideology of capitalism that Camp politics seeks to disrupt and contest? In this essay I address these two questions with regard to productions at Rockefeller Center's Radio City Music Hall, in particular the Easter Show featuring Liberace and the Rockettes.

Public acknowledgment that Liberace was gay came only shortly after his death in 1987. Liberace masked his sexual preferences from his public, and indeed in 1959 he won a libel suit against a British critic who implied he was homosexual. Not that the critic was unable to prove Liberace's sexual preferences, but rather Liberace's lawyer was able to prove that the review defamed the star's character. Liberace's audiences, largely middle- and lower-middle-class women over forty and their husbands, participated in what Michael Thompson in *Rubbish*

149

Theory (1979) has called "a conspiracy of blindness" (2, passim). An overt homosexual identity would have been unacceptable to Liberace's blue-collar, heterosexual, and homophobic audiences, who preferred *not* to view him as gay, but instead focused on his devotion to his mother, an image that Liberace himself promoted (Plate 12).[2] When Liberace was engaged to be married in the early 1950s, he publicized the purported response of his fans:

> On the day news broke of a possible wedding, the fan mail was flooded with calls from all over the country. "Is it true?" women asked, and when the news was confirmed, they broke into sobs. The outpouring of dismay overwhelmed the secretaries who handled the six thousand weekly letters sent to Liberace. Eighty percent of the writers were adamant that Liberace should remain a bachelor. . . .
>
> An aged widow in St. Paul wrote: "I feel sorry for your mother. Now she will have to share the adoration you give her." A woman in Detroit inquired: "How can you think of marriage? You belong to us." A Monroe, Louisiana, fan reasoned: "Everything a man is, he owes to his mother. A wife would never make the sacrifices a mother would." A Gardena, California, woman wrote: "Your appeal is the fact that you're single. If you have to get married, pick a plain type, not a glamour girl."
>
> (Thomas 99–100)

A 1954 fan magazine reported that Liberace had been engaged to marry three times (Thomas 93–94). As long as his gay identity was displaced to the son's devout loyalty to his mother, Liberace could represent a liberal democracy's ideal offspring: hard-working and successful, who went from rags to riches and who remained dedicated to his mother both emotionally and financially, buying her houses and clothes.

Even today, gays in the entertainment industry must remain closeted, and they must work in the interests of dominant culture. As Vito Russo put it, "Hollywood is where a gay director makes anti-homosexual films so that he can continue to work with the big boys" (322). Productions at Radio City Music Hall were not explicitly anti-homosexual. Rather they were stripped of any gay identity in order to serve capitalist interests. When corporate capitalism appropriates Camp in its own interests and then poses as its signifier, then the representation bears only the residue of Camp politics. Detached in this way from a gay subject position, Liberace's performances constituted what Moe Meyer calls residual camp or "the camp trace." Another highly successful son, long-time choreographer and originator of the Rockettes, Russell Markert, also remained single and lived with his mother. If Markert was a closeted gay man or even if he merely refused the compulsory heterosexist choice by remaining a "bachelor" (Sedgwick 193), then the Rockettes, too, can be read as residual camp.

It is in this light that I would like to reexamine the performance of Liberace and the Rockettes "in the heart of corporate capitalism" (see Drewal). First, I will explore *how* their performance served the interests of corporate capitalism through the agency of spectacle. In so doing, I deal at some length with spectacle as a replication of the authority of state and marketplace. In the second part, then, I reread these performances as indexical of the "gay regard" (Worman 1991), a subject position that holds out the possibility of subverting and extending the rhetoric of sign systems by flooding dominant discourse with Camp residues and traces that contaminate and pollute those systems through the contagious, yet subterranean, power of metonymic conjunction (Beaver 109, after Todorov; Douglas; Crocker 59). James C. Scott calls this form of resistance "the hidden transcript" (136), e.g. the mode by which marginalized groups insinuate their own voices, albeit in masked form, into official public discourse. Thus, I would like to suggest that there is not only a "straight" reception of Music Hall productions that reinscribes capitalist desire, but also a gay reception that resists compulsory heterosexuality and by extension patriarchy. Furthermore, this gay perspective is largely unavailable to a heterosexual audience participating in a conspiracy of blindness.

IN THE INTEREST OF CORPORATE CAPITALIST PATRIARCHY: READING IT "STRAIGHT"

The productions at the Music Hall have become legendary throughout the world as an expression of the joy and vitality of the American spirit.
Richard Nixon (1971)

Establishing Music Hall productions as expressions of America's spirit not only locates that spirit in the heartland of corporate capitalism, but fetishizes the performances that embody it.[3] Ideologically, then, the Music Hall, and by extension Rockefeller Center, becomes America's spiritual center. Calvinist values were transposed into the tourist environment of the Music Hall, a case that I have argued elsewhere (Drewal passim). This transposition put entertainment in the service of the work ethic. The whole was then imbued with a spiritual quality in several ways: among them, through invoking the value of hard work in themes about man's achievements that run like a leitmotif throughout the artworks in the building and the stage productions; through transposing features traditionally associated with cathedrals into the environment, thus symbolically sacralizing the site (they even went so far as to employ ushers from church-sponsored high schools and then fired them if they were found drinking in local bars [Krinsky 168]); and, equally important, through displaying advanced technology in the form of stage spectacles that stood as incontrovertible evidence of the fruits of man's labor for all to see.[4] Man's achievements were in this way objectified and fetishized. If man's salvation depends on his hard work in this life, then evidence of that salvation inheres in material success that can be measured concretely, expressed in positivistic statements,[5] and then labeled "progress." Dean MacCannell identifies this process as the main legacy of industrial society as discovered by Karl Marx (19–20).

The spectacle of vampire value: Radio City's Easter Show

In a world of hyperreal sign-values and value-signs, potentialities without end, the medium of value tends to become the frame of a flickering half-life, anemic, parasitic, and thirsty for real bodily fluids. Insubstantial, demater-ialized, dead value joins up with insubstantial, disseminated, dead power in a panic passion of resurrection through the fresh blood of desire which, upon commutative transfusion, ever recedes into a bloodless and dis-oriented desire of desire. It is not inappropriate to speak here, at least in tendency, of a culture of vampire value.

John Fekete (72)

For audience members, the Easter Show experience began at the souvenir concessions – two of them set in opposition across from each another in the Grand Foyer. There was also a smaller stand where the five-dollar program was sold. It turned out that most of the infor-mation in the program was presented in monologues by Liberace himself onstage. On the west wall of the Grand Foyer, under glass, were Liberace souvenirs, while just opposite were Music Hall mementos lying out in the open on counter tops. Liberace souvenirs, which were also pictured in the program to encourage mail orders, included two key chains – one a piano, the other a copy of an entrance ticket to the show, a white silk neck scarf with his signature and a piano stamped on it, a "special Liberace music box" that plays one of his "favorite tunes," and his record albums ("enjoy a Liberace command performance").

The latest album, entitled *The Legend Lives On*, had a picture printed right on the disk. It was the same image that served as the program cover for last year's Easter Show (Plate 13). All the key symbols were there. Liberace was in the foreground with his flashy suit, fur cape, and fingers loaded with rings. He was balanced by a big candelabrum on the opposite side. A long flowing keyboard ran under his hand and streamed into the background uniting the other symbols into one whole. There were: the famous Prometheus statue from the sunken plaza at Rockefeller Center that represents the bringer of fire to man, the Rockettes in a precision line, one of Liberace's "classic" cars, the dancing waters, the New York skyline, and the proscenium stage of the Music Hall at the center, showing the rainbow effect surrounding it. The group of symbols as a whole represented the ideas the audience should take away with them – advanced technology and progress, the value of hard work and cooperation, material wealth, and anticipation of better things to come.

In contrast to Liberace's mementos, the Music Hall's included a large assortment of cheaper key chains, bronze-colored coasters with the Rockettes kicking in low relief in the center, postcards, and piles of tee shirts. The two distinct concessions of tourist souvenirs were constructed as what might be termed "high-culture" kitsch and regular kitsch. One woman inquired, "Do you have a Liberace tee shirt?" and the salesman answered, "No, Mr. Liberace doesn't want tee shirts."

Like "high" art, the social function of this "high" kitsch is to distinguish those who distinguish it (Baudrillard 48). But most of the objects were miniature reproductions of some aspect of the stage show and thus served as further markers of what the audience could expect to see. Susan Stewart has suggested the miniature (souvenir) and the monumental (spectacle) present us with analogical modes of thought. The miniature is associated with interiority, the experience of self, the personal narrative, that which can be contained and subjugated. On the other hand, the monumentality of spectacle refers to authority, the authority of the marketplace and the state, the official collective narrative, that which contains and subjugates. In bringing these two modes together in one production, it is possible for the consumer to transfer her containment within the structure of capitalist authority to a possessor and controller of an "authentic" representative of that structure.

The show began as the sun rays turned green, then purple, and the Rockettes appeared in long pink gowns, each holding up one of Liberace's most well-known trademarks, a candelabrum, and dancing to a segment of *Swan Lake*. The routine was done in strict unison – the main focus being the stage formations. Suddenly the candles lit up as the stage lights dimmed, as the Rockettes flanked a long staircase placed upstage center. At the top a large pink Fabergé egg opened, and Liberace descended in an enormous pink fur cape with a sixteen-foot train and a high standing collar, followed by two Easter bunnies.

At the foot of the stairs, Liberace joked about his costumes being tax deductible as his chauffeur drove onstage in a "classic" pink and gray car. He introduced his driver, who was also there to remove his capes. He whirled around, spread his cape, and the driver lifted it off his shoulders, put it into the back seat of the car, and drove away. As with the rest of the show, there was an exaggerated style that superseded any content. Or, put another way, the style was the content, a style that might be termed conspicuously consumptive.

Meanwhile, Liberace told the audience that it was his fortieth anniversary in show business, that he recently won the Citizen of the Year Award in Las Vegas, that in his home town of Milwaukee there was now a Liberace Playhouse in his honor, and that he had been invited to play with the London Philharmonic. This is what MacCannell might call the naming phase in a kind of self-sacralizing process (44), authenticating himself by enumerating his honors and awards. He then told the audience he wanted to play for them what he would be playing with the Philharmonic. He proceeded to play "Rhapsody in Blue" but then turned to a medley of early popular songs that included, among others, "Embraceable You," "Swanee," "The Man I Love," and "I've Got Rhythm." As he played, a full orchestra rose from beneath the stage to become part of the *mis-en-scène*, steam flowed out around his feet, and he too rose up on a platform. Finally, the rising and sinking platforms settled back down just as the last note of the medley was struck.

The stage technology dominated the experience, even more so than the music itself, which was supposed to be the real focus. There was also an attempt to legitimize popular music by associating it with the London Philharmonic. But the effect was playful and in a way exposed the artifice of "high culture" on the one hand, at the same time preserving the distinctions for those who wanted to distinguish. These kinds of playful integrations, or juxtapositions, permeated the entire show, as was particularly evident in the next segment.

154

Liberace told the audience that many classical pieces have been turned into popular tunes, but what he wanted to do was to turn popular tunes, like "Mack the Knife," into the classics, suggesting further that this is what the "classic" composers would do if they could have their revenge. Even suggesting that a classical composer would want to turn a popular song into a classical one is a curious reversal. In truth "Mack the Knife" is a popularized song derived from Bertolt Brecht's *The Threepenny Opera*, music by Kurt Weil, itself based on John Gay's *The Beggar's Opera*. In essence, Liberace was deconstructing hierarchically structured categories. First, he played it "straight." Then he played "Mack the Knife Sonata in C Major" by Mozart, "Claire de Lune de Mack the Knife" by Debussy, and finally "Blue Mack the Knife Danube" by Strauss. In elevating a pop tune to the status of classical music, or so he would have it, he simultaneously highlighted the impact of style on content. Playing "Mack the Knife" straight before totally transforming it commented on the absurd way in which the categories themselves, which are human constructs, operate to organize attitudes and taste.

Afterward Liberace stressed how he always loved the classics, but he learned to respect pop music as he grew older. Here again is a reversal of what is thought to be the more usual process, that is, as one grows older, one becomes more sophisticated, learning to appreciate the classics. Continuing his monologue, Liberace told of his training with Polish pianist Paderewski, but also of his later admiration for Eddie Dutchin, whose most memorable dance tunes he then played. As he sat down on his piano bench in his tuxedo with tiny mirrors attached, he cracked a joke that he had to be careful in sitting, or else he could have a "shattering experience." He then played another medley – "Dancing in the Dark," "Cheek to Cheek," and so on.

At this point, Liberace danced a brief soft shoe, but said it was no fun to dance alone and so invited a woman, Bea, in the first row to come up and dance with him. After a brief fox trot, he thanked her and gave her a gift – the white silk scarf with his signature that was on sale in the lobby. She gave him a kiss. With this, he gave her a second gift – his newest album with the London Philharmonic – also on sale in the lobby. She kissed him again. Then he asked Bea if she had ever been to Las Vegas. He took this opportunity to tell the audience about the Liberace Museum. (The woman next to me said to her friend, "I've been there. It's gorgeous!")

The Museum, he said, serves as the funding arm of the nonprofit Liberace Foundation for the Performing and Creative Arts. With it, he is able to fund eleven universities with scholarship money. In the museum are Liberace's "classic" cars, his "million-dollar jeweled wardrobe," his furs, and his "unique" pianos. He stressed the workmanship in his costumes, and the program asserted that they are "elaborate works of art – created from silk, metallic and brocaded fabrics; precious and semi-precious jewels and bugle beads." The program stated further that "when one of these extravaganzas is retired from the show, it is carefully catalogued and stored. The more flamboyant end up in the Liberace Museum, where visitors can get a close-up look at their workmanship." He elevated his costumes to the status of "works of art," stressing their workmanship, and then he enshrined them in a museum, where they achieve greater status by being catalogued and either stored or displayed.[6]

Also in Las Vegas is Liberace's Tivoli Gardens Restaurant, for which he gave Bea two vouchers for dinner, making a joke of emphasizing the address. There was also a large advertisement for the restaurant printed in the program. Bea kissed him again. Then he gave her another gift – a "forever" scented silk rose. She kissed him again, but this time he said he was all out of gifts. He escorted her back to her husband and said to him in his soft nasal voice, "I got her all ready for you." Back at center stage, he reported that he heard the husband whisper to his wife, "Why didn't you get a ring?" Then he quipped, "She has to do more than dance to get a ring."

Next was an introduction to the Rockettes, who had been "having a love affair with New York City" for more than fifty years. As the orchestra played "New York, New York," a large movie screen came down and the audience saw a larger-than-life Rockettes retrospective spanning from opening night in 1932 to the 1960s. The audience saw them Paris-bound in street clothes on a boat in their precision line; on a "fleet" visit on board a U.S. Navy ship, where they perform military drills for the masters of military drill; making-up in preparation for a show; and finally onstage in glorious technicolor. Suddenly, the scrim was backlit and the audience saw the orchestra. As the scrim rose, the orchestra rolled forward to drum rolls. A large flashing "New York" sign dropped from above. The Rockettes rose from beneath the floor in a line that completely filled the width of the stage. And the orchestra sank down into its pit. Like the architectural features of the Music Hall, the build-up to the Rockettes' entrance was constructed to induce a heightened sense of anticipation in the audience.

The Rockettes did a rather static tap number in white tuxedos to "I Love New York." This time the emphasis was more on tapping, but both the tap steps and the spatial formations were simple. The focus was on uniformity and precision, but the build-up overpowered the act. The Rockettes ended their dance with the predictable downstage, high-precision kick that always gets audience applause.

Behind them, Liberace was driven onstage in a cream-colored Rolls-Royce. He told the audience that it is the only car of its kind in the world: it is the car that Michael Todd had made for Elizabeth Taylor, and it is worth a million dollars. My brother Gary turned to me to point out that a million dollars is not really a lot of money when one considered that the car the Beatles rode around in was worth several million! At that moment I realized that he was lost to the spectacle.

Liberace now wore a white *virgin* fox cape; "it took forever to get the pelts." He informed the audience that this was the cape he wore at a command performance for the royal family in London and then spun around, opening the cape so that the audience saw the inside, also spectacular, before his chauffeur took it off, put it into the Rolls, and drove off.

Liberace now told of his recent appearance at Madison Square Garden where his mentor Paderewski had played. But he did not give a concert there, rather he served as timekeeper for Saturday-night wrestling, an event that his mother always loved. Again and again, symbols of "high" and "pop" culture are systematically decontextualized and recontextualized – the place where Paderewski played classical music is where Liberace was timekeeper for wrestlers.

Next, Liberace announced that he now had an apartment in New York, thanks to Donald Trump, so he wanted to salute Broadway. He played a medley including "Lullaby of Broadway," "Body and Soul," "Forty-Second Street," "Sidewalks of New York," "Give My Regards to Broadway," and "No Business Like Show Business." With a return to the beginning, "Lullaby of Broadway," the Rockettes rose from beneath the floor in their straight line that filled the stage. Their white tuxedos matched Liberace's. He joined them center stage, and to loud applause they concluded the first half of the show with medium-high precision kicks that Liberace also mustered. In spite of all the self-aggrandizement, Liberace chose one moment to attempt to blend into the group. At intermission, an organist played popular songs on the "largest organ in the world" to entertain the crowd.

At the beginning of the second half, Liberace appeared with a piano inlaid with etched mirrors, a white cape, and a pale blue, sequined tuxedo. He paid tribute to Chopin, his "favorite" composer. Steam was pumped in to cover the floor of the stage; the colored dancing waters spouted to the rhythms of the music on a second level; and behind that another elevator rose carrying dancer Lewis, who had his partner, Kuniko, in a high lift. When the stage settled in place, they did a brief *pas de deux*, composed primarily of large, acrobatic lifts, before they disappeared again beneath the floor. The dancing waters continued, a combination of green, red, yellow, blue, orange, changing to blue and green, with concomitant changes in rhythms and textures. Liberace's piano began to turn, to thunderous applause from the audience. Kuniko and Lewis rose up again and seemed to float in the air above the piano. They performed another series of acrobatic lifts in a classical ballet genre – she wore point shoes although they functioned more as a framing device to mark the dance as ballet than a technical requirement of the choreography.

Again the intent seemed to be to contextualize markers of "high" culture in a pop frame. At the finish, Liberace introduced the "internationally famous dancing waters" and the ballet dancers. Underscoring the irony of the situation, he told the audience he was "so glad" they enjoyed listening to the music of Chopin: the visual sensory stimuli in fact diverted attention from Chopin. He followed this up by saying that, realizing the effects of running water on an audience, he appreciated that they stayed in their seats for the duration of the piece.

Introducing the Rockettes again, he asserted that he personally selected the routine they were going to perform. Called "Dance of the Diamonds," it reportedly had more kicks, and therefore was more strenuous, than any other of their numbers. The Rockettes rose from beneath the stage in long coats, framed in what was supposed to be a series of mirrors. Two lines faced each other, two women per frame, and mirrored each other as if one were the reflected image of the other. The idea played on the notion of uniformity and precision. The front line turned around, the back line stepped through the frames, and all removed their coats to expose their black leotards with silver spangles dangling off their right arms.

In this routine, the emphasis was on spatial formations and kicks, rather than tapping. First, they made a star formation that rotated, then a circle that moved as they kicked, followed by a straight line across stage from which they performed a collective wavelike motion – known as a contagion – that traveled through the line, beginning at one end and continuing to the opposite end and back. This inspired clapping. They broke into two circles that rotated, went back into a straight line, sat down on a raised platform lit from above, and did precision leg lifts, their torsos and legs turning synchronously toward different angles. Again the audience broke into applause. They did another contagion, moved to the front rim of the stage, down runways, so that they were positioned in front of the orchestra pit and then ended once more with their precision high kicks, and once more the audience applauded enthusiastically.

In drove Liberace, this time in a 1930 Boattail Auburn with red trim. He told the audience that he used this car in his show at the Hilton Hotel in Las Vegas, in which he invited the Rockettes to perform. He joked about shopping at K-Mart. And then he stroked the spectators by telling them that this is the largest theatre in the world and they are the friendliest audience. They clapped. Next he was going to play "Slaughter on Tenth Avenue" (the audience "ahhs"), accompanied by six young pianists. He began; a New York cityscape appeared in the background; and the middle stage rose out of the ground with six white pianos and six young pianists in white all playing. The raked platform eventually rotated first in one direction, then in the other. Finally their platform split into three levels, two pianos on each, Liberace's piano forming the fourth level at the bottom in the front. After this, Liberace introduced the young pianists by their first names and said where they were from. They were from all points in the U.S.A. One – only thirteen years old – he invited to play the "Warsaw Concerto." The boy asked permission from Liberace to play his piano, and as he adjusted Liberace's piano bench Liberace looked at the audience and said, "He learned how to do that from watching me." The boy's performance was the only segment of the show that was not overpowered by the stage technology. The power of the attraction was the boy's young age. The audience was in awe; the boy, some remarked, was only thirteen. Liberace was not only focusing on the youth of our country, but setting himself in the role of mentor.

When Liberace returned, he was in another cape, which was "not the loudest, but the most expensive." The audience was told it was a black diamond mink lined with Austrian rhinestones and weighed one hundred thirty-six pounds. He spun around, spread his cape (the inside was a field of rhinestones) – it was removed – and he told about his real diamond buttons that together spelled out his name. He confessed to the audience, "You know, you bought me these things. And since you bought them for me, I know you want to see me in them."

Liberace then asserted that he had been blessed with trademarks: his costumes, piano, candelabra, and rings. He knew the audience wanted to see his rings so he came up with an idea for showing them off. The movie screen came down, and on it were filmed gigantic close-ups of Liberace's two hands sporting all his rings. As he explained the source of each ring, the camera zoomed in even closer and filled the screen with each ring individually. The first was a diamond candelabrum ring. The audience "oohed." The second was in the form of a victriola with a gold record that actually spun around, given to him by his record company to commemorate his gold records. The third was a collection of diamonds given to him individually by "non-English-speaking countries." He put them together in one mounting since he did not have enough fingers to wear them separately. He called them his "European left-overs." His royal amethyst was given to him on the occasion of his command performance for the Queen in London. There was a subtle revaluing process going on here that was consistent with the ethos of the entire show. Style superseded content. Thus, the royal English-speaking amethyst was equivalent to the entire group of non-English-speaking diamonds. Baron Hilton of the Hilton Hotels presented him with a piano ring in Las Vegas, and finally his big opal came from Australia. He also showed off a bracelet and a diamond watch in the shape of a piano.

Finally, he asked the audience to make requests. He repeated what he heard and said, "okay." He repeated "Chopsticks." The audience laughed. He said, "Oh, I play all that crap." In rolled a rhinestone piano. He played another medley including "Stardust" and a boogie woogie but, when he broke into "Let Me Call You Sweetheart," the entire audience spontaneously began to sing. The acoustics in the theatre created a warm, sonorous sound so that I too was finally drawn into the spectacle. I found myself singing and feeling misty-eyed. My brother just wanted to listen, cupping his hands around the back of his ears. He was amazed that the audience knew all the words by heart. And then Liberace played "You Made Me Love You," and the audience, including myself, continued to sing. At that moment the spectacle worked even on me, even as I was analyzing and taking notes. It engendered *communitas* and broke down the bicameral roles of performer and spectator, making the spectators part of the spectacle.

Ultimately the event was under Liberace's control: he quickly reestablished bicameral roles of audience and spectators by playing "Chopsticks." This was not as spontaneous as it appeared, but part of the structure of control over the audience. The New York skyline in the background registered sundown and the rainbow effect around the proscenium showed red, like the aurora borealis. Fireworks burst out in bright colors on the backdrop. Liberace left the stage, and the orchestra slid back down into its pit. For an encore, he returned with yet another cape on, and asked, "Do you really want more?" as the audience continued to clap. He then reported that he was just informed that his show had set a box-office record in ticket sales since the Music Hall opened fifty-three years ago.

Finally, he sang "I'll Be Seeing You" to the audience and shook spectators' hands in the front row of the theatre. He came to a small boy, shook his hand, and said, "See what you can have someday if you practice." Concluding, he said, "You've been a beautiful audience, bless you," as he pulled out an aspergillum and sprinkled in the direction of the auditorium. He then got into a rhinestone car and was driven away as the curtain fell. Liberace presented himself as a conspicuous consumer; empathetic audiences responded with a disoriented desire of capitalist desire, the realm of hyperreal vampire value.

The spectacle of desire: money is blood

You know, you bought me these things. And since you bought them for me, I know you want to see me in them.

Liberace (in performance)

Liberace made his entrances in long, often pastel, capes with high-standing collars (Plate 14). With his full, slicked-back head of dark hair; his seemingly eternal youthfulness; the long, full capes with the high-standing collars; and the way he spun around and posed onstage and in publicity photographs with his cape spread out to the sides, all of these signs reference Count Dracula, or rather Bella Lugosi as Count Dracula (Plates 15 and 16). In Lugosi's Dracula, the spread black cape evoked the vampire bat and his power to transform. Things are not always what they seem! In performance, before removing his cape, Liberace confessed to his audience, "You know, you bought me these things. And since you bought them for me, I know you want to see me in them." The implication was that no one in the audience could afford to buy any one of his costumes alone, but collectively they could buy them for him. Liberace's fans, primarily the middle class, pulled together so that they could enjoy seeing one of their spiritual leaders clothed in the fruits of their collective incidental wages. As Jane M. Gaines has observed:

Dracula shows us the powers of the monopolist unchecked – he thrives on accumulation without interference – and the helplessness of others against him once he has seduced his operatives and

161

secured their properties. This is the monster produced by competition run rampant, and if Dracula doesn't stand out in metropolitan London, it is because his modes of operation, his transactions, are not significantly different from those of other entrepreneurs.

(197)

True, but the difference is, Liberace strove to *stand out* and in so doing celebrated his accumulation without interference and indeed called attention to his seduction of the audience.

Liberace's vampire image plays on the metaphor *money is blood* (after all, *you can't squeeze blood from a turnip*). As a conspicuous consumer supreme, Liberace made clear that he thrived on the earnings of his blue-collar audience. In the same way, capital thrives on its labor force. What Liberace pointed out very dramatically was the vampire nature of the capitalist system itself and the workers' desire for material wealth. As Karl Marx put it, "capital is dead labour which, vampire-like, lives only by sucking living labour, and lives the more, the more labour it sucks" (342). Accordingly, workers become vampires once they have been bitten by a vampire (capital), for that is how vampirism is perpetuated (see Barber 32). As Randy Martin has suggested, capitalism did not really take hold until the workers could afford to buy the products of their own production.

Liberace was a marginal man operating in a liminal zone. He laughed at himself, the spectators laughed with him, and at the same time they laughed at themselves and he laughed at them. What was set in relief was their mutual desires and aspirations; theirs as yet unfulfilled, his fulfilled in excess. Liberace was a symbol of capitalist potential in its extreme. How did the Rockettes figure in this capitalist scenario?

The Rocket(te)s: "They'll be straight and will go up like rockets" – Russell Markert (qtd in Roman 48)

The Rockettes were a mini-spectacle nested in a larger spectacle, part of the structure of aggrandizement. Perhaps more than any other production unit, the Rockettes reinforced the power of the Music Hall and its stage technology. The Rockettes were modeled after the Tiller Girls who were conceived by another industrialist, John Tiller, in early-twentieth-century England (Wershing 28). If the Radio City production expressed the spirit of America broadly, then that spirit was surely to be found in its most enduring component. But what did that spirit represent? According to *Webster's*, a "rockette" might be simultaneously: 1) a little rock, 2) a female rock, and 3) an imitation rock ("ette" 1969). The name carries multiple valences, all simulations of something else as were the souvenirs sold in the lobby. Someone once told James Waring that a Rockette is a little Rockefeller (71). Indeed, in 1937 when the French government awarded the Rockettes the Grand Prix of the Republic, John D. Rockefeller was on hand to receive the prize on their behalf (Roman 87). And in 1939 Rockefeller reportedly told a *New York Times* reporter that he had learned a lesson from the Rockettes – the value of working together as a group and not striving for personal aggrandizement (qtd in Kisselgoff 1). From a corporate capitalist perspective, this is the ideal attitude with which to build "tomorrow's better world" of technology.

The Rockettes' originator, Russell Markert, a Baptist and an erstwhile Wall Street financier turned choreographer, had initially named his group the American Rockets because he "liked the sharp, clear sound of the word 'rocket.' . . . They'll be straight and will go up like rockets" (Roman 48). Even after the American Rockets became the Rockettes, Markert reportedly always pronounced the name like rockets.

Critics clearly picked up on the military, if not phallic, image. Robert Roman, for example, commented that

> when they tapped, their taps had a firing-squad orderliness. Their arms, heads, hands, and legs worked in unison, and whether they moved in ruler-straight lines, circles, or precisely planned patterns to and from the footlights, each girl looked as if she had been made from the same mold.
>
> (49)

And Walter Terry asserted:

> the Rockettes were, and are, tapsters, kickers, rhythm dancers and team dancers. Their routines are rhythmic and choreographic extensions of military drills, for they move in unison as a block, break into subunits or squads with impeccable precision, change directions without a rough edge or laggard-ragged line, advance and retreat and rotate with Euclidean exactitude. In fact, one of their finest, most popular numbers, repeated again and again, was "Parade of the Wooden Soldiers". But they could be sailors, mannequins, dolls, steelworkers and riveters or any group you

care to name as they transformed the assembly line motif into theatre art.

(17)

Among Markert's special choreographic masterpieces were West Point Cadets, Israeli Paratroop Women, Can-Can Girls, Canadian Mounted Police, typewriters, dollies, soldiers, waitresses, cowgirls, and femmes fatales (Love 39). Doris Hering also observed the Rockettes pistol-leg action: "we Americans are inordinately fond of machines, and the Rockettes with their pistol leg action and their assembly line precision are as machine-like as it is possible to be" (47). Even Markert himself once commented, "nobody pays any attention to this tricky stuff. . . . It's the toughest part of the routine to do but the customers only get the thrills when the girls do their machine-gun bobbing and kicking" (qtd in Heimer n.p.). As Anson Rabinbach has pointed out, from the metaphor of machinery, or the motor, so central in the intellectual history of labor,

> it followed that society might conserve, deploy, and expand the energies of the laboring body: harmonize the movements of the body with those of the industrial machine. . . . If the working body was a motor, some scientists reasoned, it might even be possible to eliminate the stubborn resistance to perpetual work that distinguished the human body from a machine.
>
> (2)

In positivistic terms, Markert calculated that a Rockette danced fifty miles a year and wore out two pairs of shoes a month (Petrie n.p.). Elsewhere, he noted, "no stage is too large," adding, "a small stage represses the flair for work; it makes one feel small and often inadequate" (Markert n.d.: 11). The preoccupation with hard work was evident further when Markert once asserted, "my girls work too hard to spend their nights on the cabaret circuit, and they are usually too serious about their careers to be distracted by fast company" (Markert 1955: 112). The Rockettes embodied the history of labor power in Western thought and politics, what Rabinbach called "transcendental materialism" (4, 92), the union of all material being, organic and inorganic, human and machine, in their mutual subordination to work.

The Rockettes created the illusion of a machine through their focus on uniformity. In order to conceal all differences, their heights ranged no more than three inches from the shortest to the tallest, and they lined up side-by-side in such a way as to suggest that they were all the same height. Usually they wore identical hats to cover variations in hair color. As their choreographer succeeding Markert, Violet Holmes, affirmed:

> the mirror image is what I must go after all the time in rehearsal. These ladies are all individuals who, naturally, want to do things their way. But Rockettes have to conform, lose their individuality onstage, and learn to be like everybody else to the point where they work as one person.
>
> (qtd in Wentink 57)

Indeed, the emphasis on uniformity was often the reason given in the popular literature for not racially integrating the group. "A system which is indifferent to variations of form," Siegfried Kracauer has argued, "leads necessarily to the obliteration of national characteristics and to the fabrication of masses of workers who can be employed and used uniformly throughout the world" (69). The Rockettes literally stood for, and embodied, this kind of laborer.

The popular literature, most of it originating with the Music Hall's publicity department, portrayed the Rockettes as all-American girls, who work long hours, have no social life, but somehow find a husband and get married after about four years, settle down, and either have children or open a dance studio in their hometowns. And, it is asserted, they have a very low divorce rate. Typical publicity is as follows:

> While all of the girls appear glamorous (but not too "showgirl," since the Music Hall caters principally to a family trade) on stage, they actually lead a simple, almost monastic life off stage. Because there is not too much time between shows, they stay at the Music Hall, and every effort is made to keep them comfortable and happy.
>
> ("Radio City Music Hall" 1956)

By one account, Markert growled indignantly if anyone referred to his Rockettes as chorus girls, and elsewhere he asserted that he did not like "the flashy, exotic type, such as the dyed blonde with ultra-high heels or swishing sexy walk. . . . If she's cheap or common, we don't want her" (Markert 1955: 115). In other words, the Rockettes are decent, wholesome, and pure, and they embody the work ethic as well as heterosexuality admirably.[7]

It is not surprising then that the ethic of working hard as a group, assembly-line motifs, and militarism should all converge in, and be embodied by, the Rockettes. Such is the essence of tourist productions in America's corporate heartland or, perhaps more accurately, the military-industrial complex.[8] Nor is it surprising that there is a consistent ideology from the top to the bottom in the corporate hierarchy. As E. Richard Brown pointed out:

> it made little difference whether one owned a substantial share of the country's corporate wealth or whether one simply ran the factories and institutions owned by the wealthy. The actions of each group were essentially the same, and their values were quite similar. They both accepted the prevailing economic, social, and political system as given, and they sought to make the system work smoothly.
>
> (51)

Capitalist ideology and the agency of spectacle

Music Hall productions have an impact on the observer through the agency of spectacle.[9] In brief, spectacle is a genre of performance that, as John MacAloon shows, makes use of: 1) the primacy of visual sensory and symbolic codes, 2) monumentality and an aggrandizing ethos, 3) institutionalized bicameral roles of actors and spectators (that is, presentational action set in opposition to passive spectating), and 4) dynamism in the presentation that engenders excitement in the audience (243–244).

The spectacle format becomes significant in the construction of the experience. Spectacle constructs, perhaps more persuasively than any other genre, *how* the audience is to experience the performance and organizes attitudes toward that performance and toward life (MacCannell 27). It also stresses integration and the element of similarity against a background of differences (Wagner 116). The emphasis is on uniformity of action and mass appeal. As such, it constitutes what Roy Wagner calls a collectivizing, or rationalist, approach to symbolization in contrast to a differentiating one (passim). In its emphasis on uniformity, it masks all paradox and contradiction so that the ideology that flows from it has the appearance of neutrality and seems both spontaneous and genuine, as MacCannell suggests. Moreover, it also focuses and conditions awareness by abstracting out the conventional as the proper prescription for human action (Wagner 44–45) MacAloon speaks of this "strange double dynamic," concluding that

while spectacle takes the "realities" of life and defuses them by converting them into appearances to be played with like toys, then cast away, it simultaneously rescues "reality" from "mere appearances" and re-presents it in evocative form as the subject for new thought and action.

(275)

It is precisely in this double dynamic that the essential power of spectacle resides, but the viewer must subscribe to a realist conception of representation that distinguishes between reality and illusion, between depth and surface. As harmless appearance, a mere entertainment, just for show, spectacle presents itself as illusion, pure fantasy, and yet it is enormously persuasive because of its ability to focus and condition awareness and to engender *communitas* through an amassing of spectators and an overwhelming display of technology.

Spectacle operates as what Victor Turner called ideological *communitas* (132), a constructed model intended to engender a spontaneous sense of community in a group (e.g. existential *communitas*). What this means, then, is that the ideology underpinning the event is in fact persuasive without ever making the audience consciously aware of being persuaded. It is hegemonic. In effect, spectacle represents (re-presents) political ideology, but masquerades as neutrality. By saying "admire but do not be deceived by 'mere images' " in the metacommunication of the spectacle frame, the deception exposes itself as illusion at one level (MacAloon 265). But simultaneously that same illusion diverts attention (and indeed MacAloon's attention seems to have been diverted) from the ultimate deception that it successfully masks.

This more deceiving of the two deceptions is that what is actually politically loaded form and content appears neutral, merely entertaining, and therefore impotent. I should point out that Camp performance shares with spectacle the primacy of visual sensory and symbolic codes. Like spectacle, this privileging of the visual and the elaboration of surfaces in Camp has in the past led it to be theorized uncritically as apolitical, harmless appearance, merely entertaining, and thus impotent. However, the ideology of Camp as a gay signifying practice is by its very nature counterhegemonic, but I will return to this point later. Suffice it to say that the excesses of Camp subvert the depth model of identity on which dominant culture's constructions of sexuality and gender are based (Dollimore 310–311; King, this volume). As an instrument of capitalist (and heterosexist) authority, spectacle on the other hand attempts to show the surface model of identity to be false.

The illusion that spectacle promotes reveals itself as just that, a mask, but at the same time conceals the masquerader beneath. Contrary to MacAloon's suggestion that it accommodates individual choice by licensing distanced observation, or spectatorship (269–270), spectacle derives power from its potential to move its audience *en masse* and to stimulate a collective sense. The aggrandizing ethos of spectacle strives to unite the spectators into a collective and, furthermore, to unite the audience with the performance through collective but passive spectatorship.

What is more, Radio City Music Hall's conceptualizer and first producer, R. L. (Roxy) Rothafel, consciously constructed his environment to achieve this very effect. Thus, he wrote in *Variety*:

> Perhaps the most important elimination from our theaters which forms its most outstanding item of progress is the overhanging balcony. For years I have studied the reactions of crowds in balconies, and long ago decided that the balcony is not ideal for the group contact so vital in the theater. There is mass thought, emotion and confidence when a crowd is in a huddle. . . . In a huge balcony this is impossible.
>
> (1932b: 57)[10]

Rothafel thus devised three shallow mezzanines that indeed create a sense of intimacy among the spectators. Facilitating further the potential for *communitas* or, in his words, mass thought, emotion and confidence, he also inspired the extension of the stage onto the runways that extend around the sidewalls up to the first mezzanine in order to draw the audience into the production and to create a sense of unity. Thus by 1932, Rothafel was operating on ideas akin to Turner's ideological *communitas* (Turner 132) with the expressed goal of engendering existential or spontaneous *communitas* in the audience. As the above discussion suggests, much of the power of Music Hall productions stems right from the spatial organization of the theatre and its decor, a fact which Rothafel himself realized (Drewal 72; see also Francisco).

Rothafel reportedly wanted to induce in Music Hall customers "a heightened sense of tingling anticipation with every step" they took toward their seats (Karp 85). It was his general theory that the gigantic 6,200-seat theatre was a vital part of the show. From the audience's perspective, concentric ovals that are continuous with the auditorium move inward to frame the oval-shaped proscenium. This configuration is also represented in the logo of Radio City Music Hall, which shows the New York City skyline perched atop the rainbow. In a sense this is a positional inversion of the Rainbow Grill and the Rainbow Room, which literally perch atop the New York City skyline. In the auditorium, lights concealed behind the concentric panels can create a rainbow effect, a sunset, or the aurora borealis that pull together and focus the viewing masses. Or, left natural, muted beige and gold tones give a sense of sunrise. Indeed Carol Hershelle Krinsky notes that a sunrise service was often held there on Easter Sunday (176).

Thus the power of the Music Hall's design is in its ability to induce a sense of anticipation through symbolic associations with better things to come, new dawns, or new beginnings, as well as in its potential to unite the viewers with that which they view, drawing them into the event through a series of ever-decreasing ovals that flow continuously from the auditorium to the proscenium. Additionally, "the light console, far in advance of its time, can turn the great auditorium into an extension of the stage and the audience into part of the spectacle, another Roxy principle" (Karp 88). In this way, the design and the lighting minimize the bicameral roles of performers and spectators. Add to this celestial setting the world's largest organ playing as patrons enter, during intermissions, and at the conclusion, and the metaphor of tomorrow's heaven on earth is more or less complete.

Krinsky feels that the Music Hall is "unforgettable because its form is simple to understand and to describe, and because its size, its lack of intelligible scale, and its 'celestial' shape can both exalt and over-whelm" (180). Likewise, Alan Balfour suggests that the setting creates an awesome sense of anticipation, the auditorium appearing as a boundless space. He comments, "perhaps in this soaring quality that conveys a sense of almost spiritual pleasure, of entrancement, the setting and play are one" (97). But the gigantic space is only one element of the total experience.

In 1982, Walter Karp wrote that the Music Hall stage

> was – and still is – the largest and best-equipped stage in the world. Its three lengthwise sections can each be raised 13 feet above stage level and lowered 27 feet below it by huge lifts of such advanced design that the Department of War was to make use of the system during World War II and treat it as a military secret. The stage contained, in addition, a revolving circular section that is 43 feet in diameter. The seventy-five-piece orchestra, carried in a special band car, can go above the stage, below the stage, across the stage and under the stage. It can

disappear from out front and re-emerge at stage rear. The stage
has equipment that can send up towering fountains of water or
bring down cascades of rain. . . . The great stage curtain, driven
by thirteen motors, can produce so many patterned shapes that
Roxy decided to make it the first act of his opening show.

$$(88)^{11}$$

The front curtain can lift in a hundred different shapes; a second
curtain can produce a wide range of openings from door size to the size
of the proscenium arch, which is 100 feet wide.

This focus on technology in the stage productions in a curious way
paralleled the major strategy of Rockefeller philanthropies to fund
technological medicine in order to make it more effective (Brown 239).
The degree to which spectacle functions to reinscribe the capitalist
authority of the state was implied by Terry:

> the Rockettes were concluding their routine with the required
> across-the-front-of-the-stage massed unison kick. The brightest
> of lights were poured on them as they executed the kick, and the
> whole house applauded. A man sitting next to me did not. I
> leaned over to him and said, "you must be a foreigner. *In the
> United States we stand up for 'The Star-Spangled Banner' and applaud
> when the Rockettes kick together.*" Terror swept his face. *He stood up
> and applauded simultaneously!* The Rockettes, as they have for fifty
> years, deserve both tributes.
>
> (17, emphasis mine)

Reportedly standing up and applauding simultaneously, the man next to
Terry metaphorically brought the allegiance to nation-state authority
(patriotism) into contiguity with the phallocentric high kicks of
fetishized womanhood cast as a military machine. "The Rockettes,"
Terry affirmed, "deserved both tributes" (17) in the form of a standing
ovation. The Rockettes sacrificed individual aggrandizement to the
aggrandizing ethos of the whole as a more valued means to a particular
end – democratic capitalism.

Consistent with the entire Rockefeller Center environment, the basis
of the production was the work ethic and capitalist values. It was
expressed in a display of the products of man's labors. It was evident in
the display of the advanced-stage technology that had formed a central
part of Music Hall shows from its opening night in 1932, so powerful
and sophisticated that the War Department labeled it top secret during
World War II. It was evident further in the precision teamwork of the

Rockettes, the only surviving act from opening night. They supposedly taught Rockefeller the value of working together as a group instead of striving for self-aggrandizement. And the work ethic continued to be featured in one of the last versions of the Easter show through the display of Liberace's personal material wealth – all tax deductible, as he pointed out, since he used it in his work. He even enshrined the evidences of his success in his museum so that visitors may examine their workmanship up close. As he advised the boy in the front row, "See what you can have someday if you practice" – this just before he blessed all with his aspergillum. If the Rockettes embodied, as Rockefeller himself suggested, the value of working together for the good of the group in their emphasis on uniformity and conformity, then Liberace embodied their dialectical American opposite – individualism.

The key value, however, among these seemingly contradictory ones was self-reliance (Hsu 384–386). Liberace was the self-made man from humble beginnings. And even though the Rockettes were seemingly dependent on each other, that is not how their originator Markert thought of them. He looked for self-reliant women (Roman 89). And, by the same token, a lack of self-reliance could get a Rockette fired, for it was a cardinal rule that a Rockette never "hung" or "leaned" on her neighbors in line (Love 40). As in other Rockefeller organizations, the smooth workings of the whole required efficient, self-sufficient units (Brown 51).

What the Easter Show at Radio City Music Hall promoted was a break from work in order for the tourist to rediscover the spirit of work. This spirit was not merely symbolic, but was *felt*. Through the agency of spectacle, the production engendered a spontaneous sense of community in the audience, an idea that was expressed metaphorically onstage by the Rockettes. Perhaps more important – in the process it bound the collective to the ideology of corporate capitalism. This ideology was expressed at all levels in the sacrilized environment in the display of the fruits of man's labors: in material wealth, in technology, in precision teamwork. The Easter Show at Radio City Music Hall celebrated corporate capitalism as America's spiritual center, and it was persuasive through spectacle's power to engender *communitas* or, as Rothafel would have had it, mass thought and appeal (1932b).

READING THE RESIDUE

As Harold Beaver has observed, the homosexual

is a prodigious consumer [and I might add producer] of signs – of hidden meanings, hidden systems, hidden potentiality. *Exclusion from the common code impels the frenzied quest*: in the momentary glimpse, the scrambled figure, the sporadic gesture, the chance encounter, the reverse image, the sudden slippage, the lowered guard.

(104–105, emphasis mine)

What happens to representation when the signified is reattached to the gay signifier, that is, when it becomes explicitly indexical of the "gay regard"? In brief, alternative readings of Liberace and the Rockettes become available, readings not necessarily accessible to a heterosexual, lower middle-/middle-class audience seduced by the desire for material wealth. What happens then when dominant discourse is flooded with Camp residues and traces? This is the question I will address for the remainder of this essay.

Not only did Liberace's private sexual practices run counter to the dominant code, but onstage his gay identity was hidden. Both Liberace and Markert were "bachelors"; they emphasized their relationship to their mothers. They were also presented as fathers and mentors. Markert constructed himself as a father figure for the Rockettes; one of his popular articles was entitled, "My 46 Dancing Daughters" (1955). And Liberace presented boy pianists onstage as his protégés at the same time that he celebrated Paderewski as his own mentor. In this way, genealogies were configured that could serve to displace a gay identity, that is, for those who participated in "a conspiracy of blindness."

As straightforward and vacuous as they appeared, Liberace and the Rockettes were complex stage spectacles. Liberace was Count Dracula aglitter, America's blue-collar royalty, a kitsch Rockefeller, and a high priest all rolled into one (Plate 16). The Rocket(te)s on the other hand were all-American girls who represented inversions of the normal gender categories with their theatrical presentations of military drills and regimentation, machine-gun taps, and high kicks that "go up like rockets"; all typify Rockettes choreography. The military theme was also evident in the title of Captain bestowed on one Rockette.

From a feminist perspective, female bodies cast as rockets would constitute fetishism, that is, the symbolic representation of a penis on women in order to counteract a man's fear of sexual difference. Most discussions of fetishism by feminists however seem to assume not only a heterosexual gaze, but a heterosexual constructor of the fetish image as well. As Marjorie Garber has asserted, "the ideology of the fetish is the ideology of phallocentrism, the ideology of heterosexuality" (119). Conversely, in the writings of most gay men theorists the fetishization of women is a nonissue, an aporia (but see King). Once again, this absence appears to reflect an underlying assumption that fetishizers of women are by definition heterosexual subjects. Indeed Freud viewed fetishism not only as a safeguard against castration, but as a safeguard against homosexuality! (Freud 216). But were the Rockettes the fetishized objects of male heterosexual desire?

First of all, men were not the primary spectating audience of the Rockettes. If Markert turned the Rockettes into an object of capitalist desire in the form of the well-oiled military machine, he at the same time downplayed their showgirl status. Recall, he did not like "the flashy, exotic type, such as the dyed blonde with ultra-high heels or swishing sexy walk." Indeed, during one part of the show, the Rockettes wore tuxedos to dance with Liberace; the climax as usual was the uniform, downstage high kick that always got applause (actually more medium in height to accommodate Liberace! He couldn't get it up).

Transvestism unmarked: homoeroticism and the disruption of social hierarchies

Garber has called Liberace's kind of outrageous display "unmarked transvestism" (356). Technically not cross-dressing in any literal sense, unmarked transvestism nevertheless has a feminizing effect insofar as it makes the male performer into a glitzy object of the gaze. Thus Liberace made his entrances in long, often pastel, capes with high standing collars. Add to this, as I pointed out earlier, Liberace's full, slicked-back head of dark hair; his seemingly eternal youthfulness; and the way he spun around and posed onstage and in publicity photographs with his cape spread out to the sides, all referenced Bella Lugosi as Count Dracula.

Recently, Christopher Craft (1989) and Ellis Hanson (1991) have addressed the relationship between vampirism and homoeroticism. In *Dracula*, the vampire's mouth confounds the easy distinction between the masculine and the feminine. Thus,

> luring at first with an inviting orifice, a promise of red softness, but delivering instead a piercing bone, the vampire mouth fuses and confuses what Dracula's civilized nemesis, Van Helsing and his Crew of Light, works so hard to separate – the gender-based

categories of the penetrating and the receptive. . . . Furthermore, this mouth, bespeaking the subversion of the stable and lucid distinctions of gender, is the mouth of all vampires, male and female.

(Craft 218)

And:

To comprehend the vampire is to recognize that abjected space that gay men are obliged to inhabit; that space unspeakable or unnameable, itself defined as orifice, as a "dark continent" men dare not penetrate; that gap bridged over or sutured together, where men cease to play dead and yet cease to accept the normative sexual role. I am seen as the caped one, who hovers over the dreaming body of Jonathan Harker and exclaims, "This man belongs to me!" and "Yes, I too can love." I dare to speak and sin and walk abroad; and so like Lucy Westenra in her bed, Renfield in his cell, Dracula in his castle, I inhabit the space of all vampires, caught between our two twin redemptions: conversion and death.

(Hanson 325–326)

As unmarked transvestism, Liberace's vampire image signaled that redemptive space of conversion and death where dominant culture locates the homosexual. At the same time, the vampire subverted gender distinctions.

Interestingly, it was Liberace's subversion of gender codes and the ambiguity of his sexuality that drew a flagrant review from the male British critic known by the female name Cassandra, i.e. Asserter-of-Unheeded-Prophecies. About Liberace, he/she wrote:

he is the summit of sex – Masculine, Feminine and Neuter. Everything that He, She and It can ever want. I have spoken to sad but kindly men on this newspaper who have met every celebrity arriving from the United States for the past thirty years. They all say that this deadly, winking, sniggering, snuggling, giggling, fruit-flavored, mincing, ice-covered heap of mother-love has had the biggest reception and impact on London since Charlie Chaplin arrived at the same station, Waterloo, on September 12, 1921. . . .

There must be something wrong with us that our teenagers longing for sex and our middle-aged matrons fed up with sex, alike fall for such a sugary mountain of jingling clap-trap wrapped up in such a preposterous clown.

(qtd in Liberace 204–205).

This review instigated a libel suit that Liberace won. In order for Liberace's ambiguous sexual subtext to remain closeted, he was forced to confront his critic publicly.

Liberace came closest to revealing his gay identity onstage when he announced that he would play "Mack the Knife" "straight" before turning it into a "classic." "Mack the Knife" is gendered male – definitely phallic. Liberace's "classic" renditions included "Mack the Knife Sonata in C Major" by Mozart, "Claire de Lune de Mack the Knife" by Debussy, and "Blue Mack the Knife Danube" by Strauss. The very status of the identities of the music is thrown out of kilter. A stylistic cross-dresser so to speak, "Mack the Knife" was a transvestite tune. The vestments Liberace put on him were by implication hierarchically superior, that is, classical. Never mind that the music was already from an opera before it was popularized. This kind of identity fiddling is the hallmark of drag. Playing "Mack the Knife" straight before cross-dressing him commented on the absurd way in which essential identities themselves are constructed rather than given. Liberace's musical antics can be read as a critique of the depth model of identity on which gender distinctions are based.

The Rockettes in their own way confounded gender distinctions too. They were never as glitzy as Liberace. Nor did they portray any distinctive personalities. In their focus on uniformity, they were not individuated, but rather turned into a massive military machine. Nor were they icons of femininity; rather, they represented the smooth workings of industrial capitalism, male bonding, automation, and the labor force. They could do so precisely because of their phallic attributes and the denial of individuality. They were fetishized, or were they? If fetishization is the symbolic attribution of a penis to a woman out of the heterosexual man's fear of sexual difference, then the status of the Rockettes as fetish is at best problematic.

Transvestism shares with the concept of fetishism an additive procedure. That is, in male transvestism, female clothes are added literally to veil that which is present, the penis (Garber 342–344). Garber has argued, "because human sexuality is constructed through repression, the signifier of desire cannot be represented directly, but only under a veil" (343). Fetishism is also additive, in this case to displace what in psychoanalytic terms has been construed as a "lack," or an absence.

But like transvestism, the addition is never a direct representation. It is encoded through metaphor, in the case of the Rockettes, by their downstage high kicks that were "straight" and went "up like rockets" to climax their dances. Male symbolism was also encoded in their machine-gun taps and their military drills. The Rockettes were phallic, impersonal women performing tasks normally associated with the masculine. What happens to our understanding of the fetishization of the female body when the signifier is a gay man? Fetishism or transvestism? Or both?

Once the signified is attached to a gay signifier, then the Rockettes can be understood as trans-transvestites. Gender codes were in this way disrupted as women became boys in what might be conceptualized as cross-cross-dressing, that is, women cast as men – complete with phalluses and military moves – yet devoid of any personality in their veiled womanhood. I suggest that, like Liberace, the Rockettes were unmarked transvestites. Until today, gay men often remain closeted in order to secure work, and thus they must mask their object of desire. Phallic women can then stand for men masquerading as women in perpetual displacements of sexual identity. The only way gay desire can be signified within a heterosexual frame is in the guise of heterosexuality itself. Few scholars writing on fetishism have interrogated the sexual identity of the so-called "fetishizer" and what effect that would have on signification. I cannot but read one of Liberace's reported encounters with Mae West as just this kind of displacement of identity and desire:

> Finally, the big question came. One of the reporters asked, "Miss West, where are you and Liberace going after this reception?"
>
> She smiled and said, as only she could, "I'm going over to Liberace's home to see his gold organ. I've seen every other kind, but I've never seen a gold one before."
>
> . . . When it was over she did come back to my home and she loved it. As she walked into one room after another, she kept repeating, "It's me. It's me."
>
> "No," I said, "It's me!"
>
> . . . And for the finish I showed her my gold organ. I not only showed it to her . . . I played it for her.
>
> (Liberace 150–151).

CONCLUSION

The disruption of social hierarchies was a common leitmotif running throughout the Easter Show. Both Liberace and the Rockettes in their own ways served to disrupt gender codes. And Liberace consistently undermined the construction of value and taste, particularly in his blending of popular and classical music, but also in other ways as well. As America's blue-collar royalty Liberace worked hard for what he got and, with what he got, he was privileged to hobnob with the likes of Queen Elizabeth and Baron Hilton, confounding class structures. As a kitsch Rockefeller, he was a capitalist of exaggerated style and little substance. His style was his substance, but as Dick Hebdige has shown us style is a form of refusal (3, passim). With his own philanthropies, foundation, museum, and material wealth, he deconstructed "high" culture and "popular" culture categories with the same kind of vigor that the Rockefellers invested in upholding them. The place where violinist Paderewski played classical music is where Liberace was timekeeper for professional wrestling. The Liberace Museum where he had his possessions enshrined, catalogued, and displayed was surely parodic of art exhibitions that, in the words of Timothy W. Luke, "can be seen as intense semiurgic courses of aesthetic legitimation, disciplined disinformation, ideological containment, or mythological manipulation" (231). In its attack on the status of taste, the Liberace Museum serves as a glaring exposé of the ideological functioning of art exhibitions in general.

The disruption of the hierarchies of "high" and "popular" culture, art and corn, exposes taste and value as a social construction. Interrogating hierarchical arrangements more broadly, this rupture stands metonymically in subterranean conjunction with hierarchies of gender and sexual preference. Unmarked as transvestites, Liberace and the Rockettes evade disclosure and maintain a kind of overt sexual anonymity that is unthreatening to a heterosexual audience. The subterranean constructions of sexuality through unmarked transvestism, however, constitute a mode of resistance by which marginalized groups insinuate their own voices, albeit in masked form, into official public discourse (Scott 136).

The hidden transcript contaminates and pollutes dominant discourse through the contagious power of metonymic conjunction. As a gay signifying practice Camp is by its very nature counterhegemonic; it confounds gender codes, overrules compulsory heterosexuality, and undermines the very foundations on which democratic capitalism was built. The signifying subject of Camp, then, must be concealed when in the service of the corporate world lest capitalism itself be called into question. Strangely ironic that dominant discourse should appropriate Camp and turn it into a tamed expression of the American spirit. Even so, the residue attached and stuck; the camp trace lingered on.

NOTES

I am indebted to Thomas Alan King, Moe Meyer, Terri Kapsalis, Avanthi Meduri, Shannon Jackson, Gary Scott Thompson, and Henry John Drewal for many enriching discussions on various aspects of this essay and the issues they raise. Portions of this essay were published as "From Rocky's Rockettes to Liberace: The Politics of Representation in the Heart of Corporate Capitalism" (1987).

1 Following Eve Kosofky Sedgwick, I use the term "homosexual" and "gay" interchangeably.
2 As Thomas A. King pointed out to me, this identity is double-edged insofar as gay men are often socialized as caregivers for their ageing mothers and, at the same time, are viewed by society as "useless," that is, non(re)productive, as "Mama's boys." In Liberace's case, it was as if being an "artist," and thus "productive," overrode the non(re)productivity side of the "Mama's boy" identity.
3 This study is based on observation of the Spring 1985 stage show (19 April), featuring Liberace and the Rockettes; the guided tour of Rockefeller Center that included Radio City Music Hall; taped interviews and press clippings in the Dance Collection of the New York City Public Library; material from the Archives at Radio City Music Hall; secondary sources on Rockefeller Center, and Radio City Music Hall specifically; and a relatively large body of popular articles dating from the 1930s – only a few of which are quoted in the text. The latter provided insight into the consistent ideology of Radio City Music Hall productions from their inception in 1932.
4 For another study of the sacralization of a tourist environment, see Moore.
5 For example, "if the shafts of the 200 elevators of Rockefeller Center were stacked one on the other, they would reach ten miles into the sky" (qtd in *The Last Rivet* 28), a sure way to heaven? This style continues in the present. On 17 March 1985, the ad for the Liberace show announced in bold type at the head, "86,784 PEOPLE HAVE PURCHASED TICKETS TO SEE THE WORLD'S GREATEST SHOWMAN IN HIS ALL NEW EASTER SPECTACULAR!"
6 These acts parallel what Dean MacCannell identifies as the first three stages in the process of site sacralizing: naming; framing and elevating – setting off as worthy; and enshrinement. As the title of Liberace's latest record albums informs us, *The Legend Lives On*.
7 These things are all reiterated in a former Rockette's autobiography in which she describes in great detail the "gut-wretching agony" of rehearsals and long working hours (Love 7, 19–20; 27–29; 35–39).

178

8 There is a popular myth on the streets of New York that missiles are stored underground at Rockefeller Center.

9 An agency "connects a model and its influence" (MacCannell 24).

10 See also Rothafel 1932a.

11 The military use of the design for the lifts is information also presented on the guided tour of Rockefeller Center and the Music Hall. Reportedly, the War Department stationed G-men on the premises to guard the top secret.

BIBLIOGRAPHY

Balfour, Alan. 1978. *Rockefeller Center: Architecture as Theater*. New York: McGraw-Hill.

Barber, Paul. 1988. *Vampires, Burial, and Death: Folklore and Reality*. New Haven: Yale University Press.

Baudrillard, Jean. 1981. *For a Critique of the Political Economy of the Sign*. New York: Telos Press.

Beaver, Harold. 1981. "Homosexual Signs (*In Memory of Roland Barthes*)." *Critical Inquiry* 8: 99–119.

Brown, E. Richard. 1979. *Rockefeller Medicine Men: Medicine and Capitalism in America*. Berkeley: University of California Press.

Craft, Christopher. 1989. " 'Kiss Me with Those Red Lips': Gender and Inversion in Bram Stoker's *Dracula*." In Elaine Showalter (ed.). *Speaking of Gender*. New York: Routledge, 216–242.

Crocker, J. Christopher. 1977. "The Social Function of Rhetorical Forms." In J. David Sapir and J. Christopher Crocker (eds). *The Social Use of Metaphor: Essays on the Anthropology of Rhetoric*. Philadelphia: University of Pennsylvania Press, 33–66.

Dollimore, Jonathan. 1991. *Sexual Dissidence: Augustine to Wilde, Freud to Foucault*. Oxford: Clarendon Press.

Douglas, Mary. 1966. *Purity and Danger: An Analysis of the Concepts of Pollution and Taboo*. London: Routledge.

Drewal, Margaret Thompson. 1987. "From Rocky's Rockettes to Liberace: The Politics of Representation in the Heart of Corporate Capitalism." *Journal of American Culture* 10/2: 69–82.

"Ette." 1969. *Webster's Dictionary of the English Language*.

Fekete, John. 1987. "Vampire Value, Infinitive Art, and Literary Theory: A Topographic Mediation." In John Fekete (ed.). *Life after Postmodernism: Essays on Value and Culture*. New York: St. Martin's Press, 64–85.

Francisco, Charles. 1979. *The Radio City Music Hall: An Affectionate History of the World's Greatest Theater*. New York: E. P. Dutton.

Freud, Sigmund. 1963. "Fetishism." *Sexuality and the Psychology of Love*. New York: Collier Books, 214–219.

Gaines, Jane M. 1991. *Contested Culture: The Image, the Voice, and the Law*. Chapel Hill: University of North Carolina Press.

Garber, Marjorie. 1992. *Vested Interests: Cross-Dressing and Cultural Anxiety*. New York: Routledge.

Hanson, Ellis. 1991. "Undead." In Diana Fuss (ed.). *Inside/Out: Lesbian Theories, Gay Theories*. New York: Routledge, 324–340.

Hebdige, Dick. 1979. *Subculture: The Meaning of Style.* London: Methuen.

Heimer, Mel. 1948. "My New York." *The Times* (Beverly, Massachusetts) 14 December.

Hering, Doris. 1952. "The Rockettes: Pin Point Perfectionists." *Theatre Arts* May: 47.

Hsu, Francis L. K. 1975. "American Core Value and National Character." In James P. Spradley and Michael A. Rynkiewich (eds). *Readings on American Culture.* Boston: Little, Brown and Company, 378–394.

Karp, Walter. 1982. *The Center: A History and Guide to Rockefeller Center.* New York: American Heritage Publishing Company.

King, Thomas. A. 1992. " 'As if (she) were made on purpose to put the whole world into good Humour': Reconstructing the First English Actresses," *TDR: The Drama Review* 36/3: 78–102.

Kisselgoff, Anna. 1978. "Precision Dancing as Art." *The New York Times* 2 April: 2:1, 15.

Kracauer, Siegfried. 1975. "The Mass Ornament." *New German Critique* 5: 67–76.

Krinsky, Carol Hershelle. 1978. *Rockefeller Center.* New York: Oxford University Press.

The Last Rivet: The story of Rockefeller Center, a city within a city, as told at the ceremony in which John D. Rockefeller, Jr., drove the last rivet of the last building, November 1, 1939. 1940. New York: Columbia University Press.

Leavin, Paul. 1976. "Twenty-One Ways of Looking at the Rockettes." *Eddy* Spring/Summer: 66–79.

Liberace. 1973. *Liberace: An Autobiography.* New York: G. P. Putnam's Sons.

Liberace. 1985. Program booklet. Los Angeles: The James Agency.

Love, Judith Anne. 1980. *Thirty Thousand Kicks: What's It Like to Be a Rockette?* Hicksville, New York: Exposition Press.

Luke, Timothy W. 1992. *Shows of Force: Power, Politics, and Ideology in Art Exhibitions.* Durham: Duke University Press.

MacAloon, John J. 1984. "Olympic Games and the Theory of Spectacle in Modern Societies." In John J. MacAloon (ed.). *Rite, Drama, Festival, Spectacle: Rehearsals toward a Theory of Cultural Performance.* Philadelphia: Institute for the Study of Human Issues, 241–280.

MacCannell, Dean. 1976. *The Tourist: A New Theory of the Leisure Class.* New York: Schocken.

Markert, Russell. 1955. "My 46 Dancing Daughters." *The American Magazine* May: 38–41, 112, 115–117.

—— n.d. "No Stage Too Large." *Radio City Music Hall Program Magazine* 6 June: 11–12.

Martin, Randy. 1990. *Performance as Political Act: The Embodied Self.* New York: Bergin and Garvey Publishers.

Marx, Karl. 1977. *Capital, Volume One.* Trans. B. Fowkes. New York: Vintage Books.

Moore, Alexander. 1980. "Walt Disney World: Bounded Ritual Space and the Playful Pilgrimage Center." *Anthropological Quarterly* 53/4: 207–218.

Nixon, Richard. 1971. Letter to Russell Markert on the occasion of his retirement. 19 October. Archives, Radio City Music Hall.

Petrie, Ursula. 1947. "Revolt among the Rockettes." *Herald-American, Saturday Home Magazine* (Chicago) 12 July.

Rabinbach, Anson. 1992. *The Human Motor: Energy, Fatigue, and the Origins of Modernity.* Berkeley: University of California Press.

"Radio City Music Hall: Mecca and Magnet." 1956. *Dance Magazine* August: 14–23.

Roman, Robert. 1969. "Hide Your Daughters, Here Comes Russ Markert." *Dance Magazine* September: 46–49, 84, 86–87, 89–90.

Rothafel, R. L. 1932a. "The Heart Is the Target." *Woman's Home Companion* July: 13–14.

—— 1932b. *Variety* 20 December: 57–58.

Russo, Vito. 1987. *The Celluloid Closet: Homosexuality in the Movies.* New York: Harper and Row.

Scott, James C. 1990. *Domination and the Arts of Resistance: Hidden Transcripts.* New Haven: Yale University Press.

Sedgwick, Eve Kosofsky. 1990. *Epistemology of the Closet.* Berkeley: University of California Press.

Stewart, Susan. 1984. *On Longing: Narratives of the Miniature, the Gigantic, the Souvenir, the Collection.* Baltimore: Johns Hopkins University Press.

Terry, Walter. 1982. "One, Two, Three, Kick." *Ballet News* 4/2: 17.

Thomas, Bob. 1987. *Liberace: The True Story.* New York: St. Martin's Press.

Thompson, Michael. 1979. *Rubbish Theory: The Creation and Destruction of Value.* Oxford: Oxford University Press.

Turner, Victor. 1977. *The Ritual Process: Structure and Anti-Structure.* Ithaca: Cornell University Press.

Wagner, Roy. 1981. *The Invention of Culture.* Chicago: University of Chicago Press.

Waring, James. 1967. "Five Essays on Dancing." *Ballet Review* 2/1: 65–77.

Wentinck, Andrew Mark. 1981. "The Rockettes at Radio City: Gettin' Their Kicks In." *Dance Magazine* (May): 57.

Wershing, Susan. 1982. "Russell Markert: Father of Precision Dance." *Dance Teachers Now* November/December: 28–29.

Worman, Martin. 1991. "The Gay Regard." ATHE National Conference, Seattle, 8 August.

7

TAKING OUT THE TRASH
Camp and the politics of parody
Chuck Kleinhans

Our understanding of Camp changes with the evolving history of gay subculture. The conditions and contexts for Camp differ in pre-Stonewall, post-Stonewall, post-AIDS, and contemporary Queer moments. To contribute to the current discussion, I want to explore three concepts – mass culture, subculture, and parody – through several perspectives. First, using a commercial boardroom and bedroom film, *The Betsy*, for elaboration, I discuss how a parodic stand to mass culture is present in a trend I call self-aware kitsch, and how it both draws on and potentiates Camp readings. Next, I consider Camp as a parodic strategy originating from gay subculture which provides an impetus for subtextual reading. Then, a further specification emerges from examining a variety of intentional Camp which celebrates casual excess through a deliberately crude and offensive content. Films such as *Trash*, *Multiple Maniacs*, and *Thundercrack* highlight the need for a political critique of Camp and a further analysis of parody as a strategy of subcultural resistance in contemporary media.

SELF-AWARE KITSCH

At its broadest, kitsch can be taken as the popular commercial art of the modern era. Certainly this is how Clement Greenberg presented it in his well-known essay, "Avant Garde and Kitsch" (10). For Greenberg, twentieth-century art is divided into two parts: the artistic avant-garde (which he favors) and kitsch, the mechanically reproduced "ersatz culture" which depends on formulaic patterns. In his words, it is the art of "vicarious experiences and fake sensations" (10). Other commentators have also used the term kitsch in an extremely judgmental way. Gillo Dorfles calls it "the world of bad taste" (9–12), and Abraham Moles defines it as "the art of happiness." Of course a term so obviously subjective and class-biased (*whose* bad taste?) is virtually useless as a critical and analytical tool. But there is a sense in which kitsch can be used in a descriptive way, that is, when the text gives evidence that the makers themselves were aware of their "bad taste." Contemporary culture objects are often highly self-conscious of their own de-based status. I will call this self-aware kitsch.

Daniel Petrie's film *The Betsy* (1977), based on Harold Robbins's novel, is a fine example of kitsch that is totally aware of itself as kitsch. As a film version of what John Cawelti has labeled the "best-selling social melodrama" (260), the plot is familiar Robbins material – the scramble for power in the bedrooms and boardrooms of corporate America. This time we have an old patriarch of a Detroit auto dynasty who schemes to produce and dreams of a car as successful and practical as the Model T was for an earlier generation. It focuses on the success myth characteristic of work appealing to the broad mass audience, rather than the failure myth seen in work that is more appealing to the alienated petty bourgeoisie. That the film is totally self-aware can be demonstrated by mentioning that the auto tycoon is played with great gusto by Sir Laurence Olivier using a broad midwestern accent, and that we get to his ass, in long shot, as he vigorously makes love to a maid upstairs during his son's wedding celebration. This is casting against type of a rare order indeed. The lusty scene, in true melodramatic style, is secretly observed by the new daughter-in-law, underlining the film's particular method for constructing character. The characters do not *have* any psychological problems or interior life, the Oedipal situation is totally externalized; they do not *have* any fantasies, they live them. The result is a kind of behavioralist reading of the Tristan and Isolde myth – anticipation and reverie are truncated from passion, and guilt is subtracted from the love story.

A remarkable literalness infuses the entire film. At its best the directness has a comic-book simplicity as when Betsy, the granddaughter for whom the new car is to be named, goes for a naked swim. She is observed by the young hero, sees him watching, and acknowledges his glance with a smile. The neurotic voyeurism and cloying sentimentalism typical of such a shot sequence is avoided by her frankness. More typically, the film's visual style simply trades in well-worn clichés – such as lovemaking sequences that reproduce the lush cloying quality of *Penthouse* photography. Hollywood's old standby transition device, the rapid montage compressing events through time, is updated with split screen and multiple matted windows, well known to anyone who watches television commercials. This very familiarity is reassuring. Petrie's use of the virtuoso long take with a moving camera is a far cry from its use by Renoir, Welles, Sirk, Jerry Lewis, Antonioni, or Godard. In Petrie's version, a seventy-second shot that takes the daughter-in-law from bedroom door to the patriarch's bed, the camera pans and dollies to create different compositions as the woman approaches the bed. This is a bland functionalism that ends in framing the pair in long shot from the foot of the bed. Then slowly dollying and zooming in to frame the faces in a simple signification of the sexual act, it is followed by a straight cut to a long shot of the tycoon in a sunny dining room the next morning.

In a similar vein, literalness and functionalism combine in a recycled cliché when the patriarch's son, realizing that his wife is in bed with his father, commits suicide with a revolver while being watched by his own young son. We see the gun pointed at his head from the child's point of view, then a reverse shot close-up of the child's face and, as the gun goes off, a freeze frame of the child staring directly at the camera – recycling once again Truffaut's conclusion to *The 400 Blows* (1959). Of course the boy runs to find his mother and, of course, opens the door on his mother in his grandfather's arms. Could we ask for a more primal scene? Could we imagine that the film would be that obvious? But it is. Besides, the whole sequence takes place during a rainstorm – the pathetic fallacy in action. Clichés are not merely recycled in this genre, they are made more literal. For example, in *The Other Side of Midnight* (1977), faced with an unwanted pregnancy, the heroine performs a self-abortion using a wire coat hanger. Watching the film we are forced to ask ourselves, will they dare be that obvious? And of course they are, for the exaggeration, the heightening, the acceleration of clichés, underlines the situation, and the situation – the dramatic arrangement of characters and conflicts – forms the central fantasy attraction of melodrama.

For people with high-culture tastes or backgrounds, films such as *The Betsy* and *The Other Side of Midnight* can be received as total parodies. It is especially easy for media people (who can spot the formal clichés that underline the content conventions) to do so. But these films function in a different way with the general mass audience: spectators are engrossed by the situation and the exaggeration simultaneously. Fans have usually read the book and, if not, have heard the plot in advance from everyday conversations or the print and television journalism that surrounds contemporary film production, such as the *Entertainment Tonight* type of show. The experience of such self-aware kitsch demands a certain kind of willing suspension of disbelief. Identification and enjoyment of the film's visual and narrative pleasures are present, to be sure, but taken in a somewhat distanced direction. Rather than "talking down" to the audience, the makers of self-aware kitsch are "talking across" to that audience. The implicit assumption is: We all know this is fun, just a good piece of entertainment.

In a study of *Dynasty* with attention to audience responses, particularly group spectatorship in bars and clubs that made viewing a distinct event highlighted by active parodic reading, Jane Feuer linked this dual sensibility to gay consciousness:

> the camp decoding is also a preferred reading of the text. According to one critic, "*Dynasty* represents something extraordinary: the incursion of so-called gay taste into the mainstream of American culture." Camp is not a property of a text, but exists in the nature of the activations; however, not just any text can be camped, and *Dynasty* certainly facilitates the process. . . . Very early on its producers were aware of camp decodings and intended to encode them in the text by devising "outrageous plots" and "walk(ing) a fine line, just this side of camp. . . . It is important to stress that the camp attitude toward *Dynasty* in both gay and mainstream culture does not preclude emotional identification; rather, it embraces both identification and parody – attitudes normally viewed as mutually exclusive – at the same time and as part of the same sensibility. As Richard Dyer has written, the gay sensibility "holds together qualities that are elsewhere felt as antithetical: theatricality and authenticity . . . intensity and irony, a fierce assertion of extreme feeling with a deprecating sense of its absurdity."
>
> (447–448)

The characteristic parody of self-aware kitsch promotes what John Fiske has called "skeptical hedonism" in audience response to much mass-culture documentary, that is, we all know this is a fantasy, but we want in on the fun of such phenomena, for example, as television wrestling or supermarket tabloid headlines. In this duality of response, self-aware kitsch is related to, or overlaps with, Camp.

CAMP READINGS

Following Susan Sontag's provocative and original essay, "Notes on Camp," we can recognize Camp as a strategy of reading that sees the world in terms of aestheticization and style: "the essence of Camp is its love of the unnatural: of artifice and exaggeration" (105). Camp is an ironic and parodic appreciation of an extravagant form that is out of proportion to its content, especially when that content is banal or trivial. Sontag identifies pure camp as naive and unintentional, exhibiting a failed seriousness and/or passionate ambition.

A good example of failed seriousness would be the mid-1950s independently produced film about transvestism, *Glen or Glenda*, which found some success when rereleased on the midnight show and college film circuit where it is appreciated for its amazingly defensive fetishism. The defense of fantasy is so strong (a voice-over narration interprets everything we are seeing), and so mundane (the rhetoric of democratic choice and privacy of the home is constantly invoked in the style of instructional films), and so particular (we are continually reminded that male cross-dressing has absolutely nothing to do with homosexuality), that it invites the same kind of hilarity as *Reefer Madness*, the earnest anti-marijuana film of the 1930s that was recirculated to stoned audiences in the 1960s. Such work, if not actually Camp, certainly facilitates a Camp reading because it invites scornful laughter due to its ineptness.

Hollywood film often exhibits a psycho-aesthetic pluralism. Films are deliberately constructed to be open to a great deal of very different fantasizing. That is one secret of their mass appeal. What facilitates a Camp reading in this context is that possibilities for fantasizing have been so simplified that they seem isolated and ridiculous. We need our defenses. Sontag underlined the problem with this as a deliberate strategy in discussing

> the delicate relation between parody and self-parody in Camp. The films of Hitchcock are a showcase for this problem. When self-parody lacks ebullience but instead reveals (even sporadically) a contempt for one's themes and one's materials – as in *To Catch a Thief, Rear Window, North By Northwest* – the results are forced and heavy-handed, rarely Camp. Successful Camp . . . even when it reveals self-parody, reeks of self-love.
>
> (111)

Sontag, writing in 1964, minimized the links between Camp and male homosexual culture. Writing to correct Sontag, Richard Dyer and Jack Babuscio have claimed Camp as a core element of gay male subculture. As Dyer argues:

> It is just about the only style, language and culture that is

distinctively and unambiguously gay male. In a world drenched
in straightness all the images and the words of society express and
confirm the rightness of heterosexuality. Camp is the one thing
that expresses and confirms being a gay man.

(11)

Babuscio elaborates the relationship in his key essay in the developing
field of gay film criticism, "Camp and the Gay Sensibility." Arguing in
more narrow terms than Sontag, he discusses Camp as expressing a
relationship between something and the observer's gayness. Camp
constitutes a different consciousness, "a heightened awareness of
certain human complications of feeling that spring from the fact of
social oppression" (40). Babuscio elaborates in terms of four basic
features of Camp: irony, aestheticism, theatricality, and humor. Camp
irony is "any highly incongruous contrast between an individual or
thing and its context or association. The most common of incongruous
elements is that of masculine/feminine" (41). Aestheticism as part of
Camp emerges in a practical appreciation of "style as a means of self-
projection, a conveyor of meaning and an expression of emotional
tone" (43). Similarly, to take life as theatre, particularly in terms of sex
role playing, is fundamental to both Camp and gay consciousness.
Camp humor is a strategy for reconciling conflicting emotions: it is "a
means of dealing with a hostile environment and, in the process, of
defining a positive identity" (47). Significantly, Babuscio argues that
Camp humor relies on an involvement, strongly identifying with a
situation or object while comically appreciating its contradictions. In
this it is different from the detachment that facilitates mockery.

Dyer and Babuscio are right in specifying Camp as a distinct part of
gay male culture but, in making that case, they do not sufficiently grant
the broadening of concepts of Camp based on the appropriations that
took place due to the publication of Sontag's 1964 essay. "Notes on
Camp" draws many connections between Camp and the art world.
Since that time, the media world (television, radio, music, advertising,
journalism, etc.) has tended to use and even co-opt Camp, perhaps
neutralizing (by naturalizing) its subversive potential.

There is a tendency for mass-culture media to take up almost
anything that is different and turn it into an aspect of fashionable
change: something different to spice up jaded tastes. The media world's
cannibalization of subcultures is a structural feature of the culture
industry. It is staffed by people who are predominantly petty bourgeois
professionals whose very occupation implies a distance from and an

187

irony toward the personalities, programs, and products they produce – a true dissociation of sensibility. Unable to believe in what they make, to have a naive acceptance of it, mass-culture makers are often drawn to subcultures precisely for their difference, their newness, their not-as-yet-commercialized qualities. All of which, not so incidentally, can be turned back into one's work; a weekend in the subculture inspires Monday morning's new ad campaign.

If Camp is part of gay male subculture, it is certainly appropriated for nongay usage as evidenced by many of Ken Russell's films. In their extravagant theatricality, love of artifice, and extreme emotional range, they can be considered examples of what I call "Het Camp," or what Moe Meyer calls the "camp trace." Broadening a concept of Camp to encompass both kinds of phenomena – Camp originating in the gay subculture as well as its nongay appropriation – brings me back to kitsch.

CAMP WRITINGS

Camp films and videos depend on the kitsch aspect of mass culture. Originally, mass culture based itself on existing traditional culture, turning it into a system, that is, into a form able to be reproduced industrially. Today U.S. commercial culture recirculates itself. The existing culture it parodies and systematizes not only includes, but is often dominated by, previous mass culture. Current popular culture is, at its core, obsessively self-reflexive – take, for example, IBM ads that recirculate Charlie Chaplin's image or MTV's relentless recirculation of images and style figures from earlier eras.

Camp is a strategy for makers as well as for reception. It draws on and transforms mass culture. In this it critiques the dominant culture, but in the dominant culture's own terms; it seldom rests on any coherent or sustained analysis of society or history. Camp always uses parody but, more importantly, it embodies parody as a general mode of discourse. As a mode of discourse, parody typically operates within the dominant ideology, but with an internal tension. Since Camp is an especially acute ideological form containing active contradictions it can, in certain social and historical contexts, challenge dominant culture.

To some extent, Camp originates in a gay male perception that gender is, if not quite arbitrary, certainly not biologically determined or natural, but rather that gender is socially constructed, artificial, and performed (and thus open to being consciously deformed). In terms of drag, a form of gender parody, high Camp aims for the seamless illusion of female impersonation, while low Camp accepts the deconstructed gender presence of drag queens. In a closely related way, what I call trash – or deliberate low Camp – originates in the perception by some gay men and others that taste, or aesthetic sensibility, is also socially constructed. In defiance of Kantian aesthetics and high-culture prejudices, a trash imagination understands that aesthetic pleasure can be found in diverse ways, including the marginalized and excluded. When employed intentionally as a strategy for production, Camp – whether its source is gay subculture or nongay appropriation – relies for its effect on casual excess, deviant decorum, and libidinal obviousness. Camp pushes a poorly done form (poorly done by conventional standards of technique and social manners) to the limits so that its very badness is what the work is about. A classic trash moment in film appears in John Waters's *Pink Flamingoes* (1970) when the drag-queen heroine, Divine, eats dog excrement. In other words, low Camp deliberately celebrates bad taste and often intentionally offends aesthetic and social sensibilities in order to make a statement.

Minimally, Camp films embody the ethos of shocking mainstream middle-class values. Flagrant transvestites will never fit middle America's self-image. Thus by their very presence Holly Woodlawn in *Trash* (dir. Paul Morissey 1970) and Divine in *Multiple Maniacs* (dir. John Waters 1970) offend by being consistently Camp. They have the affrontery to define their own presentations: the actor as actress, not as woman. Inevitably, the audience is drawn to accept Holly Woodlawn as something more than an extended joke on gender possibilities, and to think of her seriously – not as woman, but as queen.[1] The film is subversive, not because of the initial gender confusion but because the audience is eventually lured into liking Woodlawn. She is herself always, and without excuse, a twenty-four-hour-a-day actress. The style becomes the content.

Push the point further and you have the early Divine: gross in body, gross in deed. Divine's style enters the realm where quantitative change becomes qualitative change and suddenly bad taste is celebrated as good taste. Holly and Divine interrupt and displace the usual position of the actress. Consider Rouben Mamoulian's remarks on the conclusion of *Queen Christina*:

> Garbo asked me: "What do I play in this scene?" Remember she is standing there for 150 feet of the film – 90 feet of them in close-up. I said: "Have you heard of *tabula rasa*? I want your face to be a

189

blank sheet of paper. I want the writing to be done by every member of the audience. I'd like it if you could avoid even blinking your eyes, so that you're nothing but a beautiful mask." So in fact there is *nothing* on her face: but everyone who has seen the film will tell you what she is thinking and feeling. And always it is something different.

(qtd in Milne 74–75)

Classic and contemporary Hollywood cinema uses a broad style of manipulated realism to position the actress in the narrative and in the frame as a partial metaphor, as a figure to be completed, as a Rorschach card, as an object of sexual gaze. Using a different style, one we might call sordid naturalism pushed to wittiness, *Trash* uses Joe Dallesandro in that position. Passive in the face of everything and everyone, junkie Joe offers his hustler's body to anyone and any use as long as he can shoot up. He has a blank face set against the human Muzak of such events as getting a blow job, listening to an endless monologue, or being stuck with a quarreling couple. Whatever others want him to be, he becomes. Joe is the ultimate human mask.

Although positioned in the narrative and frame as woman, he does not satisfy because he is also positioned as junkie. Just as the story line promises fulfillment, the film reverses the interplay of visual and verbal constructions. We wait out the real time of Joe's shooting up only to have the camera drift away, denying us Joe's communion with heroin by substituting the everyday and trivial. While Joe takes a dissociation of sensibility in his arm, we take it in our eyes and ears.

Arguing that the hustler and the transvestite are "linked for all their apparent difference by a common obsession with the mystery of how a man inhabits his flesh," Stephen Koch, in his book on Andy Warhol's films, finds "They are at opposite poles of a common dilemma. The transvestite, on the one hand, builds upon the denial of his anatomical reality; the hustler, on the other, proclaims himself to be 'just a body' " (122). But this observation seems to say the least important thing about Holly Woodlawn in *Trash*. Gender identity and sexuality are the least of her problems as she tries to establish a household. Much more to the point is that Holly, as a lower East Side street person, is a survivor. This garbage picker has simple and just aspirations. She only wants to make a nice home, raise a child, and attain the security of being on welfare. In the second half, as her sleazy subculture soap opera unfolds, the film invites us to approve of her self-conscious struggle for a better life. And because her cause is just, our own emotions (well-trained by old melodramas) override the simple desire for the comic when Holly faces a welfare office toad. It is funny and clever to see Holly putting on a bureaucrat, but we become annoyed when he tries to blackmail her, and we cheer when she insists on her rights and self-respect. In *Trash*, Joe is initially situated as woman and then repositioned as junkie – we can have his body, but not his mind. At first Holly is situated in the film as sacrificing woman, but then repositioned as a politically exemplary welfare mother fighting back as best she can.

In *Multiple Maniacs*, Divine fights back also, but that campaign, initiated by her assault on middle America, accumulates its momentum in a different direction – toward excess for its own sake, toward Grand Guignol, toward the grotesque. But Divine never really arrives anywhere and ends up subverting her own Camp critique. Rather than encountering the ironic interplay of style against substance that is characteristic of Camp, Divine simply assaults all audience sensibilities from a unique and inexplicable position. Shock substitutes for clever form; excess becomes its own excuse; and Divine's four-hundred-pound excess is simply bizarre, representing nothing but itself, a non sequitur raised to an initial proposition. As a result, the deliberate crudeness of Divine's behavior inhibits appreciation in the audience's response. Divine is at her best when she goes berserk after a mass murder, cannibalistic orgy, and rape by a giant lobster. But actually this story line has little to do with Divine's persona or her acting. The film never achieves the potential of Camp to transcend its own offensiveness because *Multiple Maniacs* stalls out again and again. At times Divine is disgusting only because she is dull and repetitive, not because she has genuinely assaulted anyone's sensibilities.

Multiple Maniacs underlines a problem for low Camp as an aesthetic strategy. Without narrative development, rhythmic pacing, character interest, variation, or surprise, it is difficult to sustain audience attention for the length of the film. This remains a problem in all John Waters's early work. However, by the time he gets to work with a sufficient budget for high production values – with *Polyester* and *Hairspray* in the 1980s – he decisively overcomes those problems. And not so ironically, his ongoing national reputation in film circles, coupled with a successful public persona, allowed him to become an artistic favorite son in his hometown of Baltimore. As a performer, Divine also grew artistically, and became a much stronger comic actress as well as club performer. So celebrity overcame notoriety, and financial success finally validated the early work that was explicitly intended to shock and outrage.

While Waters's earlier films are *sui generis*, some of his contemporaries such as George Kuchar and Curt McDowell have produced significant genre parodies using Camp as a strategy. Kuchar's *The Devil's Cleavage* (1975) imitates the ripest form of Hollywood domestic melodrama of the 1940s and 1950s: films that somehow made you terribly conscious of the shape of Robert Stack's mouth or Rock Hudson's jaw; films that featured actresses cast to type – Ava Gardner, Dorothy Malone, Susan Hayward, Joan Crawford, Barbara Stanwyck, Lana Turner, and Lauren Bacall.

Kuchar's lovingly farcical re-creation of those melodramas is camp parody that sometimes steals directly from the genre, sometimes burlesques it, and often travesties it. As you might expect, it soon begins to mock all kinds of cinematic references from Hitchcock to Preminger. From the opening titles with their swiggling stars and booming Hollywood orchestra, to a wonderfully inconclusive and arbitrary ending, Kuchar manages terribly well in terms of imagination and inventiveness, and just plain terribly in terms of such humdrum details of filming as using a light meter and tape recorder. Technical ineptness aside, we end up with a marvelous hybrid, as if Fuller and von Sternberg had collaborated in shooting a script by Tennessee Williams and Russ Meyer. Perhaps excess is the most basic element of Kuchar's method, even when it is an excess of cliché. Kuchar piles it on: tacky apartments are filled with sleazy characters whose conversations become confessions that, once begun, continue and continue and continue.

The result is a kind of humor often dismissed as adolescent. And it is. But it is also a joke that calls scatology what it is – shit. That is the problem. To get at the truth you have to put up with the idiosyncrasies. It is excessive. It does not always work. But when it does, it says what no one else is saying. This may help explain why George Kuchar and his twin brother Mike, who have been making films since adolescence thirty-five years ago, remain left out of most discussions of the film avant-garde. They can hardly be squeezed into formalist critiques, not with lines like, "I've read too many Arlene Dahl beauty books and Polly Bergen Oil of Turtle ads to back out now."[2]

Actually, if we want a good starting analysis of *The Devil's Cleavage*, we can look at those critics who held up for acclaim that string of 1950s weepy films by Douglas Sirk that Kuchar is parodying: *Magnificent Obsession*, *All That Heaven Allows*, *Written on the Wind*, *Tarnished Angels*, and *Imitation of Life*. Andrew Sarris says of his work that

The essence of Sirkian cinema is the direct confrontation of all material, however fanciful and improbable. Even in his most dubious projects, Sirk never shrinks away from the ridiculous, but by a full-bodied formal development, his art transcends the ridiculous, as form comments on content.

(109–110)

While Paul Willemen explains that "by altering the rhetoric of bourgeois melodrama, through stylization and parody, Sirk's films distance themselves from the bourgeois ideology" (67).

Substitute "Kuchar" for "Sirk" in the above quotes and you have a more than plausible analysis. The scene of a woman raping a man: isn't it ("however fanciful or improbable") an example of art transcending the merely "ridiculous, as form comments on content"? And does this rate as "altering the rhetoric of bourgeois melodrama": "Do you expect me to commit adultery for the sixth time this week?"[3] This is not to say that Sirk enthusiasts cannot articulate what they mean, but rather to point out that if you look at something long enough, it begins to gain qualities it never had. This is especially true with Sirk, even Kuchar. Sirk tells us, "Cinema is blood, is tears, violence, hate, death, and love" (qtd in Fassbinder 95). But the style of his melodrama is dead, and that is what Kuchar burlesques. Kuchar reminds us that cinema, like life, is also bed pans, ear wax, sleazy fantasy, ineptitude, compromise, and laughter.

Thundercrack (dir. Curt McDowell 1975) is a hard-core porn film with scenes of explicit sexual activity. It uses a trash style that undercuts most people's usual responses to porn. For example, it depicts a scene of male masturbation by machine, calculated to turn off many porn viewers. It presents a blow job in an intentionally anticlimactic way by punctuating it with a singularly banal discussion. McDowell and his script writer George Kuchar are the perfect collaborative partnership for this camp of cinematic conventions. With a stock-in-trade vulgarity of gargantuan proportions, they push their excesses to an epic length of two and a half hours. While the basic story line seems simple enough – the old reliable that brings together a group of strangers who must relate to each other and some outside danger – the film's main interest lies in depicting the constantly changing parodies of cultural conventions from the cinematic and real worlds. Thus the actor's stock piece, a narrative recital of a gruesome incident, becomes in *Thundercrack* a bizarre story about how a woman ignited her girdle at a garden party to demonstrate her freedom, only to be burned by her garment's lethal chemistry. The guests accidentally join in her immolation when the alcohol in their drinks feeds the fire instead of putting it out. The victim becomes a martyr for the women's movement and the inspiration for a terrorist attack on the girdle company that had exhibited such a typical capitalist disregard for human life by making the incendiary underwear.

The film continues in this vein, mixing shaggy dog stories, Grand Guignol, clichés of cheap magazine fiction, non sequiturs, parodies of reborn Christians, moments of soap-opera drama, and hard-core pornography. *Thundercrack* has just enough parody to construct a plausible case for redeeming social value. But any sustained attempt to justify the film on such grounds would run into the problem of the film's relentless absurdity. Can we take anything in it seriously?

I think the film does provide one anchoring reference point in the last sexual escapade. Justifying a submission to sexual blackmail, one character explains, "No greater love can a man show for a woman than to give his body to the enemy." This is a verbal defense of the one sex scene that is presented straight (well, it is a gay love scene, but without mockery). The intercourse between two men is filmed and presented as ordinary porn with an emotionally synchronized soundtrack and routine climax. This scene, as opposed to all the other sexual encounters, is privileged: it intends to be erotic.

In this way the film actually does get beyond the running gags on impotence, masturbation, voyeurism, enemas, incest, and bestiality. The women in the film are not women, but drag queens who happen to have the biological definition of female. In one sense, then, the film is an extended gay parody of heterosexuality: physically, as when one man has intercourse with an inflatable female doll; and verbally, as when both male and female characters abuse men who become impotent when faced with an invitation to heterosexual pleasure. In this sense, the whole film stands as a double entendre, one that can be fully understood only within the context of a gay male subculture.

POLITICS OF PARODY

Susan Sontag, writing in 1964, saw camp, with its rejection of morality, as "disengaged, depoliticized – or at least apolitical" (107). She argues this because "Homosexuals have pinned their integration into society on promoting the aesthetic sense. Camp is a solvent of morality. It neutralizes moral indignation, sponsors playfulness" (118). In response to Sontag, and writing within the framework of the contemporary gay movement, Jack Babuscio comments:

> Consistently followed as a comprehensive attitude, aestheticism inevitably leads to an ingrown selfishness in life, and to triviality in art. As a means to personal liberation through the exploration of experience, camp is an assertion of one's self-integrity – a temporary means of accommodation with society in which art becomes, at one and the same time, an intense mode of individualism and a form of spirited protest. And while camp advocates the dissolution of hard and inflexible moral rules, it pleads, too, for a morality of sympathy.
>
> (42)

But he does argue that "camp can be subversive – a means of illustrating those cultural ambiguities and contradictions that oppress us all, gay and straight, and in particular women" (48). Richard Dyer has elaborated this point:

> Not all gay camp is in fact progressive, but nonetheless it does have the potential for being so. What camp can do is demystify the images and world view of art and the media. . . . Camp, by drawing attention to the artifices employed by artists, can constantly remind us that what we are seeing is only a view of life. This doesn't stop us enjoying it, but it does stop us believing too readily everything we are shown.
>
> (13)

Camp, like any particular subcultural attitude in our society, operates within the larger boundaries of a racist, patriarchal, bourgeois culture. That it defines itself in difference from the dominant culture does not automatically construct Camp as radically oppositional. Only an audience and the work's exhibition context can complete that subversion. At some moments oppositionality appears more obvious than at others. For example, Waters and Divine can be rapidly recuperated into the existing system of sexist oppression. In fact, Divine's solo club act often included heavy doses of anti-woman humor.

In this perspective, *Thundercrack* came into existence in 1975 at a peculiar historical juncture. It exhibited a full flowering of the filmic Camp established in the early 1960s with Jack Smith's famous underground film *Flaming Creatures*, a polymorphous and perverse sexual romp that became a celebrated cause in breaking down reactionary censorship. At the same time, *Thundercrack* is a testament to the limited version of male consciousness without the addition of a feminist understanding of society. McDowell and Kuchar, like Waters, offer a sharp critique of dominant features of American life, but often lack a fuller view of human existence. Yet, sometimes, the subversive potential of Camp can emerge simultaneously as both ironic and sincere.

In *Trash*, Holly Woodlawn takes a class stand. Her insistence that she will keep her silver shoes and still demand the state help support her child is marvelously ironic. Similarly, in some of his shorter works, George Kuchar shows an ability to combine camp parody with sincerity as in *I, an Actress*. We find the offscreen director, after coaching an unprepared woman for a role in what must be a Kuchar camp melodrama, take center screen to show "how it should be done," in a scene of self-aware silliness as Kuchar gets passionately caught up in the role, revealing his own partisan love for the part. In *Mongreloid*, a parody of the home movie and avant-garde portrait film, Kuchar pushes the two genres' dominant code of sincerity to the point of the absurd as he portrays his dog Bocko as well as his own willingness to be foolish on screen. Giving Bocko the dog's favorite toys, Kuchar becomes the all-American father to a disinterested dog: "I buy these things for you to make you happy!" Over the grainy 8mm home movie footage he asks his pet, "We stopped in Salt Lake City. Do you remember? You made caca in Salt Lake City." Camp in its expression of social and aesthetic offensiveness can, with a prepared audience, attain a certain transcendence, providing a significant comment on art and society through a combination of parody and sincerity.

Parody can be thought of as a specific technique and also as a mode of discourse. As a technique, parody involves the articulation of a critique by expressing a meaning different to the stated or ostensible meaning through a repetition or doubling. Linda Hutcheon has elaborated, in great detail, a theory of parody in modern culture, one which – in the case of art – is often linked to self-referentiality in the text, described by Linda Hutcheon as "repetition with critical difference" (7).

Radical criticism has taken three different positions with regard to the politics of parody: as inherently apolitical, as inherently critical, and as simply a condition of contemporary art and cultural production. Those who argue that parody is inherently apolitical and regressive usually do so on an openly political basis. In its most general form, the radical argument goes: parody separates form from content, then validates that separation (a violation of organic unity), and then validates form as more important than content (formalism). It is then a species of aestheticism (or art for art's sake), of the divorce of human values from the art experience and considering art as only a matter of internal form separated from ordinary life, from the spectator. It is tied to creating a subject–text relationship that is essentially a training program for alienation.

The contrary argument, that parody is inherently progressive, rests on the assumption that parody creates an "open form" that allows for a complex experience. The text then becomes open (or free), producing a liberating effect on the audience (though we might remember that freedom can only be taken, not given). Correlative with this is a celebration of the freedom of detachment, of an indeterminate floating that was described by Roland Barthes. This celebration of indecision, of not taking sides, reflects the class position of the petty bourgeoisie. The genius of the petty bourgeoisie after all, its survival, is in working with both major classes; it floats so that it does not have to appear to be taking sides (yet to remain uncommitted during a power struggle is in reality to side with the more powerful).

Barthes, in his essays on writers, teachers, and intellectuals, urges ambiguity and floating (he makes the explicit comparison of being stoned on marijuana) as a way of foreclosing a rapid reductionism (331). This same call, which in Barthes's work seems like an attempt to interrupt the all too certain and all too rational project of traditional French intellectual life, becomes in later thinkers of 1970s France simply an excuse for maintaining privilege by refusing any totalizing thought, scorning any commitment as imperfect, and achieving an arrogant level of intellectual self-pity.[4]

We must also account for the basic feature of contemporary arts that the audience does understand parody and always has the capacity, on its own, to adopt a parodic reading of the work. At the same time, this knowledge differs in its actual social use. Audience members can use parody defensively to defuse, diffuse, and break down the assault on them (most easily done with a simple separation, which is why the formulaic quality of much mass culture lends itself so well to this kind of parodic project). On the other hand, there are those who use parody as a means of control and domination. Some maintain their political, economic, and social positions by creating and sustaining parody in the discourses of journalism, advertising, propaganda, and political rhetoric. Barthes is right to argue against authority and for complexity. But in arguing for parody and indeterminacy he finally argues against practice, commitment, risk, or even testing the idea. We cannot say that freedom is not having to decide. In fact, in the practice of everyday life, history forces decisions on us. The question of freedom is political and existential: what decision do you make, what side are you on?

A third radical position is that parody is an inherent aspect of contemporary art. Both high-culture and mass-culture forms today are heavily parodic. Art is never univocal; it always gets different responses from different people. Take the example of the cakewalk, a processional dance originating in the antebellum plantation American south. Originally the cakewalk was a show arranged for the entertainment of the white masters. The black slaves were given cast-off clothing, finery unsuitable for their ordinary labor, and thus dressed up proceeded to parade (often with a cake as the prize, hence the name of the dance). For the masters there was considerable amusement in seeing slaves in this totally "inappropriate" clothing employing extreme gestures and performing as if they had the refined manners of aristocrats. Yet for the slaves who participated, and hateful as this scorn might have been, it was also an opportunity to mock the masters' manners. After the Civil War, the cakewalk – synchronized with African rhythms – continued in various forms (including the minstrel show). From the visual evidence we have forty years later, preserved in the first silent films, we can see how blacks parodied the whites' fancy manners in a comic form that safely contained, but certainly did not eliminate, social criticism. On one level the stage representation contributed to the racist myth of the happy plantation and, on the other, it revealed the persistence of a critique within popular forms. Whites remained amused and superior, but blacks could read the subversive ridicule involved. Everyone laughed, but one side laughed differently from the other. This example should remind us that parody does not reside in the work alone, but rather derives from a stance people take toward it. All works can be read potentially as parody, though clearly some works invite a parodic reading more than others.

Parody is persistent under conditions of advanced capitalism. Parody stands as a means of accommodation to things that people think they cannot change. In that sense it is adaptive. But once people sense that history is changing and that they can change things around them, they use parody differently. It becomes deep and cutting against the past, against the status quo, against what holds people back. It is fused with anger in art and political expression. Yet in terms of everyday-life praxis, it also softens and becomes much diffused. Parody begins to function in art to indicate richness, diversity, possibility, and hope for the future precisely because it seems a whole culture can be transformed. Parody sets us the opportunity to make new connections. At its best this is how the 1960s counterculture was able to use parody. It is what is marked in Jimi Hendrix's performance of "The Star-Spangled Banner." That version of the national anthem took something totally identified with the dominant culture and magically transformed it into something that said to youth culture, "we have a right to this, too . . . we can take it over and transform it to our own ends using our own unique tools and talents." This kind of parody reveals a greater sense of the range of life and its possibilities, an awareness of the grotesque, of carnival, and of anger, sensuality, and sexuality.

Camp, as parody, has an ability to expose what the powers-that-be would like to keep neatly hidden and out of sight. Instead of acquiescing in the ideology of a disposable culture that wants to flush away its social problems, Camp can insist on a determined recycling of political agendas as well as aesthetic diversity. While the assimilationist sector of gay politics pursued a strategy of declaring "we're just like everyone else," the more radical wing – represented by *Fag Rag* in the 1970s and Queer Nation in the 1990s – often relies on Camp in its cultural production. Scott Heron's post-punk transgression, *Laff at the Fags* (1986), outrageously confirms for comic effect every prejudiced stereotype about gay men being obsessed with perverse sex. Frequently in recent years, Camp appears in conjunction with other forms serving a more explicit political agenda, as in Todd Haynes's *Poison* (1990) with one section allegorically interpreting AIDS panic through a combination of film-noir style and horror-film imagery. German political film and video maker Rosa Von Prauheim's work throughout the 1970s, 1980s, and 1990s uses and reuses Camp as a radical expressive strategy. Similarly, Canadian video artist John Greyson takes up the subject of gay men's washroom sex in *You Taste American* (1986) (with Michel Foucault and Tennessee Williams arrested by repressive police) and *Urinal* (1988) using Camp as a critical strategy. The videos indict police surveillance and harassment of gay sexuality, but also critique the gay movement's common embarrassment at this homosex ften practiced by men who do not identify with the gay community. There is a minor, but vital, tradition of radical media that takes up mass culture at its worst – not to imitate the dominant in order to attract a large audience but to work with and against its possibilities while transforming it in the process. We need richness, fullness, a sense of life's possibilities, a sense that includes the truth of Camp, if we are to create a truly popular radical culture.

NOTES

Portions of this essay appeared earlier as: Kleinhans 1976; and Kleinhans 1979. A summer fellowship from the Oregon Humanities Center, University of Oregon, provided time to revise. I would like to thank Sara Blair, Gabriel Gomez, Julia Lesage, Martha Vicinus, and Tom Waugh for their critical responses.

1 That is, if one is aesthetically receptive to the work to begin with. Which is to say that the particular and peculiar context of reception is absolutely crucial to understanding and appreciating Camp, which presents itself initially as a marginal, outré, and deviant experience, which itself is part of its attraction for its actual audience.
2 Kuchar, George (dir.). 1975. *The Devil's Cleavage.*
3 Ibid.
4 Let's name names: at the best end, Michel Foucault; at the worst: Philippe Sollers and Julia Kristeva; with Jean Baudrillard playing the Nutty Professor who bounces back and forth between these extremes.

BIBLIOGRAPHY

Babuscio, Jack. 1984. "Camp and the Gay Sensibility." In Richard Dyer (ed.). *Gays and Film.* New York: Zoetrope, 40–57.
Barthes, Roland. 1986. "Writers, Intellectuals, Teachers." *The Rustle of Language.* Trans. Richard Howard. New York: Hill and Wang, 309–331.
Cawelti, John. 1976. *Adventure, Mystery, and Romance: Formula Stories as Art and Popular Culture.* Chicago: University of Chicago Press.
Dorfles, Gillo. 1970. *Kitsch: The World of Bad Taste.* New York: Universe Books.
Dyer, Richard. 1977. "It's Being So Camp as Keeps Us Going." *Body Politic* 10: 11–13.
Fassbinder, Rainer Werner. 1972. "Six Films by Douglas Sirk." Trans. Thomas Elsaesser. In Jon Halliday and Laura Mulvey (eds). *Douglas Sirk.* Edinburgh: Edinburgh Film Festival, 95–107.
Feuer, Jane. 1989. "Reading *Dynasty*: Television and Reception Theory." *South Atlantic Quarterly* 88/2: 443–460.
Fiske, John. 1989. Comments at a Northwestern University seminar, Evanston, Illinois, April.
Greenberg, Clement. 1961. "Avant Garde and Kitsch." *Art and Culture: Critical Essays.* Boston: Beacon Press, 3–21.
Hutcheon, Linda. 1985. *A Theory of Parody: The Teachings of Twentieth-Century Art Forms.* New York: Methuen.
Kleinhans, Chuck. 1976. "The Devil's Cleavage." *Film Quarterly* 30/1: 62–64.
—— 1979. "The Actor as Actress: Holly Woodlawn in *Trash* and Divine in *Multiple Maniacs*." *The Actress on Film/Chicago.* Chicago: School of the Art Institute of Chicago, 17–18.
Koch, Stephen. 1973. *Stargazer: Andy Warhol's World and His Films.* New York: Praeger.
Milne, Tom. 1970. *Rouben Mamoulian.* Bloomington: Indiana University Press.
Moles, Abraham A. 1971. *Le Kitsch: l'art du bonheur.* Paris: Mame.

Sarris, Andrew. 1968. *The American Cinema: Directors and Directions*. New York: Dutton.

Sontag, Susan. 1964. "Notes on Camp." 1983. *A Susan Sontag Reader*. New York: Vintage Books, 105–119.

Willemen, Paul. 1971. "Distanciation and Douglas Sirk." *Screen* 12/2: 63–67.

INDEX